WHAT IS EMOTION?

# What Is Emotion?

## History, Measures, and Meanings

JEROME KAGAN

YALE UNIVERSITY PRESS NEW HAVEN AND LONDON

Set in Electra type by Tseng Information Systems, Inc., Durham, North Carolina.

Printed in the United States of America by Vail-Ballou Press, Binghamton, New York.

Library of Congress Cataloging-in-Publication Data
Kagan, Jerome.
What is emotion? : history, measures, and meanings / Jerome Kagan.
p.      cm.
Includes bibliographical references and index.
ISBN 978-0-300-12474-3 (clothbound : alk. paper)
1. Emotions. I. Title.
BF538.K34 2007
152.4–dc22      2007027381

A catalogue record for this book is available from the British Library.

∞ The paper in this book meets the guidelines for permanence and durability of the Committee on Production Guidelines for Book Longevity of the Council on Library Resources.

10  9  8  7  6  5  4  3  2  1

The disadvantage of men not knowing the past is that they do not know the present. History is a hill or high point of vantage, from which alone men see the town in which they live or the age in which they are living.
—G. K. Chesterton, 1933

Theories come and theories go. The frog remains.
—Jean Rostand, "Notebooks of a Biologist"

# CONTENTS

My decision to write a book on human emotions, considering the extraordinarily large number of dusty volumes resting in university libraries, was motivated by the recent attraction, among both American and European theorists, to the idea that emotional states with significant consequences for behavior or personal relationships had a privileged status denied to states without any function beyond the fact of their occurrence. I have always been suspicious of defining important ideas in terms of their functions, purposes, or pragmatic effects instead of by the intrinsic features that distinguish them from similar notions. Physicians diagnose diabetes by the presence of chronically high blood glucose levels, and not by the compromised visual acuity these levels can produce. The behaviorists of my generation defined a reward, which was central to all learning theories, in terms of its consequences: it was any event that strengthened a habit. This position was troubling because it meant that scientists could not know in advance whether a particular experience was a reward until they saw whether it had an effect on behavior. This is not a profitable strategy in science; theorists want to be able to predict an outcome from a prior condition and are frustrated if denied this power. Physics enjoys high respect in the academy because many of its concepts and principles meet this criterion. The concept of gravity, or deformation in space-time curvature, would be far less useful if one could not know whether this hypothetical process was operating until one threw a ball in the air and saw whether it fell to earth.

I realized, however, after reading much of the vast literature on emotion, that a more significant problem was the growing enthusiasm, following the ascendance of the neurosciences, to rely on brain states, rather than on conscious feelings or their evaluations, as definitions of emotions. The ability to record patterns of brain activity has emboldened many investigators to treat the brain profile provoked by an incentive as an emotion rather than as a possible foundation for one, because this assumption rationalized the study of emotions in animals on whom exact brain measurements under controlled conditions were easier. This position represents a serious change in the definitions of emotion proposed by scholars over the past two thousand years because animals neither appraise nor label their bodily states. Hence, this new perspective requires careful analysis. A tropical depression in the ocean off West Africa is a risk factor for a hurricane but is not labeled a storm until its size and velocity, which cannot be known in advance, assume particular values. Similarly, a changed brain state does not always lead to a feeling or an action, and when it does, any one of several feelings or behaviors could be realized.

A third problem in current discussions is the desire to divide the potentially large number of emotional states into a small, tidy category of fundamental emotions and a large, messy set of less basic states. René Descartes yielded to this temptation when he argued that all human emotions were derived from the five basic passions of gladness, sadness, love, hatred, and desire. The belief that a small set of fundamental elements or processes lies at the root of all natural phenomena remains attractive because it satisfies an aesthetic need for parsimony and seems to match the common practice of combining a few elements to compose many complex products. The right combination of wood, steel, nails, cement, tile, and plaster is all one needs to build a variety of houses. But biologists studying life phenomena have learned, on too many occasions, that just when they thought they had identified a fundamental unit, later inquiry revealed the prematurity of their conclusion. The biologists of the 1950s thought that a gene within the cell's nucleus that was the origin of a protein was the basic unit. They now appreciate that some strings of DNA do not contribute to proteins and that some are in the cytoplasm. Hence, there is lively debate over the definition of a gene. A mood of puzzlement is even more salient among those who study emotions because there is no current consensus on the states that should be called basic. This matter, too, invites scrutiny.

As I reflected on these problems and began to transform ragged thoughts into coherent sentences, the text that had been intended as a paper for a journal became a book-length manuscript that is not a synthesis but, I hope, a constructive summary of what we think we know and how we have arrived at this understanding. Because emotions are an active domain of inquiry, the completion of each chapter resembled the removal of fallen leaves from a vast lawn on a windy day in October. By the time one has cleared the last patch of earth, new leaves have fallen on the area one raked hours earlier.

Because the definition of an emotion changes when the source of evidence varies, I suggest we temporarily postpone a decision as to the best definition and turn our attention to the cascade of observations to which the abstract concept refers. Languages contain two classes of words. One refers to events, such as leaves falling from trees and stones rolling down a mountain, that create similar perceptions in all humans. The second class, higher on the abstraction ladder and not available to eyes, ears, noses, tongues, and fingers, has meanings that are continually debated. *Gravity waves, justice,* and *emotion* belong to this category. For that reason, it will prove profitable, at least at present, to cease arguing about what an emotion is and to examine the observable phenomena that are its vital components.

This suggestion would be applauded by the two scholars who happen to be my intellectual heroes—Niels Bohr and Alfred North Whitehead. Both understood the serious differences between the words we use to describe what we observe and those used to capture what we imagine is happening. The latter terms are often misleading or, worse yet, mistaken. Therefore, the observations are all we can trust. Actions, biological reactions, and, in humans, verbal descriptions are the three classes of information scientists use to infer emotional states. Each provides a distinct definition of emotions like fear, joy, or anger. This suggestion legitimizes all three classes of evidence, and three different definitions, until a future time when the relations among the types of information are better understood and an initial consensus might be possible. But we must be patient and wait to see what the future reveals.

The organization of the text is straightforward. Chapter 1 summarizes the historical changes in the conceptions of emotion and concludes that the variation is due to the selection of different criteria for classification. Chapter 2 thus considers six candidates. The reliance on language to classify human emotions is sufficiently different from the other six to warrant separate treatment in Chapter 3. The bases for variation in feelings and emotions, the theme of Chapter 4, consider social class, gender, culture, and temperamental biases. The final chapter addresses two problems that had been ignored. The first asks if brain states, behaviors, and verbal descriptions, the three signs of an emotion, are commensurable and concludes that they are not. The second probes the utility of searching for a rationale for distinguishing between basic and less fundamental emotions.

I have learned a great deal from the writings of many thoughtful psychologists, psychiatrists, biologists, and philosophers and hope that this book, which is only a scaffold, clarifies issues that have been enigmatic and, more important, motivates a new generation of social and biological scientists to enter this fascinating arena of inquiry. The answers that evade us today have profound implications for the harmony of the societies in which humans try to find satisfactions of their temporary desires and some assurance of their continuous wish for virtue.

# ACKNOWLEDGMENTS

I thank Joseph Campos, Kim Romney, Marcel Zentner, and Steven Reznick for comments on parts of early drafts and Paula Mabee, Nancy Snidman, and Robert Cant for help with the preparation of the manuscript. I am indebted, again, to Jean Black for her encouragement and critiques and to Laura Dooley for editing that reshaped awkward sentences into readable prose.

WHAT IS EMOTION?

# What Are Emotions?

Bertrand Russell once noted that scientists who thought they were studying a simple phenomenon eventually recognized that their original question, say, "Why is the sky blue?" was far more complicated than they had imagined. Although some might regard the queries "What is an emotion?" and "How can we know if a person is experiencing one?" as equally simple, the answers offered are riddled with ambiguity and do not enjoy the more consensual, transparent meanings of such concepts as velocity and heat. Most ancient writers anticipated little controversy when, after consulting intuitions that grew out of personal experiences, they defined an emotion as an appraisal of a change in feeling. Scientists' obligation to find objective signs of their concepts, however, forced them to replace the private psychological states of feeling and appraisal, which resist accurate measurement, with definitions of emotion that relied on taped verbal reports, filmed behaviors, or recordings of biological reactions. This move objectified a subjective state. But because the three sources of evidence often required different conclusions, our understanding of human emotions is more controversial today than it was when Aristotle, René Descartes, and Immanuel Kant brooded on this idea.

Although every emotion originates in brain activity, each is first and foremost a psychological phenomenon that is underdetermined by a brain state because each brain profile can give rise to an envelope of emotions. The specific emotion that emerges depends on the setting and always on the person's history and biology. Understanding how history and biology select one state from many contains the same mystery that surrounded the puzzles of why like begets like and why apples fall from trees.

The domains over which psychology is sovereign, like the three regions of Caesar's Gaul, consist of actions, cognitive processes, and bodily feelings, a division that is partially faithful to the brain's organization. However, the theoretically most fruitful concepts for each of these domains and the measurements that award validity to them remain nodes of disagreement. Should motor acts be described in terms of the muscle systems involved, their voluntary or involuntary nature, or their intended goals? Should memory be conceptualized in terms of the information that is registered or the information retrieved? Should feelings be classified in accord with their consequences, origins, brain profiles, or semantic descriptions?

Scientists trying to resolve the frustration of choosing from among alternative conceptions of a phenomenon usually select one of two strategies. One group, for whom Albert Einstein is the unchallenged hero, trusts the mind to detect the initial form of the answers through disciplined thought. These scholars first invent a set of ideas, along with their presumed referents, and then arrange experiments to affirm the validity of their a priori concepts. Physicists committed to the notion of gravity waves and psychologists convinced that the concept of a secure infant attachment is preserved from infancy to adulthood provide two examples. The second group, for whom Charles Darwin is the admired icon, are less trusting of the ambitious products of human imagination and prefer to begin with a reliable phenomenon whose causes, consequences, and contextual constraints can be probed. Only after the relevant evidence has been gathered do these investigators invent concepts to summarize what they have observed. The notions of dark matter in the cosmos and reward centers in the brain illustrate this strategy, which Francis Bacon urged as the only way to challenge the seventeenth-century Christian scholars who insisted that theological authority decided what was true.

Put plainly, the choice is between betting on a pretty idea or on a plain but reliable fact before investing energy, time, and money in experimental work. Every intellectual effort, whether in the sciences or in the humanities, balances a tension between a centrifugal force racing toward universal truths and a centripetal one grounded in the details of a concrete observation. Scientists who are certain that they have checkmated nature have learned on too many occasions of an embarrassing exception to their dazzling insight. The discovery that the malformed proteins called prions, which are neither viruses nor bacteria, can be infectious is an example of nature's stubborn reluctance to be understood too completely.

The histories of the natural sciences reveal that the second approach has a better record than the first when a discipline is in an early stage of growth. The first natural philosophers took obvious, reliable facts as the puzzles to understand. Johannes Kepler was able to infer the elliptical orbit of Mars around the sun because he had access to extensive observations gathered by Tycho Brahe and his many observers. Michael Faraday's astute observations allowed James Maxwell to construct elegant mathematical summaries of the observed relations between magnetism and electricity. Darwin's fruitful concept of evolution required the abundant evidence he gathered during the voyage of the HMS *Beagle* around South America.

These and many other examples illustrate the advantage, when theory is weak and consistent facts are sparse, of attending first to robust phenomena and postponing a premature decision on the correct explanatory concepts. Scientists laboring in less mature fields who have begun their inquiry with a favorite idea have often discovered that their beloved concept was inexact, overly abstract, or, in some cases, had no referent at all. The phlogiston that burning substances gave up to the air and the intelligence Francis Galton thought he was evaluating by measuring sensory acuity and speed of motor response turned out to have no coherent actualizations in nature. Initial explanations in immature disciplines are often flawed because they support ideas that have pleasing connotations. Because Kepler accommodated to the evidence, he was forced to reject the aesthetic assumption that the planets moved with a constant velocity in a circular orbit.

Despite this less than illustrious record for an a priori strategy in young fields, some psychologists and most philosophers seized the bull by its horns and imposed definitions on popular, but ill-defined, concepts before exploring the full range of observations to which the words were supposed to refer. Some examples include *consciousness, stress, intelligence,* and, the theme of this book, *emotion.* It will be fruitful to desist from the semantic bickering and begin the more difficult task of figuring out the relations among the six constituents of this concept: provocative events, brain states, detected feelings, appraisals, semantic labels, and actions. Only after this goal has been achieved will we be able to decide how useful the idea of emotion is and how best to define it.

## The Meanings of Human Emotion

Nouns representing things and verbs representing their functions are the heart of language. The languages of the sciences vary in their emphasis on the structures of things or functions. Particle physicists rely heavily on mathematical functions. Biologists and chemists are far more interested in the structures of genes, cells, and molecules. The major ideas in psychology, such as habits, perceptions, memories, and emotions, are functions, rather than material things. The emotions have recruited the attention of many scholars because they serve many functions. Some states are bold punctuation marks that seize control of consciousness and force it to attend to an event or bodily state that requires immediate action. Others help the individual control behaviors that are violations of the community's ethical code or the person's private conscience. Still others guarantee perseverance in sustained attempts to gain desired goals, aid the registration of experiences in long-term memory, facilitate learning about events to avoid, motivate sexual reproduction, and permit the intimate bonding between persons that is necessary for the successful rearing of the next generation. Some emotions, however, are less obviously adaptive. The states created by an encounter with a beautiful scene, a reflection on past pleasures, an hour of exercise, or a glass of wine possess many of the features of the more urgent emotions but seem less necessary for survival.

The corpus of scholarly writing on emotions is so extensive that it would seem presumptuous for anyone to assume they could add to the existing record of wisdom. Because the meanings of words change with history and vary across cultures, however, each historical moment invites an analysis of the meanings of popular terms. The word *university* originally referred to collections of teachers, mainly recent residents of cities like Bologna, Paris, and Oxford who, needing protection and mutual support, organized themselves into a form of local guild. Biologists are debating the traditional definitions of species, and astronomers are quarreling over the definition of a planet. The task of semantic analysis is usually assigned to philosophers, but on occasion, scientists take on this responsibility.

A review of the changing understandings of the concept of emotion is especially relevant today because, as I noted, older definitions regarded emotions as the appraisals of consciously detected feeling states named with familiar words. This consensus, which lasted for almost two thousand years, was challenged when the ability to measure brain activity led some scientists to claim that a brain profile, usually produced by an incentive, represented an emotional state, even if the agent failed to detect any consequences of the biological response, did not engage in any appraisal, and displayed no change in behavior. A brain state and a subjective interpretation of a change in feeling that originated in a brain state are distinct phenomena. The former has the potential to become an emotion but has not yet attained that status. Although the brain state created by seeing a crying child on a playground eliminates a large number of possible feeling states, a small envelope of potential feelings remains. And although the one that is finally selected eliminates a large number of possible appraisals, an envelope of potential interpretations remains. The one eventually chosen is determined by the person's understanding of the local context, which in turn is influenced by his or her life history, culture, and temperament. The same principle applies to the meaning of sentences. A friend hearing me say, "Bill cut the grass," can immediately eliminate many thousands of intended meanings, but at least two possible meanings remain. I could have intended to say that Bill used a mower to cut his lawn or a knife to cut some marijuana. The listener's knowledge of Bill, me, and the context of the utterance is needed to permit my friend to extract the intended meaning.

The indeterminacy inherent in an incentive and an accompanying change in brain state and feeling is especially obvious for the emotions of anxiety and anger. The detection of a change in heart rate by a college student who received a poor grade on a paper, a young scientist whose article was rejected, or a motorist who hears the persistent honking of a car horn from the automobile behind her or him could be followed by the emotions of anxiety or anger. Psychologists invented the terms *internalizing* for those who are biased to become anxious and *externalizing* for those who are apt to become angry. Similarly, the emotion induced by an act that violated a personal standard will depend on the combination of two contextual factors: Was the action accidental or willed and are others aware of or ignorant of the violation? Accidents that others witnessed, or might learn about, elicit the emotion English calls shame; acts that could have been suppressed that are not known by others evoke guilt; if others are aware of the act, the emotion will be a blend of shame and guilt. And an emotion is least likely if the violation was an accident and the person believes no one knows it occurred. Few emotions always follow a particular originating event.

The cascade of processes, from incentive to brain profile to feeling to appraisal, resembles the game of twenty questions. Once a player knows that the secret object is an animal, and not a vegetable or a mineral, she or he still has to exclude a great many possible alternatives before finally inferring the correct answer. Analogously, a cascade of phases is involved in someone's perception of an object, say a cup. During the initial stage in the primary visual cortex, the orientations of the contours and their spatial frequencies are detected. There is no representation of a cup at this first stage, and no measurement of the neuronal activity in this area would allow a scientist to infer that the person was gazing at a cup.

The important point is that every change in brain state to an incentive that might lead to an emotion does not produce a feeling or an emotion. There are $10^{12}$ cell divisions in the human body each day and a non-zero probability of a change in a DNA string during each division. But the vast majority of these alterations in the genome have no consequences for the phenotype. Analogously, the vast majority of changes in brain that occur in every person each day have little or no implications for an altered psychological state. They are like the unfelt motions of the air molecules that swirl continually around my face.

Before scientists could detect individual genes, the actual presence of symptoms, not the possibility of developing them, defined a disease. The possession of a gene that places a person at risk for diabetes is not equivalent to possessing the symptoms of the illness. Many adults harbor colonies of the alien bacterium *H. pylori* in their stomachs. But because a majority do not experience any distress, their biological state is not called a disease until con-

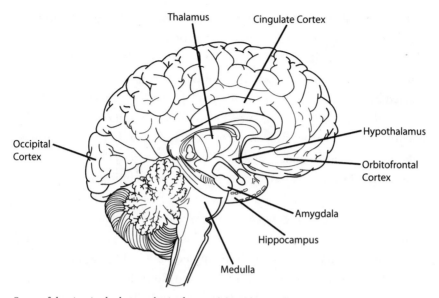

Thalamus

Cingulate Cortex

Hypothalamus

Occipital
Cortex

Orbitofrontal
Cortex

Amygdala

Hippocampus

Medulla

Some of the sites in the human brain that participate in emotions

ditions in the stomach wall change and the bacteria produce an ulcer. Analogously, a brain state, unaccompanied by any measurable change in feeling
or behavior, possesses none of the features of the traditional understanding
of the concept "emotion" and, like a gene, is only a "risk factor" for an emotional state.

Technological advances that create new sources of evidence are usually
followed by the invention of novel concepts. For example, the observations
electron microscopes provided required the invention of terms for the extremely small structures in living cells. The powerful techniques of molecular biologists also produced information that demanded new constructs,
such as anti-sense RNA.[1] It is time for investigators to invent special terms for
brain states that could, but do not always, become emotions. A serious problem trailing the practice of treating a brain state as an emotion is that the
specific state created by an event always depends on the agent's past history.
Unfortunately, scientists who rely only on brain states to infer an emotion
often ignore this fact. A ball thrown in the air a dozen times falls to earth
every time with a velocity that is in accord with a reliable equation. The ball
does not alter the form of its fall because it had eleven prior trajectories.

But a brain state does change with repetitions of the same experience. The profile evoked by the twelfth presentation of a photograph of a snake will differ from the profile shown to the first presentation because the object is now expected. If scientists who use brain scanners to measure the emotion created by pictures of snakes, spiders, and faces with fearful expressions first showed their subjects these pictures before they placed them in the scanner and told them what they were about to see (which they do not do), the brain pattern to the snakes, spiders, and faces would differ from the ones displayed when these illustrations were unexpected. Neuroscientists are attracted to the epistemology of the physics of Newton, but they are studying life-forms, and the reactions of living things are always affected by their past.

Before presenting a selective review of historical changes in the meaning of human emotion, it is important to appreciate that both agents, and the scientists who study them, are dependent on words to describe emotional states. Unfortunately, most of these terms, especially in English, name single categories rather than blends of two or more states. As a result, agents, observers, and scientists are often forced to select one term from a set of mutually exclusive categories, such as afraid, sad, happy, guilty, surprised, or angry, even though individuals often experience a combination of the states that these abstract concepts name. For example, many young women who had just eaten a chocolate bar reported an increase in a blend that combined joy and guilt.[2] Or consider a woman who has just learned that her ninety-year-old mother, who had been suffering from a painful cancer for three years, died. If asked to describe her state she is likely to say "sad" or "relieved," depending on the more salient feeling, when her actual state is a blend of both emotions. However, if the same woman lost her infant because of a physician's incompetence, she would experience a blend of sadness and anger. This state, which occurs often among the socially disadvantaged, arises when a personal loss is interpreted as an unfair consequence of unjust conditions in a society. The state of a young, unmarried woman who is about to murder her newborn infant because she feels she cannot care for it combines guilt over planning the violent act, shame over her failure to avoid the pregnancy, and anger at the biological father who abandoned her. No English word captures this coherent experience.

The Iranian film *Leila* supplies a fictional but not necessarily unrealistic example. Leila is a young Muslim wife who, having discovered she cannot conceive, feels ashamed and guilty because she has failed to meet one of the imperatives of her community. Leila's mother-in-law asks her to permit her husband to take a second wife who might provide the desired son. Leila vacillates but agrees, and the night the new bride arrives in her home to consummate the marriage she flees, crying, to her parents' home. No English or Farsi word could describe Leila's emotional state, which combined feelings of virtue for being loyal to her society's standards, anger at the second wife as well as her husband, anxiety over her new, less-advantaged position in the household, and shame over her infertility. The existence of other equally complex blends highlights the inadequacy of most languages to capture the range of intensity and quality of frequent human experiences.

Blends are coherent states, and not additive combinations of elementary states. Sulfuric acid has a special structure and set of functions that cannot be understood by describing the molecule as the sum of the properties of oxygen, hydrogen, and sulfur. The existence of blends, like the discovery of irrational numbers by early Greek mathematicians, mars the beauty of a view of nature that loves elementary states named with single words. The rational numbers 1, 2, 3, and 4 have an aesthetic quality that is shared with the purity of the terms *sad, angry, fearful,* and *happy,* tempting us to assume that each word names only one phenomenon. It is not clear why the existence of a word continues to seduce us into believing that it has a unitary referent, even though many philosophers have commented for centuries on this flaw in human thought. But, as with the common cold, no cure for this handicap has been found.

Scholars writing about emotion with popular words confront the frustration of having a vehicle that is poorly suited to the phenomena the terms are intended to describe, not unlike an artist wishing to paint a canvas of a spring garden who has only three pigments and two large brushes normally used for painting walls. Humans invented languages to communicate required behaviors, to persuade others of the desirability of a course of action, to teach skills, and to indicate the location and nature of resources and dangers in the world. The accurate description of private feelings was not intended as a primary function of speech for two reasons. First, it is not adaptive to reveal the anger, jealousy, envy, sexual feelings, guilt, or intimidation felt with respect to another. Second, the brain sites that are primary foundations for feelings are less fully connected with the sites that represent language than the cortical locations that represent objects and locations in the environment. Perhaps this is why most physicists, echoing Galileo, believe that only mathematical statements can capture the complexity of natural phenomena. Unfortunately, there is no mathematics that comes close to describing the simplest emotion.

The problems raised by using categorical terms, such as *sad, angry,* or *happy,* to describe events that vary on continua of valence (pleasant to unpleasant) and salience (low to high intensity) are not restricted to the social sciences. Although biologists recognize that the members of each species vary in genetic pedigree, the terms for species are also categories. It is cumbersome, however, to write about a dog whose sire was a wolfhound and dam a labrador, even though the behavioral characteristics of this animal would differ from one whose sire was a beagle and dam a dalmatian. Readers should remain cognizant of this issue while reflecting on the themes to be considered.

## A Brief History

It is not a coincidence that ancient Greek and Roman commentators wrote far more extensively than Islamic scholars about emotions. Humans, nature, and the Divine were the three great mysteries. Emotions are the domain of the individual, which Athens and Rome celebrated, whereas Islamic philosophers celebrated the Divine. Greek and Roman writers brooded on the cascade of processes that begins with an emotional incentive and proceeds to a pattern of brain activity, a conscious feeling, the interpretation of that feeling, and a possible action focused on the cognitive appraisal of a changed feeling. They did so because their societies were concerned with each individual's ability to restrain actions accompanying emotions that might disrupt the community. Most but not all Greek philosophers assumed that this control was possible because, unlike Freud and some students of evolution, they believed that on balance nature was more benevolent than malevolent. Therefore, if individuals lived in accord with what felt natural, they would be able to regulate their passions.[3] It cannot be a coincidence that the vast number of essays and books on emotion written over the past two millennia almost competes with the number devoted to morality. The idea that links these two domains is the need for and concern with maintaining social harmony.

There are far fewer books on human motor skills and ways to prepare food than on morality and emotion because the former talents have less obvious implications for the civility of social life. Thus, it is not surprising that the first factor in Aristotle's list of fourteen emotions contrasts ethically good with bad states, for the list is easily divided into the feelings that the Greeks judged as praiseworthy (confidence, joy, friendliness) and those that were subject to criticism (fear, envy, hatred, disgrace). *Eudaimonia*, a special form of happiness that shares features with the contemporary idea of subjective well-bring, was absent from Aristotle's list because he regarded this state, attained through a life of virtue, contemplation, and the control of strong emotion, as both a mood and a primary human goal, analogous to the revered state of nirvana in Indian philosophies.

A subtle ethical judgment also permeates the currently popular contrast between *positive* and *negative affect*, with anger, fear, and sadness nominated as prototypes for the latter state because of the implicit premise that negative affect interferes with happiness and health. I suggest, however, that medieval Christians committed to their faith would have reported a feeling of positive affect that existed simultaneously with justified anger at Jews, Muslims, and atheists, a fear of God's punishment should they commit a sin, and sadness over the loss of a young child. Thus, the specific affects judged as positive or negative, which vary with time and culture, are ethical categories linked to the concepts "good" and "bad," and are not particular biological or psychological states that assume the same form across the world. Hence, it is not obvious that they are any more useful as scientific concepts than the notions "pretty" and "plain."

Subsequent generations of European commentators writing on emotion, especially those reluctant to reject the tenets of Christian philosophy, focused on the earlier phase in the cascade that represented the feelings accompanying sexual arousal and anger because these states were disruptive and difficult to regulate. Most medieval Christian theologians affirmed the fourth-century assertion by Augustine that, before the Fall, Adam and Eve were free of sexual desire and in full control of the responsiveness of their genitals. God's punishment for their disobedience was to burden humans with sexual urges that came on suddenly and were difficult to ignore.

Thomas Aquinas's division of the soul's passions, a word implying that agents were necessarily passive to their intense feelings, into states of arousal modulated by states of restraint retained the evaluative connotation implicit in the desirability of controlling one's emotions. This opposition was preserved through the nineteenth century in the contrast between uncontrollable emotion and reflective reason until Freud turned the tables on the past by arguing that the restraint dictated by reason, in the form of repression, was the cause of, rather than the cure for, unhappiness and mental illness.[4] Aquinas called the appetites, whose feelings were difficult to ignore, the concupiscible passions, with love, desire, hate, and pleasure as exemplars. His second class of irascible passions involved appraisal and the possibility of regulation. Some were celebrated because they modulated the irrepressible appetites; for example, hope and courage, but this category also included despair, fear, and anger because of their dependence on appraisal and their amenability to control. Nathan McCall, an African-American writer who grew up in a poor, ethnically segregated neighborhood, phrased Aquinas's concupiscible category in plainer prose: "The heart is a stubborn thing. It don't give a shit what you tell it to do. It does what it wants, and it can't be trained to do otherwise."[5] It is worth noting that some Chinese living in the second century BCE appeared to regard sexual arousal as more controllable, for the sexual act required certain preparations. Men were advised to exercise, eat certain foods, and apply a poultice to the penis and saliva to the woman's wrists before beginning the rituals of love.

It is not surprising that Aristotle and Aquinas would be preoccupied with the consequences of an imbalance between the socially dangerous emotions of excessive anger, greed, lust, and ambition, which were difficult to suppress and often disrupted community life, and the benevolent states that engendered a feeling of virtue and preserved social harmony. Synonyms for anger and guilt, representing the opposition between arousal and restraint, are present in most languages. A number of eighteenth-century philosophers believed that civil society could be preserved only if individuals redirected the energy behind the socially disruptive emotions into a desire to make money. Freud's concept of sublimation is one derivative of this psychological alchemy. Modern readers, who celebrate the emotions of exuberant joy, intense love, and justified anger, may find it hard to believe that less than seventy-five years ago P. T. Young, a respected expert on motivation, resurrected the nineteenth century's dark view of emotions by defining them as states that were always accompanied by a disintegration of behavior.[6]

Darwin's ideas were a watershed in European discussions of emotion because his treatises on evolution and emotions introduced two ideas missing from most analyses written during the prior two centuries. Darwin suggested, first, that there were profound biological continuities between animals and humans that were stripped of ethical connotations. Hence, scientists could illuminate the mystery of human affects by observing and performing experiments on animals. Sixteenth-century religious Europeans, but not necessarily Buddhists or Hindus, would have rejected this notion as absurd. Darwin's second suggestion, in his famous book *The Expression of the Emotions in Man and Animals* (1872), was that emotional states found expression in distinct arrangements of facial muscles provoked by a "nerve force." This claim implied that emotions were potentially localizable in brain activity. Both assumptions are alive and well in contemporary writings that attribute select emotions to animals (for example, anxiety in mice, fear in rats, anger in monkeys, empathy in chimpanzees) and nominate particular brain circuits as the biological foundation of specific states (for example, fear mediated by the amygdala, disgust by the insula and orbitofrontal cortex).

Freud's conception of anxiety added a significant element to Darwin's semantic network for emotion. Many nineteenth-century physicians treating patients with serious forms of depression, psychosis, alcoholism, and criminality regarded the symptoms as qualitatively distinct phenomena that were the direct consequence of a compromised brain, just as the symptoms of smallpox were the result of the toxic products of a microbe. Freud inserted an undifferentiated state of "neurotic anxiety" between brain and symptom and implied that this state, which could range from mild to intense, was provoked when the person repressed sexual urges or encountered a threat reminiscent of an earlier experiences of "loss." Because these experiences occur to almost everyone, every individual was potentially vulnerable to the development of a phobia of animals or crowds, a melancholic mood, or a delusion.

Historical changes in Western communities, from the Renaissance through the Industrial Revolution to the present moment, added an evaluation of excessive timidity, caution, and concern with the opinions of others as less adaptive in an increasingly competitive, mobile, industrialized, urban society than these traits had been several centuries earlier in a rural, agricultural economy of villages and towns. History also created large communities of strangers who held diverse values that, nonetheless, were entitled to respect. As a result, a different kind of uncomfortable feeling was evoked by reflection on the adequacy of self's skills or status and the validity of one's moral premises. These feelings, which were labeled anxiety, ascended to the position of the alpha emotion in the hierarchy of human affects, replacing anger, lust, shame, guilt, and an insatiable desire for power as the enemies of happiness. Not surprisingly, psychologists and psychiatrists redirected their attention to its measurement and alleviation.

And then, as often occurs in science, a single experiment with rats coalesced the intuitions of many around a unifying idea. In this case, a trio of psychologists at the University of Iowa performed a conditioning experiment with rats in 1951 that became the model for many hundreds of studies with rats or mice designed to clarify the nature and causes of human fear or anxiety. The Iowa scientists first presented rats with the combination of a light and buzzer sound followed quickly by an electric shock to the paws, which rendered the light and buzzer capable of evoking a state of anticipated electric shock. When they later presented the light-buzzer combination without the shock, followed by a very loud sound that naturally causes a rat to show a reflex body startle, the magnitude of the body startle response was greater than it was in animals who had not learned that the light-buzzer signaled shock.[7] These psychologists, apparently relying on their intuition of how they would feel, assumed that the animals expecting an electric shock should be in a state of fear. Hence, the larger than normal startle to the loud sound that was preceded by the light-buzzer was a sign of that emotional state, just as Darwin inferred a state of fear in a monkey who grimaced at the approach of a larger animal. This idea had aesthetic appeal because it promised a simple way to measure a complex human state. It quickly acquired credibility because many assumed that the rat was a good representative of all mammals. The Iowa scientists ignored the fact that the white rat was chosen in the 1890s as a useful model because of its convenience as a laboratory animal and not because its brain physiology was very similar to that of primates.

It is useful to analyze the logic behind the Iowa conclusion. The seminal premise, which is reasonable, is that receipt of electric shock is an aversive experience; hence, anticipation of this event should evoke an unpleasant feeling. The second, more questionable premise, traceable to Freud, is that the anticipation of an aversive event usually generates anxiety or fear. This assumption is vulnerable because most aversive events—a bitter taste, cold fingers, loud noise, nausea, cramped posture, or acrid smell—provoke not fear or anxiety but annoyance or anger. That is why the unpleasant sound of metal scraping on slate is as effective an unconditioned stimulus as electric shock in the classical conditioning of heart rate or a sweat reaction in humans.[8] There is no reason to be afraid of the sound of metal on slate. Furthermore, if the aversive event were unexpected, which was true for the rats that were unprepared to be shocked, the likely emotion in humans would be vigilance or surprise but not fear.

The final element in the argument was that the behaviors conditioned to a signal for an aversive event could be regarded as sensitive signs of the emotions of fear or anxiety. Ivan Pavlov did not make this mistake, for he did not assume that the salivary secretions he conditioned in dogs by presenting them food powder after a sound reflected a state of hunger in the animals. Konrad Lorenz, too, would have criticized the Iowa premise because he did not attribute an emotion of affection or affiliation to the newly hatched goslings that followed him. Rather, he argued that their trailing was a biologically prepared reaction to a moving object, a fixed action pattern released by their perception of Lorenz's motion. A larger than average startle to a loud sound that was preceded by a signal for an aversive event, say a blast of air to the throat, is also a biologically prepared response. But it is not obvious that fear is the best name for the state created by the signal. Alert, surprised, or vigilant seem to be better names; none is a synonym for fear. An unexpected streak of bright lightning across the night sky evokes an alert state of vigilance for the coming clap of thunder without necessarily provoking fear.

Moreover, research a half-century later challenged the interpretation of the Iowa psychologists. Rats that had been exposed to a cat, their natural predator, showed increased excitability in the brain areas assumed to be the bases of fear and a reluctance to explore an unfamiliar area, but these animals did not show enhanced body startles. Because it is unreasonable to argue that the rats that saw the cat were not in a fear state, their failure to show large startles to a signal for shock implies that exaggerated startles are not reliable signs of that state.[9] Indeed, rats exposed to several minutes of bright light, as well as humans sitting in a dark laboratory room, showed enhanced startles to a loud sound, suggesting that the anticipation of pain or other form of harm is not the only cause of a potentiated startle. The claim that adults, who encounter darkness every night when they enter their unlit bedrooms, are in a state of fear when the lights in a laboratory are turned off for a few minutes strains credibility.

Despite this evidence, many experiments with animals over the next half-century continued to assume that the varied behaviors animals display to aversive stimuli or settings, such as a rat's reluctance to explore an unfamiliar arena, enhanced startles, or immobility to a signal for an aversive event, are sensitive indexes of a state that shares important features with the emotions of fear or anxiety in humans. This questionable line of reasoning would be less troubling if scientists had not proceeded to the next step and assumed that any drug or genetic polymorphism that reduced, or increased, the magnitude of these responses in animals had implications for human anxiety. It is an obvious error to conclude that a drug that reduced the magnitude of enhanced startle to a loud sound in humans (measured by the vigor of the eyeblink reflex to the sound) would mute human anxiety if the startle is not a reliable sign of that state. A great deal of evidence indicates that the human startle to a loud sound is enhanced by how much "cognitive work" the person is engaged in when the sound occurs.[10] Thus, Darwin's assumption of psychobiological continuity between animals and humans, Freud's twin beliefs that aversive events generate anxiety and that anxiety is the primary cause of neurotic symptoms, and the Iowa study came together to create the conviction that understanding the causes of animals' reactions to conditions that, intuitively, seem unpleasant will contribute to an understanding of the varieties of human anxiety. This assumption is pretty because it is simple, has broad implications, and allows scientists to use rats and mice to illuminate human emotions, but unfortunately it soars high above the facts.

It is worth noting that rats can be conditioned to avoid eating a particular food, but no one has argued that this fact provides a useful model for understanding women who avoid eating fats and carbohydrates because they want to be physically more attractive. Although animals can be conditioned to avoid mating with the opposite sex, no scientist has suggested that this observation might help to explain homosexuality. Nor can chronic fatigue syndrome in humans be understood by noting that rats can be conditioned to press a bar continually until exhausted in order to receive electrical stimulation in the so-called reward areas of the brain. Thus, it is not obvious that a rat's display of an enhanced startle reaction or body immobility to a signal for shock are fruitful models for all human anxiety states. Anxiety is no less complex a human emotion than shame or guilt, which are as potent causes of the symptoms of depression, melancholy, post-traumatic stress disorder, and anorexia as anxiety. The insomnia and nightmares that some drivers develop following an automobile accident that caused minimal pain to them but severely injured (or killed) one of the passengers are the products of guilt over feeling responsible for injuring another and are not conditioned fear reactions. But because there is no animal model for shame or guilt these states are ignored and their study is relegated to clinicians and students of personality who rely almost exclusively on questionnaires and interviews as their sources of evidence rather than on behaviors or biological information. Sadly, there is too little communication between these investigators and the behavioral biologists who study fear or anxiety in animals.

It is instructive to reflect on the differences between Darwin's discussion of emotions and John Dewey's conceptualization of feelings in his text *Psychology* (1886). Darwin, with his characteristic caution, never defined emotion. Instead he described with great care a number of involuntary muscular profiles that were presumed to be signs of more than three dozen emotional states, including grief, anxiety, despair, joy, and love, in animals, humans, or both groups. Dewey, the philosopher who did not have to worry about amenability to measurement, awarded significance to the conscious feelings of a psychologically active agent rather than to observable muscle patterns. Although William James was attracted to Darwinian ideas and Descartes's earlier notion that emotions automatically followed the perception of bodily changes, he was reluctant to parse these perceptions into categories based on a theoretical rationale.[11] Dewey, however, did divide emotional experiences into three types.

The *organic* feelings originated in the senses and biological appetites; these are Aquinas's concupiscible passions. The *formal* feelings consisted of a long list of abstract semantic terms, without a target or context, naming states that could be categorized as hedonically pleasant or unpleasant (for example, despair and disgust compared with surprise and love). The third class of *qualitative* feelings supplied a target for each of the many formal feelings and, in addition, contrasted appraisals of events in the world with appraisals of psychologically constructed, ideal states of affairs. The difference between formal and qualitative feelings is analogous to the distinct perspectives of Paris by a passenger in a plane hovering over the city and a pedestrian walking its boulevards, streets, and alleys. Dewey's categories, which were relatively indifferent to the Greek concern with controlling passions, seemed to be a compromise between a wish to accommodate to the ethical neutrality of Darwinian ideas while simultaneously honoring the traditional philosophical concerns with morality and the rules of language usage. All of these early schemes, with the exception of Darwin's, emphasized conscious feeling states based on the writer's intuitions, rather than systematic observations of behavior or brain function, honed by the premises of each scholar's culture.

A little over a century later, when biological measurements were routine, neuroscience was flourishing, and sociobiology was popular, scientists turned their attention to the brain activity that represented the initial phase of the emotional cascade. Paul Ekman and Richard Davidson edited essays on emotion written by twenty-three social scientists. The nodes of disagreement centered on three issues: (1) Is it useful to posit a small set of basic, compared with a larger set of less basic, emotions? (2) Should a brain state that does not pierce consciousness to produce a feeling be regarded as an emotion? and (3) Should the concept of emotion be restricted to states that have consequences for behavior or the quality of social relationships? None of these questions explicitly engaged the ancient preoccupation with good versus bad states or the importance of controlling overpowering feelings in order to preserve community harmony. Some neuroscientists, however, surreptitiously sneak an evaluative notion into their definition of emotion by using concepts that readers might not recognize immediately as proxies for good and bad. Joseph Le Doux defines an emotion as a brain process that computes the *value* of an experience. Although the term *value* is not explained, most readers will implicitly assume that this concept refers to events that are either good or bad for the individual.[12]

The most significant historical change in the conceptualization of emotions by Western commentators has been a replacement of the implications of an agent's feelings for the integrity of, and their relation to, others in the community as the criterion for classifying emotions with each individual's sensory pleasures and biological fitness. Instead of celebrating the emotions that sustained courage, restraint, honesty, cooperation, loyalty, and modesty, the feelings that maintained sexual arousal, justified anger, and accompanied the seeking and receipt of sensory delights and dominance were nominated as being in closer accord with human biology. Few evolutionary psychologists would concur with Plato's advice that each person should continually try to maximize his or her wisdom, courage, temperance, and sense of justice. Nor did John Updike agree when he advised twentieth-century readers, "When in doubt we should behave, if not like monkeys, like savages—that our instincts and appetites are better guides, for a healthy life, than the advice of other human beings."[13] A tipping point occurred at some time during the two centuries between Adam Smith and E. O. Wilson when feeling happy because self's sensory pleasures and potency were enhanced replaced feeling happy because self had earned the respect of friends and neighbors by adhering to norms that guaranteed community harmony, a view held by many French citizens at the end of the nineteenth century. Carl Jung is the notable exception in this historical sequence. Jung's ideological rupture with Freud in 1912 was caused, in part, by his belief that desires for feelings of virtue and spirituality were more urgent for humans than the need for sexual gratification. Freud either did not understand or could not accept this argument.

We should not forget that individuals in ancient Greek and Roman societies, who had clearly defined statuses (citizens, women, slaves), were continually concerned with losing the respect of those in a similar position.[14] The spread of Christianity, and especially Martin Luther's Reformation doctrine emphasizing private feelings of faith and worry over God's, rather than a neighbor's, acceptance of self, made it easier for each individual to become the judge of his or her own character. When guilt over failing to honor one's private standards was married two centuries later to an emergent egalitarian ethos, the hierarchy of human emotions experienced by Europeans and Americans seriously diverged from the hierarchy present in many other cultures. Specifically, guilt assumed precedence over shame; anxiety over personal failure dominated worry over another's gossip; tolerance toward those holding deviant values subdued moral outrage toward those who ignored local norms; sensory delights and self-aggrandizement lost their ethical taint; and a gnawing uncertainty over the ethical premises demanding unquestioned loyalty rose to more prominent positions.

Each commentator on human nature is entangled in a web of social facts whose strands are linked by premises that make it easy to decide that the ideas and social arrangements of their era contain a deep truth. Thus we cannot fault Aquinas for using ease of regulation as a principle for classifying emotions nor snicker at Freud for claiming that sexual conflict was the foundation of all neurotic symptoms. It is unlikely that today's scholars have arrived at permanently true conclusions and that the end of inquiry has arrived.

## The Present Situation

In light of the empirically lean and theoretically contentious understanding of emotional phenomena, any proposed definition is unlikely to escape controversy or be permanently correct. It is disheartening to read the papers presented less than sixty years ago at the famous Mooseheart Symposium on feelings and emotions because the fuzzy definitions of feelings and emotions that penetrated those discussions remain a source of frustration. Eleven contemporary theorists, writing decades after the Mooseheart meeting, hold different opinions regarding the states that should be treated as distinct emotions. For example, only seven of the eleven nominate guilt, shame, or surprise, and surprisingly, five theorists do not think that the emotion accompanying sexual feelings toward a loved partner warrants distinct status.[15] These scholars should read Egyptian love songs composed three thousand years ago as well as Homer's *Odyssey*, which contains almost as many references to sexual desire as to anger and sadness because the Greeks regarded eros as one of the most powerful feelings humans could experience. I suspect that one reason for this omission is that the uncertainty that used to hover over imagined sexual pleasures has been replaced with the mystery of acute self-consciousness.

A chapter in the *Annual Review of Psychology* illustrates the uncertainty that surrounds the most productive definition of *emotion*. The authors, apparently reluctant to incite controversy, do not define this concept, leaving this decision up to the reader, and treat biological, behavioral, and semantic evidence as equivalently useful signs of emotions. This laissez-faire stance is reminiscent of the list of eleven emotions posited by Alexander Bain, the fierce nineteenth-century advocate of associationism, that is a potpourri of sensations (a sweet taste), motives (a desire for power), and appraised feelings (terror, sexual arousal).[16]

The lack of consensus means that any discussion of emotion must acknowledge the legitimacy of the various definitions proposed during this historical era. My decision to nominate a detected change in feeling as a necessary, but not sufficient, feature of an emotion awards potency to the contrast between an agent's present state of consciousness and the states that characterize most moments of each day. The mind is continually prepared to contrast events that differ in a salient feature and to invent separate categories for them; heaven–earth, animate–inanimate, good–bad, body–mind, and feeling–reason are classic examples. The acute emotions are products of feelings whose perceptual properties are clearly discrepant from those experienced most of the time. College students who wrote down each evening for sixty days the two most memorable experiences of the day usually described a routine social or work-related event rather than one characterized by a salient emotion. Similarly, average middle-aged Americans who stopped to reflect on their present emotion most often decided that they were calm or mildly happy. Yet if asked a year later to recall the most memorable emotions of the past twelve months, both groups would not have mentioned these gentle states but would have recollected those occasions when they felt fear, anger, or sadness.[17]

Because the emotions that accompany the blocking of a goal-directed action, a personal insult, an encounter with a dangerous animal, an object, or a person, the loss of a cherished relationship, and the experience of a foul odor, a bitter taste, or a mutilated body are both less frequent and more salient than the more frequent, subtle, and pleasing states that accompany task involvement, anticipation of dinner, meeting an obligation, and affectionate social interactions, most individuals remember more unpleasant than pleasant past experiences.[18]

The attraction to feelings that contrast with a prior state makes it likely that individuals will recall an unpleasant past experience if they are currently feeling happy (because they received a good grade or the day was sunny) rather than unhappy (because of a poor grade or a cloudy day). Humans reflecting on the difference between the past and the present moment tend to exaggerate the more salient emotional state. This principle applies to judgments of others as well as to many perceptual phenomena.[19] Emotions are like the weather. There is always some form of weather, but we award special status to the infrequent, distinct arrangements of humidity, temperature, and wind velocity called hurricanes, blizzards, and thunderstorms.

Every judgment of a state of mind, which represents the selection of one category from a number of possibilities, depends on the person's current state, the immediate context, and the event chosen for comparison. The answer to the query, "Are you happy?" will depend on whether the previous minute, day, month, year, or the composite memory of childhood was the buoy that served as referent for appraising the present moment. If I were answering this question the morning I was writing this paragraph, my replies would be yes, yes, no, no, yes for each of the five comparisons. The judgment that one is happy at any particular moment resembles the perception of the ends of a rainbow which changes whenever the observer moves to a different location.

## Current Views

A large number of psychologists regard the idea of human emotion as an abstract, value-free construct referring to four different, imperfectly related phenomena: (1) a change in brain activity to select incentives, (2) a consciously detected change in feeling that has sensory qualities; (3) cognitive processes that interpret and/or label the feeling with words; and (4) a preparedness for, or display of, a behavioral response. Scholars vary, however, in the significance they award to each of these four components and in their assumptions about the strength of the associations among them.[20]

I shall use the term "feeling" for the second phenomenon and "emotion" for the third in order to aid comprehension, but recognize that this decision is not consensual and do not expect it to be acceptable to everyone. Because the quality and intensity of a feeling before a semantic appraisal are difficult to quantify, this part of the cascade encounters resistance among scientists unwilling to acknowledge the legitimacy of ideas that cannot be measured accurately. Many respected physicists working at the turn of the last century were skeptical of the validity of the concept of the atom for the same reason. Einstein's famous 1905 paper on Brownian movement, which provided support for this idea, failed to persuade all the skeptics.

A critical advantage of focusing on the separate components of emotions is that investigators, as well as the public, will appreciate that most generalizations are restricted to the evidence that was their source. Statements about an emotion based only on measures of brain do not necessarily apply to statements based on semantic appraisals or actions. Hence, all conclusions about emotional processes should append the source of evidence so that readers will know whether the basis for the claim was (1) a biological profile, whether brain or autonomic activity; (2) a detected change in feeling; (3) a symbolic appraisal of the feeling, often semantic in form; or (4) a motor reaction. This state of affairs is reminiscent of Akira Kurosawa's film *Rashomon* (1950) in which a wife, husband, thief, and onlooker offer different descriptions of the same sequence of violent events.

Scientists who call a brain profile an emotion (for example, activation of the amygdala to a photo of an angry face) when the neural activity is not accompanied by a detected change in feeling, facial expression, heart rate, or muscle tension, should acknowledge that an emotional term has a special meaning when a brain state is the sole referent. A young woman who suffered serious brain damage in a traffic accident was diagnosed as being in a vegetative state because she was behaviorally unresponsive to stimulation. However, the speech areas of her brain became active when sentences were read to her and the motor cortex became active when she was asked to imagine playing tennis. Even though her brain responded appropriately to these incentives, it is not obvious that she was in an emotional state. Adults exposed to the olfactory stimuli extracted from the sweat of a fearful person did not detect any change in feeling, even though their performance on a word association test improved. Theoretical clarity would be gained if scientists invented a term for the brain state produced by the olfactory event that permitted the improved performance. This new word should differ, however, from the one used when the stimulus actually evoked a change in feeling. The meaning of the construct "fearful" when attributed to mice who display a pattern of brain activity to the smell of a predator should not be equated with the meaning attributed to adults who have just learned they have a malignant tumor of the pancreas.[21] Neuroscientists who write that amygdalar activation to a picture of a spider represents fear resemble physicists who claim that time can be imaginary and, when combined with space, curved. The meaning of time in these statements is a mathematical notation that is not equivalent in meaning to the declaration, "Time passed quickly on our holiday." Physical time is not synonymous with psychological time. Analogously, the neuroscientists' definition of fear is not synonymous with the social scientists' understanding.

An analysis of the relation between feelings and the interpretive labels imposed on them reveals substantial individual and cultural variety in the terms chosen to name states that appear to have similar origins. The experimental induction of a high heart rate following the administration of epinephrine should produce a similar change in feeling, but individuals use different names for their emotional states depending on the context. It is critical to distinguish between a feeling, which is a perception, and a semantic concept. All humans, infants to senile adults, can feel a loss of energy at the end of a long workday, but the semantic label used to describe the perception varies across cultures and times. For the same reason, we must distinguish between the universal ability to perceive quantity (which many animals can do) and the concept of number (1, 2, 3); the ability to perceive the duration of an event and the concepts "minute," "hour," and "day"; and the capacity to perceive the linear extension of an object and the concepts "centimeter," "meter," and "kilometer." Moreover, humans have semantic concepts for imagined events that do not exist (for example, elves) and perceptual representations for experiences that do not have a consensual semantic name (for example, the smell of a forest floor in late October or the sound when standing alone on the top of a mountain on a windless day). Finally, the attainment of a particular feeling is an important motive. Individuals say they want money, dominance, status, celebrity, friendships, or sexual liaisons, but they strive for these events in order to experience the feelings that achieving those goals permits. College students from fifteen cultures reported that the feelings that accompany self-acceptance and a transcendental spirituality possessed particular salience.[22] Depressed adults fail to work toward the goals prized by their society because their biology is a barrier to the feelings normally released by attaining these prizes. If a raise in salary or status did not produce a pleasant feeling, people would stop working so hard.

## Contemporary Definitions

Social scientists have offered different definitions of emotion over the past thirty-five years. George Mandler, who wrote before the new discoveries in neuroscience, defined an emotion as the interpretation of a change in level of "arousal." Lisa Barrett calls the interpretation of such a biological state a *core affect*. These contemporary concepts bear a remarkable resemblance to the ancient Greek term *thumos*, which referred to a biological capacity for an intense feeling that could become any one of a number of emotions depending on the setting. Robert Zajonc is willing to regard a simple preference for one event over another—choosing vanilla over chocolate ice cream—as sufficient evidence of an emotion, even if the person did not experience any change in feeling as a choice was made. Antonio Damasio, writing with the perspective of the neuroscientist, has defined emotions as "complicated collections of chemical and neural responses . . . [with] some kind of regulatory role to play." This unusually permissive definition, with which Michael Lewis agrees, permits almost every moment to be an occasion for an emotion. Damasio's decision to treat a brain state as an emotion is not consensual. Although the brains of patients in a vegetative coma displayed a distinct waveform in the electroencephalogram on hearing their own names but not other names, it is not obvious that attributing an emotion to these comatose patients, or to their brains, is useful theoretically.[23] Physicists do not use the term *ice* for water that is being cooled until the temperature reaches a critical value and crystals form. However, this notion is attractive because it implies that measures of brain activity will allow us to "see" what an emotion is. The ability to visualize an abstract idea has extraordinary power to persuade us of the reality of the idea. But a colored photograph of a brain state created with the help of a brain scanner is no more equivalent to an emotion than a picture of an apple represents the texture and taste of the fruit.

Clinicians who conceptualize their patients' emotionally based symptoms as originating in their neurobiology are biased to excuse them from responsibility for their distress. By contrast, clinicians who regard the same symptoms as psychological products of experience are more likely to hold them responsible for their problems. Thus, the ethical dimension that penetrated earlier schemes explicitly is implied in more subtle ways in contemporary theory.[24]

Although feelings, their interpretations, and the behaviors that might follow have a foundation in brain activity, each of these three components can occur without the others, and the strengths of the associations among them are quite modest. For example, the detection of a brief feeling of dizziness need not be labeled or followed by an action. A response, such as a brief smile, need not be accompanied by a detected change in feeling or symbolic interpretation. And a change in brain activity need not provoke any change in conscious feeling or behavior.[25] The brain's phasic reaction to an emotional incentive is incorporated into the person's immediately prior state, which varies seriously across individuals. Therefore, any one of a large number of brain profiles, and subsequent feelings, is possible, and it is difficult to predict which one will be actualized. A stone thrown into ponds of differing turbulence and viscosity provides an analogy: the pattern of ripples in the water produced by the stone striking the surface will vary across the ponds.

Some social scientists want to restrict emotions to states that have some utilitarian function, such as contributing to survival or a better adaptation. A number of contemporary philosophers, including Jean-Paul Sartre and Martha Nussbaum, share this preference. Joseph Campos, Carl Frankel, and Linda Camras wish to limit the concept emotion to those states that alter the relations between the individual and his or her circumstances on matters of personal significance, a position shared with Richard Lazarus. E. T. Rolls is more restrictive, limiting emotions to those states elicited by events that have functioned as rewards or punishers.[26] Rolls's definition, which is loyal to the spirit of Darwinian adaptation, appears to eliminate many states that most psychologists would regard as emotions; for example, the state evoked by a whining puppy, learning that a neighbor was rude to the postal carrier, reading that a predicted blizzard was not going to occur, and being notified that a distant relative won first prize in an art contest. However, Rolls's position awards significance to disgust, fear, and the anticipation or consummation of food, water, and sexual activity. Although many emotions do have significant consequences, I shall argue in the next chapter that this fact is not a sound reason for exiling a large number of states that lack this feature.

## Questions to Answer

This book considers several controversial issues and offers an opinion on each. I shall argue that a brain state that fails to produce a conscious feeling or action should not be regarded as an emotion, question the advantages of restricting the term *emotion* to states that have functional consequences, critique the assumption that facial expressions always reflect emotional states, and adopt a skeptical stance toward the existence of a small set of basic emotions.

I believe that future investigators will be forced by evidence to invent different constructs for the separate components of the cascade that characterizes an emotion. This view is shared by Andrew Ortony and T. J. Turner and is in accord with the practice of the ancient Greeks, who distinguished between the automatic increase in heart rate and facial warmth following an insult, on one hand, and the emotions of anger and desire for revenge that follow an appraisal of the bodily feeling, on the other.[27] One set of terms will describe the distinct brain states provoked by a long, but nonetheless restricted, list of incentives that were not accompanied by a change in conscious feeling or motor response. The brain produces a reliable waveform in the EEG to faces with emotional expressions, whether or not the person detected any change in feeling.[28] This state needs a name. A second set of terms will apply to the brain states that were not accompanied by a consciously detected feeling but, nonetheless, produced an involuntary behavioral or autonomic response (for example, a smile or a slight rise in heart rate). A third set will name the brain states that resulted in detected feelings that were not interpreted; a fourth set will name the combination of a brain state, a detected feeling, and an interpretation; and a fifth set will apply to the combination of the four components: a brain state, detected feeling, appraisal, and some response. This last state is the ideal that is often presumed by contemporary scientists who usually measure only one of the constituents. Biologists invented distinct vocabularies for the DNA strings that are the sources of proteins, called exons, and the introns that are not, as well as for the brain cells that make myelin and those that do not.

I support the current distinction between acute emotional states that persist for a limited time and chronic moods, such as dysphoria, exuberance, or serenity, that are maintained for longer periods of time. The psychiatric definition of anxiety as a painful state that renders individuals "helpless in the face of an impending threat to his or her psychological well-being" fails to specify the duration of the emotion and, therefore, leaves this state midway between an emotion and a mood.[29] By contrast, the ancient Galenic categories of sanguine, choleric, phlegmatic, and melancholic were moods created by imbalances in body humors. This distinction is in accord with the biologists' differentiation between the brief (phasic) reaction to an event and the longer lasting (tonic) state. It is adaptive to be alerted by an unexpected sound from the basement but less adaptive to remain vigilant for days in anticipation of an uncommon sound.

It is surprising that most theorists ignore the mood that accompanies a person's awareness of their continuing obligations. One must search a long time to find an individual who does not carry the burden of some obligations to family, lover, friend, employer, or community. Cicero wrote his son, "There can be no state of life . . . that is without obligations. In the due discharge of that consists of all the dignity, and in its neglect all the disgrace of life."[30] The Greeks invented *eudaimonia* for the state experienced when a person met his or her responsibilities, but they failed to coin a term for the state that blends the feeling accompanying recognition of the obligation, the striving to satisfy it, and concern over the critical thoughts of others, or a moment of self-blame should the individual fail to honor his or her obligations effectively. One reason theorists ignore this state is that historical changes in industrialized societies have eroded its salience.

The themes in many contemporary novels, plays, and songs, compared with those a century earlier, center on loss: loss of meaning in daily life, loss of loyalty in relationships, loss of faith in authority and the absolute goodness of knowledge, and loss of the idealistic dream of attaining a perfect society. This mood is the product of half a dozen generations of geographic mobility, inexpensive contraceptives, large, bureaucratic workplaces, dense urban centers that leave residents free of the social restraints that family and friendships impose, and too many wars and massacres that, on reflection, seem senseless because they solved no problems. These changes persuaded a majority that the best life strategy was sole reliance on an autonomous self free of external constraints. But this freedom exacts a price. Most humans also want to be members of stable groups that award the pleasures of affection, assurance, and protection in return for loyalty. In less than a hundred years, historical events in Western communities turned upside-down Freud's declaration that the demands of the superego were the origins of anxiety. Too many individuals in modern societies feel anxious because they are not quite certain what their superegos are whispering. Jung may have understood aspects of the human condition that were opaque to Freud.

## The Emotions of Infants and Animals

Finally, special concepts will be required for the states of human infants and animals because neither impose symbolic interpretations on their sensory states. Newborns swaddled in a blanket are likely to cry when someone opens the blanket to expose them to the cooler temperature of the room. This cry should not be regarded as a sign of fear or anger because it is a biologically prepared reaction to the change in temperature. Moreover, genes whose products influence limbic sites are not yet active in newborns. Nor should we call a crying six-month-old who dropped her rattle *angry* because this emotion presumes knowledge of the cause of a distressed state. Charles Darwin, who kept a diary on his child, made that mistake when his seven-month-old son screamed after the lemon he was playing with slipped away. The father of evolutionary theory assumed a biological continuity between animals and infants and projected the state he felt when he lost a valuable object on to both animals and his young son.[31] Many contemporary psychologists attribute a state of fear to seven-month-olds who cry at the approach of a stranger and to forty-year-olds who notice a large amount of clotted blood in their saliva. But the states of these two agents cannot be the same because of the profound biological and psychological differences between infants and adults. The infant's distress is an automatic reaction to the inability to relate the unfamiliar features of the stranger to his or her knowledge; the adult's state follows an appraisal of the meaning of the blood for his or her health.

The infant's behavioral reactions to emotional incentives are either biologically prepared responses or acquired habits, and the responses are signs of a change in internal state that is free of appraisal. The structural immaturity of the infant brain means that the emotions that require thought, such as guilt, pride, despair, shame, and empathy, cannot be experienced in the first year because the cognitive abilities necessary for their emergence have not yet developed.

The restriction on possible emotions extends beyond infancy. Children less than a year old cannot experience empathy with another or shame, whereas all three-year-olds are capable of these states because of the emergence of the ability to infer the state of others and to be conscious of one's feelings and intentions. This extremely important developmental change, due to brain maturation, adds a qualitatively new reason for actions, especially the desire to preserve a conception of self as a good person. This motive, which has an emotional component, is a seminal basis for later behaviors that are called altruistic. Furthermore, children less than four years old find it difficult to retrieve the past and relate it to the present and, therefore, cannot experience the emotions of regret or nostalgia.[32] Even preadolescents have some difficulty manipulating several representations simultaneously in working memory because of incomplete maturation of the connectivity of the dorsolateral prefrontal cortex to other sites. This fact implies that seven- to ten-year-olds are protected from the emotions that emerge from a thoughtful examination of the logical inconsistency among their personal beliefs. Older adolescents, by contrast, are susceptible to the uncertainty that follows recognition of the inconsistency between their experiences and their childhood premises about sexuality, loyalty, God, or the heroic stature of their parents. The desire to repair the inconsistency requires some alteration in the earlier beliefs and the evocation of emotions denied to younger children. The cognitive immaturity also means that ten-year-olds are protected from arriving at the conclusion that they have explored every possible coping response to a crisis and no adaptive action is possible. As a result they cannot experience the emotion of hopelessness that can provoke a suicide attempt. Hence, we need to invent a vocabulary for the repertoire of states experienced by infants and young children. These terms do not exist.

A similar skepticism applies to the states of most animal species. I say "most," rather than "all," because some investigators believe that primates, and especially chimpanzees, are capable of some emotions that seem to resemble human experiences. Dog owners are certain that their beloved pets are capable of empathy and guilt. However, the symbolic appraisal of feelings is absent in rodents, and investigators should not use the words *fear* or *anxiety* as interpretations of their behaviors but invent special terms for the brain or psychological states of mice or rats who fail to enter a brightly lit alley, become immobile to fox odor, or display an exaggerated startle to a tone that signals electric shock. I make this suggestion not only because mice and rats do not assign symbolic interpretations to their sensory states but also because of the likelihood that the neural circuits activated in these animals when they are in these situations differ from the brain states of humans who feel afraid in crowds, in high places, when ill, or when speaking before an audience. The brain's two hemispheres are connected by a band of fibers called the corpus callosum. The size of the callosum, relative to the whole brain, is larger in monkeys and chimps than in humans. This fact means that the two hemispheres have more autonomy in humans and activation of the right hemisphere, which plays an important role in the perception of bodily feeling, is not always accompanied by equivalent activation of the left, which is more relevant for the appraisals of feelings.

The Pavlovian conditioning of body immobility or startle can occur without extensive cortical involvement; these phenomena resemble the involuntary blink a person might show when entering a crowd of strangers. However, the reluctance to speak in public because of anticipated distress requires extensive cortical activity. Furthermore, mice and rats have great difficulty learning an association between two events, say a tone and a subsequent shock, if the second event is delayed by a few seconds. Humans have no such difficulty because they always ask of an event: What caused it? Hence, humans can learn to fear an intention to steal if they came down with an illness several days after stealing some money from a friend if they decided that the illness was a punishment for the ethical violation. Some parents are capable of developing intense guilt after learning that their twenty-year-old son has a drug addiction if they conclude that the son's symptoms were caused by their sending him to a day-care center when he was an infant. These emotional consequences are simply not possible in animals. Few students of emotion comment on the remarkable ability of some individuals to dispel a bout of extreme fear or anger experienced in one setting when a different setting requires adaptive functioning. Some adolescents who feel fear of and rage toward a father who unjustly punished them are able to suppress this blend of states an hour later in the classroom. A rat who has encountered a cat for one minute will continue to display signs of fear for several days.

Vasopressin and oxytocin are two brain molecules that have profound effects on emotional states, especially on the establishment of close emotional bonds to others. But the brain locations where these molecules are active in rats and mice differ from their active locations in humans. Thus, the emotion of maternal love in humans should not be equated with the state of nursing mother rats. Some adults anticipating a painful event show a distinct brain profile that accompanies their fear that they might become anxious; this profile is different from the one seen when they actually feel the painful event.[33] Animals might be capable of the latter, but not of the former, state.

Although the brain states of animals and humans might be similar to certain provocations, the absence of appraisal in animals means that their emotions will often be qualitatively different. Consider again the molecule oxytocin. The hypothalamus produces a surge of oxytocin when rat and human mothers nurse their infants; hence the brain states of the two species share some properties. However, only the human mother appraises her feeling for her child and the importance of her care for its future. For that reason her emotional state has to differ seriously from that of the rat. Similarly, male and female prairie voles, a small rodent species, pair bond to each other for life following a half-dozen sexual couplings over a period of hours. Human couples also develop strong mutual attachments following episodes of sexual gratification. But I trust no scientist would attribute to voles the emotion we assign to human couples in love. Nor can we assume that the state of a male chimpanzee approaching a female for sex is similar to the state of a twenty-five-year-old from Helsinki who, with a dozen friends looking for excitement and a break in their daily routine, are on a ferry to Talinn in Estonia anticipating a night of sex and drinking in a brothel. Because prostitutes are available in Helsinki the change in setting and camaraderie are as important as the sexual pleasure. Thus, there are important differences between animals and humans for a function as significant as sexuality.

I confess to a feeling of surprise after reading three papers that used words naming distinctly human properties as descriptors for other organisms. One paper attributed the properties of *cooperation* and *conflict* to single-cell yeast; the second argued that chimpanzees experience *subjective well-being*; the third claimed that meerkats (a species of mongoose) *teach* young pups how to kill prey.[34]

Poets possess the license to use a predicate any way they wish, as long as an aesthetic effect is produced. Sylvia Plath can write that swans are brazen and pots can bloom, but scientists are denied this creative freedom because the meaning of a predicate for a process, action, or function always depends on the objects participating in the process. The same predicate cannot be used with qualitatively different classes of objects without altering its meaning in a serious way. The predicate "crossing over" applies to a pair of chromosomes that exchange genetic material during the phase of cell division and is not used to describe what happens when two corporations merge and exchange their assets. An essential feature of the meaning of the predicate "teach" is a conscious intention on the part of the tutor to instruct a learner about a skill to be mastered. Scientists cannot assume that the meanings of words, such as *cooperate, teach,* or *subjective well-being,* when applied to yeast or animals, remain unchanged when the seminal features of their meanings when they describe humans are missing. Would anyone describe as gay a male giraffe with an erection mounting another male?

Furthermore, the borrowing of terms is usually one-way. Students of animal behavior regularly borrow concepts invented to describe humans; students of human behavior rarely borrow words invented specifically for animals and apply them to humans. No human hibernates, swarms, or molts, even though we sleep more during the winter, come together in crowds, and shed our wool coats in summer. Students of animal behavior commit this semantic error because they usually lack a vocabulary to describe the observed animal pattern. No single word or phrase captures what the meerkats are doing with their pups. These scientists borrow the concept "teach" because they uncritically accept the Darwinian hypothesis of a close continuity between animals and humans and presume that the brain state created by an event that provokes an emotion in humans probably creates a similar state in animals. They assume, for example, that the brain profile of a rat hearing a tone that signals an electric shock is essentially the same as the brain state of a person seeing a coiled cobra about to strike in order to rationalize the use of animal models to illuminate human characteristics, especially mental illnesses.

This strategy is an example of a more general scientific habit of using the properties of a better-understood phenomenon to explain one that is less well understood when the two seem to share a few features. Renaissance scholars assumed that some plants had some of the properties of human bodies. Hence, a plant that happened to have the shape of a heart was presumed to be therapeutic for patients with cardiac problems.[35] Later generations nominated the clock, the steam engine, and more recently the gene as models for human functioning. Each metaphor evokes a different image. The clock implies a linear connectivity among fixed mechanical components and turns the mind away from the whole and its dynamic changes. The steam engine invites the idea of a continuum of energy exploited for different purposes. The gene returns the mind to material entities but has the advantage, denied to clocks and steam engines, of acknowledging a ballet with environmental events. I suspect that the Internet will eventually replace the gene, and information will become an important metric. But information assumes that receivers have different properties and a communication does not have the same meaning for all recipients. This metaphor is more appropriate for emotions because it requires accommodation to the fact that no uniform feeling or appraisal follows a particular event.

The influence of Darwin's ideas cannot be overestimated because it permits confidence in the belief that principles derived from research with animals will usually inform the human condition. A mouse that becomes immobile at the sight of a cat or fails to explore a brightly lit alley seems to share features with a social phobic who is reluctant to attend a party of strangers; hence, it seems reasonable to attribute anxiety to both forms. But an apparent similarity in behavior between two distant species, which is easy to infer, can be based on very different mechanisms.[36] The brain and psychological states that provoke female monkeys to mate with a half-dozen males over the course of a day are very different from those of women who engage in exactly the same behavior. Put plainly, behaviors that appear to share similar elements can be the product of different brain states. Humans differ from chimpanzees in a number of biological features, including an upright posture, long, thin leg bones, opposable thumb and index finger, absence of fur, number of sweat glands, a closed vagina that is tipped forward, and several brain properties, including a disproportionate increase in myelinated fibers from the frontal lobe to other parts of the brain that permit more effective modulation of impulsive behaviors or intense emotions. And the differences between apes and humans in the ability to retrieve the distant past, anticipate the far future, infer the thoughts of others as well as similarities in relations between objects, compare self's properties with those of others on a good-bad dimension, and categorize and communicate with a symbolic language are well documented. Humans rely on two comparisons when they evaluate their personal characteristics. They compare their features and resources with the small number of others with whom they interact regularly but also with their understanding of the features and material advantages possessed by the much larger group in their society. Thus, a middle-class adolescent in a high-achieving school that sends all its graduates to good colleges who knows he is only in the seventieth percentile in academic accomplishment in his school is also aware of the fact that he would be in the ninety-fifth percentile with respect to all youths in his large city. This second evaluation allows him to control his uncertainty. Chimpanzees are capable of only the first comparison. Hence, there is ample justification for questioning the belief that the psychological states of animals and humans encountering the same incentive are sufficiently similar to warrant strong conclusions about human emotions from the study of animals.

Jeffrey Gray and Neil McNaughton mounted an ambitious argument claiming that the balance between approaching or avoiding events or settings that do not match a rodent's past experience or expectations is a useful model for understanding human anxiety.[37] Their seminal premise was that an animal's reluctance to approach less familiar settings reflects activity in a brain circuit that is the biological foundation of anxiety. This bold position has three problems. The most serious is the assumption that human anxiety is automatically evoked by activation of a specific brain circuit rather than the product of a symbolic interpretation of a detected change in feeling. Second, many persons who report intense anxiety do not appear to be in conflict over approaching a person or a situation. Patients who have panic attacks are anxious over the possibility of having a heart attack or "going crazy." Patients diagnosed with generalized anxiety disorder report that the source of their distress is the inability to predict the future, not a conflict between approaching or avoiding a person or setting. I suggest that two frequent human emotions are a state of uncertainty over what event might occur in the future and uncertainty over what behavior to display when choice is possible. These are not frequent states in rats.

A final problem is that the empirical support for this theory comes from the effects on animal behavior, and on the brain circuits controlling approach or avoidance, of drugs that reduce reports of anxiety in patients. However, these brain circuits, which are the immediate cause of the animal's behavior in a novel situation, might not represent the more fundamental origins of the varied forms of human anxiety. For example, compromised function of the prefrontal cortex, which modulates the amygdala, can be accompanied by increased feelings of anxiety in humans. But this circuitry is not the one Gray and McNaughton nominated as the foundation of anxiety. Most laxatives work by increasing the motility of the muscles of the large intestine, but the basic causes of constipation are a diet low in fiber and a sedentary lifestyle.

Some emotions are unique to humans. There is no experimental manipulation with mice, rats, or chimpanzees that could simulate the emotional consequences of being insulted because of membership in an economically disadvantaged ethnic minority, learning that one is the valedictorian of a high school graduating class, expecting a malevolent wish or act by another because one has a resource the other wants, or being the victim of incest. The Roman statesman Seneca should be nodding in assent, for he insisted that only humans could judge whether an action by another was deliberate and therefore people, but not, animals, were capable of anger.[38] Although there are a great many significant biological continuities across animal species, especially within sensory and motor competences, there are also a few important discontinuities. For example, only in human embryos is there a migration of neurons from the anterior part of the developing brain to an area that will become part of the thalamus. Because the thalamus is the primary way station for most sensory information before it reaches the cortex, and an indispensable component of consciousness, this unique anatomical arrangement implies an intimate connection in humans between sensations and the evaluative functions of the frontal lobe.

Many human emotional states are discontinuous with the states experienced by animals because the appraisal process, which often involves inferences about the meaning of an event and the thoughts and feelings of others, is integral to these emotions and is not simply an epiphenomenon. That is why the likelihood of developing the symptoms of post-traumatic stress disorder following a catastrophic event, such as a cyclone or an automobile accident, is primarily a function of the person's later appraisal of the cause and consequence of the event rather than a conditioned reaction to the features of the threatening experience as it was happening. Adolescents who blame their carelessness for a car accident or interpret the loss of their home during a cyclone as meaning that life is unpredictable are most vulnerable to the disorder. Appraisal processes are also needed to explain the satisfactory psychological adjustment of all but one person who had spent their first three to eleven years in a Nazi concentration camp before being flown to England as the Second World War ended. Sarah Moskovitz, who interviewed twenty-four of these middle-aged adults, concluded that most were happy, productive, and free of excessive anxiety, anger, or depression, despite harsh deprivation during their early years. "In spite of the anxiety and fear, and the tortuous detours often used to deflect them, a most striking quality about this diverse group of people is their affirmation of life."[39] There is no animal model that could simulate this phenomenon because it requires an evaluative comparison of one's childhood years with the present moment. The interpretation of an event or a feeling, which often involves a comparison of past with present and of one's current state with the presumed states of others, creates a special class of phenomena that is absent in all other animals. The possible sounds that varied musical instruments can produce might be a useful metaphor to capture the different capacities for emotions across animal species. Pianos can generate many more patterns than kettledrums.

The assumption that many animal and human emotions are similar is related to the dogmatic insistence by evolutionary biologists that the urge to maximize one's reproductive fitness is the only important factor regulating the preservation of a biological or behavioral property over long periods. The behaviorists made a similar error when they declared that no animal would exert the energy required for an action unless there was a material reward for the response. As a result, they were puzzled by the observation that animals and humans regularly acted in order to produce a slight change in stimulation. Monkeys in a closed space, for example, press a lever just to get a brief peek at the outside world.

Evolutionists are puzzled by the fact that humans expend energy when they aid or cooperate with strangers who do not share the genomes of their family pedigree. Display of these behaviors is presumably inconsistent with the premise that no person should do anything that is psychologically costly if it does not contribute to their inclusive fitness. Since many people do regularly engage in such acts, biologists have tried to construct formal arguments that will explain why reciprocal altruism and cooperation do aid fitness. But these arguments ignore the fact that the evolution of the human brain was accompanied by the ability to infer the private state of another, self-awareness, symbolic representations, the habit of categorizing self as good or bad, the capacity for shame and guilt, and the tendency to impose greater symbolic value on goals that require great effort to obtain, such as a university education, a celebrated cello recital, or a position on an Olympic sports team. Freud relied on this principle when he defended the practice of patients paying therapists for their treatment. Economists often fail to appreciate that the psychological benefit to be gained from attaining some goals is enhanced, not reduced or balanced, by the cost involved in their attainment.

Altruistic or cooperative acts that help unrelated strangers can be the product of several quite different conditions. In some cases the agent also benefits (a child joins another on a seesaw). In other instances the behavior serves a psychological motive to adhere to an ethical standard in order to regard self as good and to provide protection against guilt and shame (a child helps with the dinner dishes). And on some occasions these acts are biologically prepared reactions to the inference that another needs help (a child opens the door for a person who is holding many packages). These behaviors are traceable not to genes for altruism or cooperation but to the many genes that made inference, empathy, self-awareness, symbolism, the categories good and bad, and the moral emotions possible. Altrusim and cooperation were inevitable by-products of these human properties that do contribute to fitness. Altruistic behaviors emerged as derivatives of these more fundamental characteristics, as the shape of the human chin was a necessary by-product of adaptive changes in the bones and teeth of the human facial skeleton. Evolutionary biologists focus only on the apparently altruistic behaviors because they are more easily measured than the private state of virtue that is the fundamental reason for the acts. Many nineteenth-century scientists, including the brilliant Ernst Mach, resisted the concept of the atom because they could not see it.

Furthermore, historical changes altered the salience of the first two reasons for cooperation, especially in European societies after the Renaissance, by rewarding the successful efforts of the individual rather than the groups to which the individual belonged. Hunter-gatherers had to be cooperative to survive. Modern societies created specialized roles (professional armies, police, agricultural conglomerates, doctors, and public health experts) to deal with potential threats to health and survival. Finally, I suspect that, on many occasions, altruistic behaviors do not contribute to an agent's fitness, even though the potential for this behavioral category has been preserved. An unselfish act of charity can generate anger if the recipient cannot reciprocate the kindness or feels denigrated by its receipt. The Spanish director Luis Buñuel captured this dynamic in the film *Viridiana* (1961). The movie describes the growing resentment of a group of beggars toward a nun who treated them charitably and whom they attack violently in the last scene. It is likely that depression, insomnia, fainting, addiction to alcohol and tobacco, incestuous relations, and premature births have been preserved as human properties for as long a time as cooperation and altruism, but it is tortuous to argue that these properties aid fitness. Seeking food, water, and sex, as proximate motives, and enhancing the health, fecundity, and welfare of self and self's genetic relatives, as ultimate urges, are not the only bases for human behavior. Inclusive fitness is not the only factor determining the preservation of a human trait over many generations, and not all traits that are preserved contribute to fitness. These latter two claims are heretical only to orthodox Darwinians who do not like multiple causes for a phenomenon; they seem perfectly reasonable to the average citizen and a good many writers and social scientists.

## The Relevant Relations

The broad domain of human emotion consists of four sets of loosely connected, underdetermined relations among: (1) incentive events and changes in brain state, (2) changes in brain state and feelings, with or without an involuntary motor response, (3) detected feelings and the symbolic interpretations imposed on them, and (4) interpreted feelings and behaviors. A persuasive example of the effect of a brain state on an involuntary motor reaction is the influence of a status differential between an agent and another person on the acoustic qualities of the voice. Two scientists performed spectral analyses of speech samples recorded during twenty-five interviews that Larry King, a television talk-show host, conducted with different guests. When individuals of differing status interact, the person of relatively lower status begins to match the acoustic profile of his or her voice (especially for lower frequencies) to the profile characteristic of the person with higher status. When Larry King was talking with guests of high status (such as former presidents George Bush and Bill Clinton) he began to match his voice to that of his guests. But when King was interacting with individuals who had somewhat less eminence (for example, Dan Quayle and Robert Strauss), the guests began to match their voices to his profile.[40] It is unlikely that King was aware of the subtle variation in his voice as he spoke with different guests, and he might not have been aware of experiencing different emotional states during the two types of interviews. Although the second claim is harder to defend than the first, if King did experience different emotions with high- and lower-status guests the terms we might use to describe these states are absent from most lists of emotional concepts.

A sibling or spouse who feels less talented or less virtuous than his or her counterpart frequently displays behaviors that are the result of brain states that do not pierce consciousness and feelings that are ignored or misinterpreted. Some theorists might call their state unconscious "jealousy." However, it would be better to invent a new term for their psychological state. The permissive practice of applying the same emotional term (for example, *anxiety*) to feelings (the sensation of a racing heart or tense muscles before entering a crowd of strangers), semantic descriptions (a report of worry over meeting strangers), behaviors (tense facial expression in a social situation), brain states (activation of the amygdala to angry faces), or a chronic mood of worry (general anxiety disorder) is retarding progress.

We should not begin our inquiries into emotions with popular words that come packaged with the stamp of authority and should restrain the temptation to legislate the meaning of *emotion*. Word meanings are always subject to historical change. Both Virginia Woolf and Ludwig Wittgenstein, echoing Francis Bacon, understood that words are free agents that can assume different meanings across time and language communities because the meaning of a word is whatever the community decides it is.[41] No meaning lasts forever. Samuel Beckett phrased the mischievous quality of words more poetically when he urged readers and listeners "to bore one hole after another" into every statement "until what lurks behind it—be it something or nothing—begins to seep through." Hence, it should be useful to set aside disagreements over the one correct definition of *emotion*, as philosophers now do for truth, and return to the phenomena that most scientists agree are critical constituents of the generic domain called "emotional." This open frame of mind allows brain states, detected feelings, appraisals, and behaviors to be called "emotions," as long as the signatories to this truce acknowledge that the meaning of this concept is not the same across these four sources of evidence. How a scientist decides that a person is happy is part of the meaning of the declaration that she or he is happy.

## The Importance of Detected Feelings

Although the origin of every emotion is a change in brain state, the brain is continually changing from moment to moment. Hence, an additional property must be added to distinguish emotional states from the majority that accompany the hours of each day. The critical extra feature is the conscious detection of a change in feeling. A changed feeling is the primary reason for inventing the concept emotion, and every known language contains a term for "feeling."[42]

I like Lawrence Weiskrantz's uncomplicated definition of conscious awareness as the "ability to make a commentary." Michel de Montaigne wrote, almost four hundred years ago, "I judge myself only by actual sensations, not by reasoning." Damasio agrees, for he, too, declares that consciousness begins as a feeling. The etymological origins of many emotional terms in Sanskrit, Greek, Latin, and the Germanic languages were originally names for parts of the body whose actions were associated with a feeling.[43] For example, *greed* was derived from the word for grasping, *fear* from trembling, *anger* from grinding of teeth, and *distress* from prolonged hours of manual labor.

Individuals who direct their attention to a perceived change in feeling can ignore it or appraise its meaning. If they choose to appraise it and are motivated to name the experience, the words selected will be influenced by the immediate context, ongoing actions or thoughts, and the folk theory and language of the culture. Americans and Europeans are biased to interpret a rise in heart rate and facial warmth as signifying anxiety but are less likely to do so for heartburn, back pain, headache, dizziness, or tingling sensations. Members of other cultures might impose different interpretations on these bodily feelings. There is even variation in the appraisal of painful sensations, for pain is a "perceptual experience whose quality and intensity are influenced by the unique past history of the individual, by the meaning he gives to the pain-producing situation, and by his state of mind at the moment." That is why there is considerable variation among individuals in their tolerance for pain and discomfort. The level of neuronal activity in two brain sites activated by pain (the medial prefrontal cortex and anterior cingulate) in adults anticipating electric shock was less when they were engaged in a difficult, compared with an easy, cognitive task. College students reported more, not less, intense pain when their hand was immersed in ice-cold water if they were exposed, simultaneously, to either a pleasant or an unpleasant odor. Hispanic adults with serious health problems (for example, diabetes, or cardiac, stomach, or kidney disease) reported more frequent and intense pain than non-Hispanic Caucasians plagued with the same problems. One reason is that complaints of pain in Hispanic communities usually bring a great deal of sympathy from family and friends. Thus, the feeling of pain is not a simple sensation but one that is modulated by many psychological conditions.[44]

The evidence also indicates that the meaning and, therefore, the psychological significance, of a detected feeling can vary with the local setting. The profile of neuronal activity in the anterior cingulate to the pain produced by intense heat varied as a function of whether the individual or the experimenter administered the heated probe. Even the frequency and salience of frightening dreams are affected by the setting; a person's dream content contained more fearful images when sleep occurred at home than when it occurred in a laboratory. Women who were unaware of being exposed to a male pheromone reported a change in feeling only when tested by a man rather than a woman. The increase in sexual arousal reported by women presented with the olfactory components of a breast pad from a lactating mother was greater if the women were about to ovulate than if they were menstruating. Girls between five and twelve years of age displayed smiles to unpleasant odors only if they were with others and did not do so when alone. Infants are more likely to become distressed if their mother leaves them alone in an unfamiliar laboratory room than if she exits from the familiar living room.[45] The emotions of "outsiders" whose beliefs or physical features prevent them from feeling part of the majority culture with power and privilege are always dependent on the historical context. Christians were outsiders in the first century CE in Rome; Jews were outsiders centuries later; scientists, like Galileo, who probed nature were outsiders in the fifteenth century but are insiders today.

The importance of the context for the emotion eventually realized has an obvious parallel in the effect of the setting on the symbolic significance attributed to an object. The network of representations evoked by a butcher knife lying on a counter is different from the network provoked by seeing the same object in the hand of a one-year-old or in the clenched fist of a man with a raised arm and a sneer on his face. The meaning of a photograph of a face with an angry expression appearing on a monitor in a laboratory is not the meaning evoked when someone sees the same face attached to a body on a city street. The profile of brain activity in women who see a man's angry face on a screen differs from the profile produced by a woman's face with the same expression because male and female facial poses of anger provoke different associations.[46]

The context is always an essential component of every event, a principle ignored by many scientists who present faces and scenes on monitors to individuals lying supine in a magnetic scanner. The element in the foreground, without specification of its background context, should never be treated as the origin of an emotional experience that would occur across varied settings. The significance of the context is analogous to the importance of the reference frame in determining the simultaneity of two events, as Einstein realized in 1905.

Feelings refer to detected sensory changes that originate in spontaneous brain processes or activity in the cardiovascular system, gut, muscles, genitals, and vestibular apparatus that is transmitted to the brain. One of every three randomly selected Japanese adults reported frequent feelings of a stiff neck or shoulder, backache, or fatigue.[47] Homer frequently mentioned a detected change in heart rate as a regular accompaniment to the fear and anger Odysseus experienced during his long heroic voyage.

I exclude no feeling from consideration; increased muscle tension, energy level, heart rate, stomach motility, sweaty palms, tingling sensations, headache, numbness, dry mouth, skin temperature, breathing difficulty, dizziness, satiety, genital tumescence, and orgasm are all legitimate members of this category. Carolyn Saarni and colleagues make cognitive appraisal a component of their definition of a feeling.[48] I emphasize its sensory qualities, which, like the redness of an apple, can be accompanied by, but do not require, appraisal. Both definitions are defensible, given the immature state of theory and evidence.

However, the sensations that contribute to a detected feeling—cold fingers on a winter evening—are not automatically appraised as pleasant or unpleasant. That decision requires an additional judgment. Jean-Jacques Rousseau describes a childhood experience in *The Confessions* (1781), in which the sensation of pain following a harsh spanking from the attractive woman caring for him created a feeling that he judged as sexually pleasant.[49] Hence, he had to control an urge to disobey in order to reexperience the pleasant feeling the punishment created. If I were to stop writing this paragraph and attend to the increased muscle tension in my posture as I sit bent over my computer in a quiet room at home, I might choose words like "aroused" or "engaged" to describe my feeling. But I would select the same words if I attended to my feelings while playing tennis or having a heated discussion with a friend over a controversial book. Hence, it is necessary to specify the context in which a semantic interpretation is applied in order to differentiate the arousal felt while writing from the arousal of a lively discussion or a close tennis match. The interpretation of a feeling is like the mutually exclusive perceptions of either a young or an old woman in the ambiguous figure often illustrated in psychology texts.[50]

Most of the sensations that originate in the environment—sights, sounds, and touches—usually do not provoke feelings if they are not intense. But sensations originating in the body do so more often. The brain honors this distinction, for activities originating within the body are processed initially by a neuronal cluster in the medulla before being sent to the thalamus and cortex, whereas sights, sounds, and tactile sensations are initially processed by the thalamus. The visceral pain accompanying a distended rectum is mediated by a circuit different from the one that mediates the sensation of a painful stimulus applied to the skin, and the former is more salient.[51] Smells have a special status, even though they originate in the environment, because they can activate the cortex without requiring prior processing by the thalamus. The emotional power of perfume is not accidental.

Each person when awake is always in some feeling state. But because the state is the usual or expected one in the context in which the agent is acting, it fails to recruit attention and escapes appraisal. A feeling that is unexpected or unfamiliar, however, attracts attention and, if interpreted, generates an emotion. I shall deal later with the differences between the subjective state of an agent and the hypothetical state investigators infer from measurements.

The quality of a feeling, like the perception of an object, is influenced by a small number of features. Contour, motion, curvature, continuity of line, closure, and symmetry are among the important determinants of the perceptual representation of, or schema for, visual events. For example, a circular form and the black-white contour contrast between the dark pupil and the white sclera of the eyes are the most critical features of faces that activate neurons in specific areas of the monkey brain.[52] The critical features of a feeling include intensity, duration, familiarity, expectedness, punctateness, apparent location in the body, and a sixth, subtle property called "quality" that is difficult to define because of the lack of appropriate words. Informants from five cultures reported the body sensations (from a list of twelve) most likely to occur to the names of seven emotional states. Although there were cultural differences, the similarities across societies were more impressive. The informants agreed that anger and fear were accompanied by an increased heart rate and changes in breathing, disgust by stomach sensations, and shame by the facial warmth that accompanies blushing. James Russell and Lisa Barrett call detected feelings *core affects* and contrast this concept with *prototypical emotional episodes*, which combine a core affect with actions and a target in a specific context.[53] To my surprise, however, they suggest that the same word can name a core affect and a prototypical emotional episode. This is not a wise decision because the referents for the two concepts are not at all similar.

Individuals can vary in the frequency and salience of particular feelings because of temperamental biases that originate in the excitability of limbic sites, muscles, and peripheral targets of the autonomic nervous system. These biases are biologically prepared susceptibilities for particular feelings. A small proportion of adults, for example, occasionally feel that they are floating. Individuals with a labile cardiovascular system, who are susceptible to a racing heart, are better able to detect their heartbeats and as a result report more intense levels of anxiety. Those with greater parasympathetic tone, who have lower heart rates and blood pressures, are vulnerable to feeling faint or dizzy.[54]

Because the sensory foundations of a change in feeling are more fully elaborated in the right hemisphere, and the left hemisphere normally modulates the right, individuals possessing a more active right hemisphere might be susceptible to more frequent or more salient changes in feeling. The right hemisphere is more responsive to the features of an event that have a relatively lower frequency (for example, the changing loudness and rhythm of a voice), whereas the left hemisphere is more responsive to elements with a relatively higher frequency (for example, rapid but brief changes in facial muscles or the ratio of the amount of white sclera to dark pupil).[55] Hence, individuals with a more dominant right hemisphere might be more sensitive to the emotional implications contained in a speaker's voice than to changes in facial muscles or eyes.

History, culture, and, therefore, personal ideology also influence the prevalence of certain feelings as well as the interpretations imposed on them. American women born after the Second World War regarded the feelings that give rise to anger toward a spouse as more acceptable than nineteenth-century wives. Members of Chinese and Indian societies have traditionally celebrated a state of low arousal or calmness, whereas Europeans and Americans placed greater value on states of excitement. Some individuals regard a feeling of low energy as a sign of fatigue; others interpret the same feeling as meaning the absence of pleasure in their lives.[56]

Consider the conditions existing among residents of northern Europe during the Middle Ages when many lived on agricultural estates with no central heating and no effective treatment for infectious diseases, worked and slept with large numbers of genetically unrelated peasants, and had an expected life span less than forty years. I suggest that feeling cold in winter, fatigue at the end of each workday, the bodily distresses of illness, and a loss of appetite and energy following the premature death of a child or spouse were frequent incentives for emotions. By contrast, the most common feelings for contemporary residents of this region, who are likely to have a heated residence, access to medical care, and a sedentary occupation, are varied qualities of tension provoked by thinking about possible task failure (academic or vocational), friends and neighbors who have more material resources, and the ethical values that deserve a loyal commitment. Further, contemporary Europeans as well as Americans regard their status as more malleable than did medieval peasants. As a result, anger over a failure to rise in rank is more salient among today's citizens than anxiety over losing self's position in the group, especially among those in the bottom half of the social hierarchy who believe that their disadvantaged position is not their fault. Finally, although few contemporary adults traveling to conduct a commercial agreement worry about being robbed, most medieval European merchants on their way to a client feared an attack during each day of their journey.

Most cultures have a semantic concept whose meaning resembles that of the English term *love* because humans are biologically prepared to impose the evaluation "ideal" on select people, activities, or ideas and strive to posses these targets in order to feel a special quality of pleasure, however momentary, that is not strictly sensual. That is why the sensory pleasure a person or activity provides is distinguished from a feeling of love for those targets. However, the quality of the emotion of love varies with the feelings evoked by different targets. If the feelings were sexual the Greeks called the emotion felt toward the target *eros*. If they accompanied the knowledge that another valued self and the feeling was reciprocated, the emotion felt toward the other was called *philia*. If acceptance of the ethical norms of the society permitted a feeling of enhanced virtue, the emotion felt toward these values was called *nomos*. And if the feeling originated in the belief that a divine force had a benevolent feeling toward self, the emotion was *agape*. These four emotions share two critical features: the symbolic notion of an idealized state and the unique pleasure created by an experience that matched the ideal. It is obvious, therefore, that the varied states of love are deeply symbolic. Voles who pair bond after several matings are not in love. Humans do not "love" every partner with whom an orgasm was experienced, every sweet-tasting chocolate mousse, or every warm bedroom on cold evenings because the target must share some features with the lover's conception of the ideal. That is why, as one writer noted, the lover takes more pleasure from an intimate relationship than the beloved.

The emotion experienced by those who believe they are "loved" by another, the beloved, probably varies with time and across cultures because the knowledge that self is valued serves different psychological functions.

As long as hunger, thirst, and protection from the elements and physical attack are not salient concerns, a condition denied to a great many contemporary populations, uncertainty over self's virtue is a dominant preoccupation. Each person wishes to believe that their collection of talents, beliefs, intentions, and appearances belongs to the sprawling symbolic category "good." A section on semantic labels in Chapter 3 notes that the contrast between good and bad is the cardinal axis around which all emotional words revolve. Individuals who believe in the validity of some ethical premises governing proper behaviors and intentions can reduce moments of uncertainty over their virtue by displaying one of the required actions or rehearsing an approved intention. A husband who accepts, as a moral imperative, the responsibility of providing for his family is permitted some degree of satisfaction. A woman who is certain that bearing and nurturing a child is an ethical requirement experiences an equally pleasant feeling. That is why Søren Kierkegaard wrote that loyalty to one's obligations is an absolute requirement for psychological health.

There are intervals in history, however, when large numbers of individuals lose their faith in the absolute validity of any ethical proposition. This state of affairs may have occurred in Rome during the final century of the empire before it fell to invaders. It is present today in a fair proportion of Americans and Europeans. Contemporary novels, plays, films, and even cartoons affirm this claim. These skeptics are not able to mute uncertainty over their virtue by adhering to an ethical demand because they do not believe in the inherent or absolute goodness of the demand or the action it requires. Hence, an important source of assurance for these individuals is the belief that they are valued by some other person. Being loved is a more critical requirement for this group than for those who believe in the validity of their obligations. Of course, the latter group extract joy from knowing that their parent, spouse, or partner loves them, but they assume that every parent, spouse, and partner should be loving. Hence, the sense of desperation felt by the skeptics is muted in the emotional patina of those who hold unquestioned ethical imperatives. The sating of hunger following starvation for three days is unlike the state that occurs each day after eating lunch.

The intensity of fear to imminent harm is also modulated by loyalty to an ethical premise. Youth or adults regularly exposed to violence (for example, residents of Israel or the West Bank) varied in the intensity of the feelings they interpreted as fear as a function of their ideological commitment to Israeli or Palestinian causes or their religiosity. Even victims of repeated torture held in Turkish prisons reported feeling less distress if political activity, in the service of an ethical ideal, was the reason for their imprisonment rather than a crime.[57] The availability of a symbolic rationale for states of distress can mute the intensity of fear or anxiety that accompanies the threat of physical harm.

## The Significance of Thought

A change in feeling can follow a thought, an external event, or a spontaneous activity in brain sites or in bodily targets projecting to the brain. Although most scientists emphasize the potency of the latter two incentives, one of Carl Jung's recollections illustrates the power of thought to provoke a salient feeling and intense emotion. On returning from school on an unusually lovely day, Jung recalls being overwhelmed by the aesthetic pattern of light and shadow on a church roof. As he reflected on the beauty of the scene and its source in God's actions, he experienced a sudden numbness and an urge to cease all mental activity: "Don't go on thinking now! Something terrible is coming. Something I do not want to think, something I dare not approach." Jung recalls feeling afraid that he was about to have a sinful thought that would offend God. It may not be a coincidence that Jung was a Protestant for, among religious American college students, Protestants are far more likely than Jews to believe that a bad thought is as immoral as a bad action.[58]

The state of those in an inferior social position in society depends on their private explanation of their disadvantaged role. Shame is likely if individuals believe they had no control over their plight; guilt is more likely if they believe that their decisions and actions were the cause of their status; anger is likely if they conclude that their status was the result of hostile or unjust actions by others. Similar variation occurs among some victims of rape who develop health complaints years after their attack. Some upper-middle-class adolescents feel guilty over the privileged lives they enjoy, but did not earn, when they think about the states of many in economically less developed nations. Victims of a crime are more likely to develop symptoms of post-traumatic stress disorder if they blame themselves and ruminate on their feelings of shame for allowing themselves to be victimized. Men who attribute their weak erectile response to an erotic film to the poor quality of the movie are less likely to worry about their sexual potency than those who decide that their genital reaction implies a compromise in personal adequacy.[59]

The emotion experienced by ancient Greek youth who permitted their older tutors to embrace them sexually depended on whether the adolescents believed they were erotically aroused or not. If not, their state of philia probably resembled that of adolescents who spent their savings to purchase an expensive gift for a parent celebrating a birthday. However, the same youth felt shame if they interpreted the feelings provoked by the tutor's embrace as the emotion of eros, even though the observed behavior and the context were identical. Medieval Christian theologians held a similar belief. They approved sexual relations between a husband and wife if sexual desire was absent but classified coitus as a sin if carnal lust were present. Many ordinary citizens of that era, however, held the opposite premise. An illicit or adulterous sexual act was less likely to evoke guilt if it was accompanied by strong sexual passion. A thirteenth-century woman living in a small French village said of her sexual affair with a priest: "In those days it pleased me and it pleased the priest, that he should know me carnally and be known by me; and so I did not think I was sinning and neither did he. But now, with him it does not please me any more. And so now, if he knew me carnally, I should think it is a sin."[60] When inexpensive contraceptives became available toward the end of the nineteenth century, American religious leaders began to celebrate the passion of sexual gratification between married partners. Removal of some of the fear of pregnancy permitted sexual desires easier access to consciousness. Jung understood the significance of this historical change and, in a letter to Freud, suggested that this was one reason for the intense conflict over sexuality in nineteenth-century Europe. Freud rejected this idea.

The depressed state of older adults with a chronic medical condition is distinguished from the depression of psychiatric patients by the more frequent intrusions of thoughts of self-blame in the latter group. American college students who reported a brief period of depression were likely to have experienced an awkward social interaction or a feeling of "neediness" the previous day. These experiences were inconsistent with the standards they held for their ego-ideal. When adults recalled past experiences that exemplified each of ten emotional concepts, the thoughts, not the causal conditions, accompanying the events best distinguished among the emotions. That is why patients with depression, chronic pain, or Parkinson's disease who receive a placebo but believe that the pill or injection will alleviate their distress not only report feeling better but also show patterns of brain activation that resemble those observed when they receive a clinically effective therapeutic drug.[61]

The emotions provoked by events occurring to those with whom the agent is identified, called vicarious affect, provide persuasive proof of the potency of thought to evoke feeling and emotion. Individuals who regard themselves as sharing psychologically significant features with another are susceptible to an emotion when the other experiences some desirable or undesirable event, or possesses a praiseworthy or unappealing feature. This phenomenon, called identification, is most likely when self and others share a genetic pedigree or membership in the same ethnic, religious, or national category. A vicarious emotion is more salient if the shared category is distinctive in some way; therefore, being a member of a group that is a minority in the community is always distinctive. American adolescent girls who took a pledge to remain virgins until marriage were most likely to honor their vow if it awarded them distinctiveness and less likely if a majority of girls in their community also took the pledge. Classic examples of vicarious emotion include the pride felt when the other is celebrated or the shame experienced when the other violates a community norm. Many contemporary, middle-class American parents who decided to have only one child invest an inordinate amount of effort and material resources in their daughter or son and experience vicarious pride in the child's accomplishments. Some adolescents recognize that this source of parental pleasure depends, in part, on their achievements. This dynamic can lead to an infantilization of the adolescent who, reluctant to lose the parental affection and the sense of importance it brings, is anxious over separating from the family. Of course, parents of prior generations enjoyed their children's victories, but these families often had many children, and therefore, no single one felt the burden experienced by the only child.

Vicarious pride, shame, and anger, which can last a lifetime, originate in the agent's acquired representations, even though the emotion can occur without much reflective thought. Obviously, neither infants nor animals can exploit this basis for emotion.

A change in feeling, following the brain's reaction to an event, represents an early stage in a cascade of events. The appraisal of the feeling, the semantic label applied, and any motor response, which occur later, can alter it. The brain circuits that make a major contribution to the generation of feelings differ from those that modulate and integrate them.[62] Still other circuits are activated when semantic labeling or a behavioral reaction occurs. This state of affairs does not mean that undetected brain activity, semantic labeling, and motor responses are unimportant, only that the detected change in feeling requires a special vocabulary and strategy of inquiry.

## A Summary Statement

Although all four components of the concept emotion are influenced by origins, contexts, and the agent's personal characteristics, changes in feeling, characterized by variation in perceptual salience, quality, bodily location, expectedness, and familiarity, deserve special attention and are not always knowable from the underlying brain state. Although neuronal clusters respond to some of these properties in incentives, they are not the defining attributes of neurons, circuits, or profiles of brain activity. Molecular biology supplies a possible analogy. The strings of nucleotides transmitted together, called haplotypes and often consisting of several hundred genes, are analogous to the very large number of brain states that could follow an emotional incentive. The much smaller number of amino acids (there are only twenty), derived from combinations of nucleotides, is analogous to the limited number of conscious feelings. The much larger number of proteins (more than a hundred thousand), constructed from the amino acids, is analogous to the very large number of possible emotional states that can follow a detected feeling. Finally, the functions of the many different tissues, constructed from proteins, are analogous to the varied decisions and acts that agents living in different cultures and historical eras implement when they are in an emotional state. At each transition in the cascade, from brain profile to feeling to appraisal to action, there is a loss of determinism and the possibility of more than one outcome. That is why the string of DNA that, if transcribed, would become the neurotransmitter serotonin is not called serotonin. Remember, the same string of DNA does not yield serotonin in every part of the body. For the same reason, a brain state should not be given an emotional name because it is not possible to predict the feelings, thoughts, or actions that will follow a brain profile created by an emotional incentive.

TWO

# Classifying Human Emotions

The conditions able to provoke a feeling that invites an appraisal are too numerous to list. The most frequent incentives are the anticipation or realization of physical harm, blocking of a goal-directed action, coercive command, or threat to a cherished belief; the loss of property, relationship, or status; lack of food, water, or warmth; violation of a moral standard by self or another; witnessing distress in another; learning that a desirable or undesirable experience has occurred to a target of identification; investing sustained effort in order to obtain a goal; attaining a goal after sustained effort; and, of course, sweet tastes, soft touches, a warm fire on a cold night, sexual satisfaction, exercise, and physical affection. And this list is not exhaustive. Faced with such a long, diverse set of possible bases for emotions, scientists searched for ways to eliminate or to group some of them to create a small, more manageable number of categories. Philosophers writing on morality adopt the same strategy.[1]

The ways we think about emotions depend on the criteria used to classify them. In this chapter I discuss six of seven possible criteria: origin, biological profile, expectancy and familiarity of the incentive or feeling, consequences, pleasant or unpleasant quality (called valence), and salience (or intensity). The seventh, the semantic label applied to the appraised feeling, is the theme of Chapter 3. It is not a coincidence that the same features are used to classify stressful events.[2] Most ancient classifications relied on the valence and perceptual salience of the emotion; modern scholars rely more often on profiles of brain activity and behavioral consequences. Far fewer theorists regard the origin or the expectedness of the incentive or detected feeling as worthy of special consideration.

## Origin

I begin with the source of, or incentive for, a feeling because the history of the biological sciences contains an instructive lesson. As understanding of a phenomenon became deeper, including its origin as part of the description became more probable. Species classifications that had been based in the past on similarities in anatomy now include the genetic features of ancestor groups. Diseases that had been categorized on the basis of symptoms added their origins once the causes had been determined. The inability to walk caused by infection with the polio virus is now distinguished from other different reasons for the same handicap. Contemporary physicians rely on at least six distinct origins to classify most diseases: infections, cancers, cardiovascular, endocrine, and immune disorders, and toxicities. A headache caused by high blood pressure is distinguished from the same symptom when it is the result of a viral infection. Biologists do not like positing disease spectra, such as a stomach pain spectrum. Psychologists and psychiatrists, however, are attracted to the idea of a continuum of symptom severity, such as the autistic spectrum, which ignores the many distinct causal conditions and attends only to the symptoms and their consequences.

The meanings of most words for objects, people, and actions are contained in the representations of the distinctive features of the things being named. The meaning of "apple," for example, is contained primarily in the representations of its shape, color, texture, and taste and only secondarily by knowledge of its origin on a tree. However, a person's understanding of an emotional word does require a representation of the cause of the feeling that is the foundation of the emotion. A rise in heart rate and muscle tension cannot be the meaning of anger or fear because too many different incentives can cause these reactions. One must add the reason for, or cause of, the bodily feelings, especially the distinctions among an external event (which includes an act by another person), a conscious thought, an action, or a bodily activity. Furthermore, among the feelings that follow violation of a community norm or private standard, we should specify whether the act was involuntary or under the person's control, whether the act did or did not hurt another, and whether the agent believed others observed (or would learn of) the act or it was known only to the actor. The combination of these three conditions creates eight different emotions. I suspect that each of the eight would evoke different profiles of brain activity, feeling, and facial and bodily responses, even though English has only three words—embarrassment, shame, and guilt—to cover all eight states.

The advantage gained by attending to the originating condition is seen in a comparison of two very different reasons for an emotion that agents describe as unworthiness, polluted, or worthlessness. Medieval Christians were vulnerable to this emotion if they lost their faith in God or had violated one of his imperatives. Contemporary adults are susceptible to this state if they had been childhood victims of sexual abuse by a relative. These are not the same states because a feeling of betrayal is a component of the emotion felt by victims of abuse, whereas fear of an eternity of pain in purgatory is a critical element of the emotion experienced by the medieval nonbeliever.

The emotions evoked in those who have less of a prized resource than another provides a more persuasive example. Instead of arguing over the meaning of envy, we should focus on the intersection of two originating conditions: Was the desired object potentially available to all or only to some, and was its possession justly earned or unjustly awarded? I suggest that a unique emotion occurs when the resource is limited and its possession by another is judged unjust. For example, actors, writers, and scientists who were not awarded a prize they believed they had earned are prone to feel an emotion toward the prize-winner. Envy is the name usually given to this state. This emotion is much less likely, however, when the award is frequent and deserved. Envy may be less common in America and Europe today than it was a century earlier because a majority of citizens believe that wealth, status, and a professional education are potentially achievable if one is willing to work for them. The main point is that progress is more likely if we begin with an analysis of the originating conditions for an emotion rather than begin with a word and bicker over its definition. George Orwell understood a deep truth when he warned readers of the danger of surrendering to words.

The languages of many cultures honor the origin of the emotion English calls "anger" by using different words to distinguish between a justified anger provoked by an insult or the inappropriate behavior of another and the less justifiable state that accompanies dislike of another, the accidental behavior of another, or a personal mistake. A seventeenth-century English commentator distinguished between the abomination felt toward a person who violated an ethical norm and the anger experienced when another blocked an agent's goal-directed behavior or challenged his dignity.[3]

The case for acknowledging origins is easy to defend because the appraisal of a feeling is usually influenced by its presumed cause. Humans automatically ask of most events, "What conditions preceded it?" The emotion evoked by a photograph of a scene differs, albeit in subtle ways, from the state provoked by a painting of the same scene because the viewer is aware of the different origins of the creative product. Salient olfactory stimuli, especially in modern communities with plumbing and sewers, are more likely to evoke a feeling than salient auditory or visual events and, in addition, are better remembered for longer periods. The biological reaction to an incentive is also affected by its cause. For example, the heritability of the change in systolic blood pressure to the stress of placing a hand in ice-cold water for one minute differed from the heritability of the rise in blood pressure to the stress of counting backwards by sevens from the number 999. Even the brain state evoked by a liquid with a distinct taste, which was used as a conditioned stimulus for an unpleasant bodily state, depended on whether the animal licked the substance from a bottle or the liquid was injected directly into the mouth. If this minor variation in the origin of a taste is important, it is more than likely that the origin of most feelings has significant implications for the emotion that will emerge.[4]

Most individuals can distinguish among the feelings produced by a direct insult, thinking about the same insult at a later date, and an unexpected and apparently unprovoked increase in muscle tension that, following reflection, is interpreted as the remnant of a rude encounter that occurred several hours earlier.[5] Even though English-speaking individuals would use the same semantic term to describe their emotion (for example, "mad" or "angry"), the feelings are distinctive, and equally important, the brain states and consequences for action would be different. These states should therefore be given different names. There are at least four origins of states with distinct brain profiles and feeling tones that would lead individuals to decide that they were happy or feeling pleasure: (1) the reduction in the uncertainty that is generated while working toward an uncertain goal when the goal is attained; (2) the feeling that accompanies meeting a personal standard of excellence; (3) learning that a parent had been awarded a prestigious prize; and (4) savoring a delicious piece of chocolate cake. Pleasure is a many-splendored phenomenon. Parents who attributed the death of their child to personal negligence would experience emotions unlike the states that would occur if they attributed the loss to a witch, the incompetence of a physician, or chance factors over which they believed they had no control. Historical events have made the last appraisal more frequent among Americans and Europeans over the last century. Few members of any ancient society would have nodded in assent to the phrase, occasionally seen on automobile bumpers, "Shit happens."

The languages used by residents of the small atoll of Ifaluk in the Western Caroline Islands of Micronesia and the Utku Eskimo of Hudson Bay honor the origins of many emotions that English terms do not. The Utku, for example, have three distinct terms for anxiety that specify whether the feared event was physical harm, rejection by another, or being startled and four different words for the emotion English calls "loneliness" that allow them to specify the experience the agent lacks but wishes to command.[6]

Most English terms for emotions are ambiguous with respect to origin because the primary concern is with the agent's feeling rather than the provocative setting or the consequences of the state. The term *fear* provides a clear example of the problems this linguistic restriction creates. Several years ago I saw in my laboratory a three-year-old boy who had been exposed to painful medical procedures for serious burns. Thus, it was not surprising that he cried in fear when the examiner tried to place electrodes on his chest to record his heart rate. But only minutes later he showed absolutely no fear to a toy snake and a person in a clown costume and mask, which evoke a cry of fear in many three-year-olds. Fear, as well as anxiety, should not be treated as free-floating states that have the same biology and phenomenology independent of their causes. These concepts acquire scientifically useful meanings only when their origin is specified. For example, patients with panic disorder are anxious over an unpredictable feeling of suffocation or rise in heart rate, whereas social phobics are anxious over an inability to control signs of nervous behavior in public.[7] These are very different worries. The attempt by some scientists to find the brain circuit that is the foundation of "fear" or "anxiety," independent of its cause, is reminiscent of a saying attributed to Confucius: "The hardest thing of all is to find a black cat in a dark room, especially if there is no cat."

The reasons why English and some other European languages are indifferent to the origin of an emotion are unknown. The ascendance of Christianity when these languages were being created may have been a contributing factor. The imperative for medieval Christians was to love and to fear God. These profoundly personal emotional states are not limited to a specific setting. Latin and Greek, invented before the establishment of Christianity, more often specified an origin, often in a bodily organ or setting, or named the target of the emotion. For example, most references to emotions in Homer's *Odyssey* specify the object of a feeling. Odysseus hungers for home; Kalypso craves Odysseus; Poseidon bears a grudge toward Odysseus; and Athena loves the sea. If the target changed (Athena loves wisdom), presumably the emotion would be different.

The central concern for members of some non-European cultures at the same time in history was to establish and maintain harmonious relationships with others in the community. However, because the age, gender, biological relatedness, and status of the other have implications for one's feelings and actions, the specific social context assumes an importance that is missing for those who are preoccupied with loving and fearing God. This difference might help to explain the absence of contextual information for most English emotional words but cannot explain why modern students of emotion continue this practice.

I suspect that this habit is partly attributable to the admiration of, and temptation to mimic, classical physics. The laws of electricity that relate voltage, current, and resistance are valid across different sources of electrons—small batteries, waterfalls, and nuclear plants. The famous Newtonian equation stating that force is the product of mass and acceleration holds for an adolescent who has kicked a heavy boulder down a mountainside and a pitcher who has thrown a baseball at a batter. The same force can emerge from different combinations of mass and acceleration. Einstein's equation

$E = mc^2$ does not specify whether the energy comes from the sun, a burning log, or a uranium atom. But biology has no equations of this type. Roses and rats produce and use energy in different ways.

The origin of an emotion has become almost irrelevant to contemporary clinicians treating patients with a form of anxiety or depression because most therapists use the same drugs, independent of what caused a patient's symptoms. This practice is rife with error. The recognition that the anomalous emotions and actions of children diagnosed as autistic are the result of qualitatively different biological conditions, and represent distinct diseases, may lead, eventually, to different therapeutic regimens. The "depression" of adolescents living in poverty with a single parent will eventually be distinguished from the "depression" of middle-class adolescents living with nurturing parents in an affluent suburb and, perhaps, treated differently. When future clinicians and investigators acknowledge the origin of an emotional state, the currently popular English terms will be replaced with new concepts that specify the cause of the various members of an emotional family. Put plainly, there is not one state of happiness, anger, anxiety, fear, or sadness but many. Although contemporary investigators usually ignore origin in their categorizations of emotions, I suspect that one day they will follow the Ifaluk and the Utku Eskimo and treat this feature as theoretically useful. This prediction is affirmed in select instances because psychiatrists do distinguish among the "anxiety" of patients who are worried about a panic attack, meeting a stranger, giving a speech, boarding a plane, or leaving home to attend college. This wisdom should be applied to other emotions as well.

## The Unexpected and the Unfamiliar

Each person is always in a state of anticipation of the next moment. And most of the time that expectation is confirmed. On the infrequent occasions when an event disconfirms the expectation (the sound of an airplane breaks the early morning silence), the unexpected event is understood almost at once. On rarer occasions the unexpected event is unfamiliar and not understood immediately. The brain reacts immediately to both of these experiences (about two hundred milliseconds earlier to the first than to the second) to create special states that contribute to the emotional patina normally associated with the incentive. Hence, unexpected and unfamiliar experiences, which are components of some origins, deserve special attention. For example, the perception of a rise in heart rate after running fifty yards to catch a bus would be ignored because it is both expected and familiar. However, the same sensation would not be dismissed by someone planning to fly the next morning who has just heard a meteorologist report that a blizzard is in the forecast. This individual is likely to reflect on the reasons for the unexpected rise in heart rate, decide he is worried about cancellation of the flight, and interrupt his ongoing activity to inquire about alternative travel plans.

The death of a ninety-year-old parent, the embrace of a lover, repeated coughing by a patron during a concert, and scenes of bloodied soldiers on television can provoke emotions, even though these events are neither unexpected nor unfamiliar. However, a preadolescent's suicide, a letter announcing the inheritance of a large sum of money from a distant relative, and the receipt of a telephone call threatening to set fire to one's home are both unexpected and unfamiliar provocations that add a psychological and biological element to the sadness, joy, and fear typically evoked by these events. Unexpected-familiar or unexpected-unfamiliar events evoke related states of surprise that are blended with the state normally induced by the event. The residents of Ifaluk, for example, say that they feel *rus*, translated as fearful, to rare, unexpected events, such as a fight or typhoon, that harm a person but use a different word for a fear state produced by an expected event with dangerous consequences. Americans are likely to say that they feel sad or empathic, rather than afraid, on learning of a fight between two rival gangs because the media inform them of frequent instances of these events.

An *unexpected event* refers to an experience that an agent does not anticipate. An *unfamiliar event* is one that the person cannot immediately assimilate to existing knowledge. Most unfamiliar events are also unexpected, for example, the sound of chirping birds when one picks up the telephone. Both properties are inherently quantitative, even though agents usually treat them as binary categories. It is important to distinguish between an unexpected event that does not engage the person's long-term store of knowledge and one that engages such knowledge. Many laboratory experiments present individuals with a series of tones in which an unexpected, deviant sound occurs only 15 percent of the time (called an oddball procedure). The unexpected sound creates a brain state at about 200 to 250 milliseconds that can be distinguished from the state that occurs to an unexpected event that is novel or bears only a partial relation to the person's understanding of the world and therefore is both unexpected and unfamiliar (for example, seeing a face with one eye or hearing the sentence, "The boy wore a sleeveless mountain"). These events create a brain state between 300 and 400 milliseconds.

Although most unfamiliar events are unexpected, there are exceptions. An unfamiliar odor presented in a laboratory setting in which the investigator told the participants ahead of time that they would experience novel smells is an example. Some unexpected events involve familiar objects (for example, finding the back door ajar in the early morning), and some expected events have unfamiliar features (seeing the early morning sun with a pale green cast). Consider the different feelings evoked by encountering a familiar friend at an appointed time and place with the feelings evoked by unexpectedly seeing the same friend in a distant city or seeing the friend at the appointed time and place but wearing an eye patch and walking on crutches.

Unexpected and unfamiliar events have profound effects on the brain. They replace the usual tonic activity of neurons in the thalamus (a structure that is the way station between all sensory information, except smell, and the cortex) with intervals of burst firing that create a special form of excitation in sensory areas of the cortex, recruit brain activity in many locations, especially the amygdala, hippocampus, and rhinal and prefrontal cortex, and are accompanied by immediate increases in brain dopamine and norepinephrine. The most vivid memories of college students refer to unexpected events, such as an accident to a friend or relative, the surprising outcome of a sports event, or the unanticipated encounter with an animal.[8]

Adults judging whether the facial expression of a male or female face was happy or fearful took longer to decide whether a man's face was fearful because they did not expect to see photos of fearful men. Even the profile of autonomic activity and the subjective feeling of discomfort produced by a painful stimulus depend on whether the pain was anticipated or unexpected.[9] Although many anatomical and physiological features have been altered through evolution, a small number have been preserved for millions of years. Bilateral symmetry of the body and eyes are two obvious examples. A sensitivity to unexpected and unfamiliar events is a psychobiological characteristic that has been preserved from the simplest animals that lived more than several hundred million years ago to humans. If such experiences induce synchronous discharge of neuronal clusters at a similar frequency, which is a possibility, these clusters would be bound together to represent a class of event distinct from expected, familiar ones. It is not surprising, therefore, that unfamiliar events motivate the invention of special categories.

Sixteenth-century alchemists, for example, classified sulfur and mercury as unique substances because their properties were discrepant from those possessed by other metals (sulfur has an unusual odor and burns and mercury is a liquid).[10] The monsters medieval citizens imagined and feared were always drawn with unfamiliar or deviant body features. Indeed, human faces with a slight deviation from the average face in a society are usually judged as less attractive than faces that share the usual arrangement and proportions of eyes, nose, mouth, and ears. Adults with a name whose three initials connoted an undesirable feature, which occurs infrequently (for example, A. P. E., B. A. D., or B. U. M.), were a little more likely to die prematurely, due to suicide or an accident, than persons whose initials implied a desirable characteristic (A. C. E., G. O. D., or J. O. Y.).[11] The fear and hostility directed at Jews living in the Roman Empire during the first century CE were fueled by the many unfamiliar practices that placed Jews in a unique category. The members of this small sect worshipped an abstract God with no iconic form, refused to eat pork or marry outside their religion, circumcised their sons, observed the Sabbath, and proselytized others.[12]

A familiar event in a familiar context, characteristic of most moments of every day, is quickly assimilated to existing knowledge, and no change in feeling occurs. If, however, an event is unfamiliar (a child is walking with an ostrich on a leash) or familiar but in an unfamiliar context (a robin is resting on a dining room table set for dinner), an immediate change in feeling is followed by a train of thought attempting to explain the discrepant experience. If an explanation is forthcoming within a second or two, the prior, less perturbed state returns.

However, unfamiliarity is not a yes–no experience. Events vary in their degree of unfamiliarity based on the number of features they share with the person's knowledge. A child walking with an ostrich on a leash is more discrepant from the past experiences of most Americans than a child walking with a small puppy but less discrepant than a child riding on the back of a leopard. The degree of discrepancy, or difference, between what the individual expects and what occurs influences the level of attentiveness it recruits, its aesthetic consequences, and the likelihood of its evoking a humorous reaction. Events that are moderately unfamiliar (that is, events that share some features with what is known) elicit the longest bout of attention. Seeing a child walking on a busy street with an ostrich on a leash would recruit a longer bout of attention than seeing a new machine (for example, a particle accelerator) because the former scene shares features with many past encounters of children walking with cats or dogs.

This principle has implications for the jokes that provoke the heartiest laughs and the musical structures that many composers prefer. An analysis of the first sixteen measures of a large number of Western musical compositions, both classical and jazz, revealed that the most common pattern was one repetition of the initial theme (that is, AA), followed by a new theme (B). This pattern occurred about 60 percent of the time, compared with 28 percent for an AB pattern and just 12 percent for an AAAB pattern. The opening bars of Beethoven's Fifth Symphony are a classic example of the AAB pattern. Maurice Ravel's compositions are exceptions, for they often violate the AAB pattern. The same pattern is present in the number of ideas that precede a joke's punch line: an AAB pattern occurs 72 percent of the time. That is, the first two ideas, which are similar and do not violate expectations, are followed by a discrepancy in the punch line. This pattern was judged funnier than jokes with an AB or AAAB pattern.[13] The many jokes involving a priest, a minister, and a rabbi are loyal to the AAB pattern.

Many celebrated poets and artists employ the same principle. The first six lines of T. S. Eliot's famous poem "The Love Song of J. Alfred Prufrock" provide an example. Lines 1 and 2 end with the same sound ("I" and "sky"), but line 3 ends with the word "table"; lines 4 and 5 also end with a rhyme ("streets" and "retreats"), but line 6 ends with "hotels." The six lines of the child's poem "Jack and Jill" fit the same pattern. Seamus Heaney's short poem "Digging" begins with three ideas ("Between my finger and my thumb / The squat pen rests / snug as a gun"). The poem's last three lines repeat the first two ideas but end with "I'll dig with it"—an AAB pattern. Shakespeare, however, preferred an AAAB pattern in many of his sonnets.

Painters often create an AAB pattern by varying the color, shape, or location of one object compared with two others on the canvas. Claude Monet's painting *Garden at Sainte-Adresse* (1867), which depicts a veranda with chairs, people, and flowers in the foreground and the sea in the background, contains three AAB patterns. The eye is drawn to a pair of adults seated in the foreground (A), another pair standing in the background (A), and a large bed of flowers in the center of the veranda (the B element). The second instance is defined by a pair of chairs in the foreground on the left side (A), a second pair of chairs in the foreground on the right (A), and a pair of tall flags at the edge of the veranda (B). The third, more subtle occasion contrasts a group of boats in the distant background on the right side (A), another group of distant boats on the left (A), and a prominent sailboat closer to the viewer (B). Monet often placed one object in an eccentric position or with a distinct color in opposition to a pair of similar objects nearby.

Obviously, an AAB structure is not always present in works of art, music, and poetry, and many other features contribute to an aesthetic feeling. But it is worth noting, nonetheless, that the mind seems to have a slight preference for the occurrence of two, rather than three or four, similar events before the introduction of a change. The expectation of an "A" after three occurrences of "A" is stronger than it is after two occurrences; hence, the preference for AAB implies that an aesthetic feeling is a little more likely after a moderate, gentler violation of what is expected than after a more abrupt, more surprising change that might distract the agent's attention from the creative product.

A distinctly different emotion emerges, however, if assimilation of the event is not possible. For example, a man who is usually empathic when he learns that a friend or relative is distressed will be surprised if he does not experience this emotion when a close colleague dies. A young mother who fails to feel the anticipated, powerful surge of affection for her first infant, and does not know why, is vulnerable to a bout of depression. The writer Octavio Paz, who had been friendly to the ideology of the Soviet Union when he was twenty-five, felt surprise when he learned in 1939 that Stalin had made a pact with Hitler. Paz confessed that his strong emotional reaction to this unexpected, and inexplicable, event produced a dramatic alteration in his philosophy.[14]

The different attitudes of Americans and Europeans toward devout Muslims reveal the influence of unfamiliarity on emotion. Because more Americans than Europeans are deeply committed to a religious faith, the presence of Muslims in American communities is not perceived as discrepant—one-third of American adults told an interviewer that the theory of evolution was absolutely false, compared with only 7 percent of Danes.[15] This may be one reason why there has been minimal prejudice toward Muslims, despite the events of September 11. Many more Europeans are agnostics or atheists who find it hard to understand the minds of those who have a profound belief in a spiritual force. Hence, the British and French are slightly more likely to be suspicious and fearful of their Muslim citizens. But their group memory of the dark prejudices that brought the Nazis to power and led to the Second World War provokes a counterphobic reaction to an emotional blend characterized by condescension toward marginalized Muslim youth and an extraordinary tolerance of asocial acts committed by a few members of this group.

The regular media announcements of the coming rise in the sea level, depletion of oil reserves, a pandemic influenza, and dirty nuclear bombs blowing up urban centers are having a similar emotional effect on older Americans born between 1925 and 1945 for whom the adolescent years were more predictable. Urban citizens are exposed to a denser set of unexpected events than rural ones, and this fact can mute the reaction to deviant experiences. It is reasonable, therefore, to award special status to the events and feelings that are infrequent in a particular society. A fear of serious illness in an infant was far more common in colonial America than it is today and, I suspect, generated a less salient emotion. By contrast, anxiety over "identity theft" did not exist in seventeenth-century Massachusetts. Furthermore, the assimilation of an unexpected or unfamiliar event may be a special source of pleasure because a special class of opioid receptors are unusually dense in a brain region (called the parahippocampal cortex) that participates in the retrieval of an agent's knowledge in the service of understanding a new experience.[16]

An unexpected or unfamiliar event instigates a cascade of reactions involving many brain structures that eventuates in the first component of a state that, although not yet a feeling, may become one. Select neurons in the human hippocampus and amygdala are altered by the single occurrence of an unfamiliar event and can remain sensitive for as long as twenty-four hours. The unexpected appearance of a face with a fearful expression or an unexpected change in posture is usually accompanied by a distinct waveform in the electroencephalogram and activation of the amygdala. Adults who do not play violent videogames had a stronger cortical reaction to the presentation of violent scenes than those who played these games frequently because the scenes were more discrepant for the former group.[17]

Because the first components of the cascade are not yet feelings, most scientists interested in human emotions typically ignore these brief initial phases and apply emotional terms only to the later, longer lasting feeling that is interpreted. For example, the perception at midnight of a sound produced by the motion of a bedroom door creates a state of alertness, which is followed by a train of thought directed at accounting for the unexpected sound and a subsequent emotion that some might call uncertainty.[18] The emotion that defines the next phase of the cascade will depend on whether the person (1) arrives at an explanation that is free of threat (for example, a breeze through an open window moved the door, which was not fully closed at bedtime); (2) fails to arrive at any reasonable account; or (3) invents an account implying imminent danger (a thief in the room). Each conclusion is accompanied by a different brain state and feeling, and each would probably invite a different semantic label (for example, relieved, concerned, or afraid).

Unexpected and unfamiliar events can produce one of four feelings for which there are no consensual names: (1) an unexpected, but familiar, event is assimilated quickly (the ring of a telephone after midnight); (2) an unfamiliar, unexpected event is assimilated quickly (seeing an unusually colored jellyfish on a beach); (3) an unexpected but familiar event is not assimilated (seeing a half-dozen friends with gifts on opening the back door); and, finally, (4) an unfamiliar, unexpected event is not assimilated (intermittent cries and growling sounds coming from within the chimney). I suspect that event-related potentials and profiles of blood flow measured in a magnetic resonance scanner would reveal a distinctive pattern for each of these states.

The emotion that English calls "uncertainty" has two origins that have distinct brain and psychological profiles. Up to now I have considered the state generated by an unfamiliar or unexpected event, which we might call "stimulus uncertainty." However, a second state, characterized by an unsureness over what decision to make, what idea to believe, or what behavior to display when alternatives are available, might be called "response uncertainty." Response uncertainty is both more prevalent, and probably more salient, in cultures where individuals have considerable choice regarding their beliefs, values, mating partners, and life's work. These conditions are more frequent in modern industrialized democracies than they are in third world villages or were in medieval farming communities. Perhaps this is why Aquinas did not posit uncertainty as an important emotion, whereas contemporary psychologists have constructed a questionnaire to measure this emotion.[19] The questionnaire items endorsed most often, which refer to response uncertainty, affirm the suggestion that this state thrives when persons are free to decide what to believe and what to do each day; for example, "It frustrates me not having all the information I need," "Uncertainty stops me from having a strong opinion," and "I can't stand being undecided about my future." An inability to tolerate the uncertainty that always hovers over how to prepare for the future is characteristic of patients diagnosed with generalized anxiety or obsessive compulsive disorder. W. H. Auden called the twentieth century "The Age of Anxiety" because of the response uncertainty engendered by a profound confusion over what to believe and, therefore, what goals to pursue.

Response uncertainty, especially when chronic, is an unpleasant state that individuals try to eliminate. All cultures generate sources of uncertainty, and the experiences presumed to mute this emotion become prized goals to obtain. Thus, uncertainties are the origins of some motives with extraordinary salience. Many medieval European Christians tried to act in ways that would please God because of their continual uncertainty over his approval. Uncertainty over critical community gossip made preservation of a family's reputation a prominent motive in the villages and towns of eighteenth-century Europe. Historical events in the succeeding two centuries removed a great deal of uncertainty over God's love, gossip, sexuality, and a host of other concerns that formed the ethical tapestry of European and North American societies. The result, which Freud would not have anticipated, is that many adults are not certain what they should want, believe, or do. The caption of a New Yorker cartoon in 2007 illustrating two homeless men sitting on a sidewalk with beer cans and a whiskey bottle reads, "Then, I thought, Hey, hold on a minute—maybe failure is an option."

## Unfamiliarity and the Amygdala

Although both unexpected and unfamiliar events activate many brain sites and are accompanied by changes in brain chemistry, the amygdala invites special attention because of its contribution to the acquisition or expression of behaviors that are presumed to be signs of fear in animals. These include body immobility, a larger than usual body startle, and reluctance to explore an unfamiliar area. Many investigators, influenced by the Iowa study described in Chapter 1, interpret increased amygdalar activity to any event that could be regarded as aversive or symbolic of threat as reflecting a fear state. The problem with this inference is that much of the time the aversive or threatening event is also unexpected, unfamiliar, or both. Darwin made this error when he interpreted his young son's signs of "alarm" toward unfamiliar caged zoo animals as fear. Rather than conclude that the scene's unfamiliarity was the incentive, Darwin perceived the child's reaction as a vestigial remnant of an antelope's reaction to a lion preparing to strike.

The presumption that a state of fear or anxiety is evoked simply because the amygdala was activated by an event that the scientist judged as threatening is vulnerable to a critique because most brain structures serve many functions. It is just as likely that the amygdala's response to the unexpected appearance of faces with fearful expressions represents a blend of stimulus and response uncertainty created by the cognitive effort needed to classify the face or to understand why it was presented. The credibility of this suggestion is supported by many facts. First, individuals with social anxiety show increased amygdalar activity to neutral faces if they have to decide whether the facial expression has a positive or negative valence. Because the correct answer is not obvious, they feel uncertain as to what they should do, and the amygdalar activity reflects that state and not the fact that the neutral face evoked anxiety.

Second, the amygdala is activated by a very brief presentation of a pair of eyes with a large amount of white tissue (called the sclera) surrounding a dark pupil (a feature of fearful expressions) and no other facial features.[20] It is unlikely that this simple stimulus provokes fear and more likely that the amygdala is activated by the contour contrast between the white sclera and the dark pupil. This claim is affirmed by the observation that the amygdala responds to pictures of fear faces within 30 milliseconds but requires five times as long, 150 milliseconds, to respond to angry faces, even though an angry face is more likely than a fearful one to induce a feeling of being threatened.[21]

The perception of a fearful facial expression requires the processing of the higher spatial frequencies characteristic of the contrast between the dark pupil and the white sclera. Adults looking at fearful faces that retain only the low spatial frequencies, with the higher frequencies removed, do not recognize them as fearful because the contrast is missing and the eyes appear as blurred spots. Moreover, the magnitude of amygdalar activation to faces with fearful expressions, presented at exposure times so short that they could not be seen, was larger when the subjects thought they saw a fearful face but one was not present than when a fearful expression was actually present but they did not perceive it consciously. Furthermore, the amygdala is more active when adults are trying to learn whether a meaningless design will be followed by the appearance of a face with a fearful or neutral expression than when a fearful face is presented without a requirement to learn anything. That is, the response uncertainty linked to the wish to solve a cognitive problem was more potent than the fear face per se in inducing amygdalar activity because the amygdala is reliably activated when a person is trying to resolve an ambiguous situation. That is why adults report more intense anxiety, and show larger eyeblink startles to an unexpected, loud noise (a reflex potentiated by the amygdala) when they do not know whether an electric shock will be administered than when the electric shock is predictable.[22] This evidence, along with others, implies the tortuousness of arguments claiming that individuals must be experiencing fear if the amygdala is activated when they are looking at faces with fearful expressions. Heart muscles become activated and heart rates rise when individuals are suffocating or trying to remember a string of ten numbers. It would be a serious error to conclude that the increased activity of cardiac muscles always means that a person is trying to stay alive.

Equally relevant is the fact that angry and fearful faces (or scenes) are encountered less often in natural settings than either neutral or happy ones, and faces with fearful expressions, without a supporting context, are ambiguous and create response uncertainty regarding the correct emotion displayed on the face. A fearful face without an attached body or background, which occurs only in research laboratories, produces a larger waveform in the electroencephalogram (called the N170) than a fearful face in an appropriate background. When the person knows that an unpleasant picture is about to appear, there is no large increase in amygdalar activity. Adults were asked to select one of seven emotional terms as the most appropriate name for fifty faces, both male and female, posing varied emotional states. The words were *angry, disgust, fear, happy, sad, surprise,* and *neutral.* The adults were least accurate in naming the faces the scientists had classified as fearful; one-third of the time they thought this face was expressing surprise. This ambiguity is absent when people read sentences describing fearful or aggressive events and the amygdalar reaction is muted. Because the circuit involving the amygdala and a certain region of the prefrontal cortex (called the ventromedial prefrontal cortex) are also activated by stimulus or response uncertainty, it is eminently reasonable to reject the claim that amygdalar activation to a fearful face reflects a state of fear in the viewer and to argue instead that it is a sign of stimulus or response uncertainty.[23]

Equally important, the amygdalae of monkeys and humans are activated by the unexpected presentation of events that have absolutely no relation to fear or anxiety. The amygdala is activated by neutral, sad, or happy faces; uncommon but pleasant words, like *ecstatic,* that imply very high arousal; pleasant pictures, cartoons, odors, and tastes; erotic scenes; minor or irregular musical chords; a video clip in which the person sees himself or herself being deceived; scenes of food in hungry adults; and short vignettes that attribute to a person the intentional commission of an act that violated a community norm (for example, spitting out food at a dinner party). It is unlikely that the individuals reading these statements became fearful and more likely that they felt either shame or surprise. The argument that amygdalar activity accompanies a form of surprise, or stimulus uncertainty, is supported by the fact that this neural activity disappears or is reduced after repeated exposure to events that are unfamiliar or signal electric shock, even though the shock retains its aversive properties.[24] This important fact means that the initial encounter with an unfamiliar experience automatically activates the amygdala.

Rhesus monkeys with bilateral lesions of the amygdala and normal control animals were exposed over a series of days to unfamiliar but harmless metal objects (for example, a padlock, keys on a ring) as well as to the approach of an unfamiliar adult. The animals without an amygdala spent more time exploring the objects and remaining at the front of the cage near the adult on the first three days of testing, implying a reduced restraint to unfamiliarity. But by the fourth day, when these events had lost their novelty, there were no behavioral differences between these surgically altered animals and normal monkeys. The authors concluded that an important function of the amygdala was to induce a state of caution to the initial encounters with novel objects or ambiguous situations.[25]

The significance of unfamiliarity for amygdala functioning is revealed in the behaviors of eighteen-month-old monkeys whose amygdalae had been removed when they were two weeks old as they interacted with other familiar monkeys. The animals without an amygdala, compared with unaltered controls, were less dominant and less aggressive with their peers but displayed the vocal screams and facial grimaces that are usual signs of fear in healthy monkeys. If the amygdala is required for a state of fear, the operated animals should not have shown these reactions. The behaviors of monkeys whose amygdalae had been removed at puberty led to a similar conclusion, for these animals also showed more avoidant behavior than controls when interacting with other familiar animals. The characteristic common to both groups of monkeys without an amygdala was not the absence of signs of fear but inappropriate reactions to familiar animals or unfamiliar humans.[26] This evidence implies that the ability to recognize the psychological significance of the unexpected actions of others and/or the ability to select the most appropriate response are cardinal functions of the primate amgydala.[27]

Social play among healthy young primates requires suppression of the usual behavioral restraint that accompanyies initial encounters with an unfamiliar animal. Two-year-old children show the same restraint. Chimpanzees, who engage in far more social play than monkeys, have a significantly smaller amygdala (controlling for brain size), even though chimpanzees must remain as vigilant as monkeys for the possibility of dangerous events.[28] It appears that evolution rendered the amygdala an early component of the brain's response to any unexpected or unfamiliar experience. The emergence of fear is dependent on brain processes accompanying a subsequent evaluation of the event.

The corpus of evidence suggests that a primary function of the amygdala is to respond to unexpected, unfamiliar, or ambiguous events, whether they are safe, pleasant, aversive, or potentially dangerous. A section of the frontal lobe called the orbitofrontal prefrontal cortex, which modulates the amygdala, plays the more important role in discriminating between pleasant or safe events, compared with unpleasant or dangerous ones. That is why both heterosexual women and homosexual men showed stronger activation of this region of the frontal cortex to attractive male faces than did heterosexual men and homosexual women. However, the amygdala and orbitofrontal cortex are not the only sites activated by unfamiliar events; perhaps that is why Caucasian and Japanese adults displayed different profiles of brain activation to the same set of fearful faces.[29]

Because the unexpectedness or unfamiliarity of an event, not only its symbolic meaning, always influences the initial brain profile, it is surprising that some investigators have not accommodated to this fact in the design of their experiments and their reflections on the evidence. There are two very different ways to interpret a relation between an emotional incentive and a brain profile—for example, a face with a fearful expression and activity in the amygdala. The popular view attributes the relation to the induction of a state in the person that matches the symbolic meaning of the incentive; therefore, the viewer is afraid. A second, equally reasonable explanation is that the brain reacted to an event that was unexpected or unfamiliar and the viewer was surprised or experienced response uncertainty.

I noted earlier that the concept of reward, a central idea in theories of learning, is defined functionally. An event is called a reward if its occurrence increases any response that preceded it. A monkey in a closed space with no windows will continue to strike a lever if that response is followed by the opportunity to peek at the outside world; hence, the outside scene is a reward. Although most theorists assume that rewards are hedonically pleasant experiences, it turns out that many desirable events that deviate from the present moment or from expectation, and are not obviously "hedonically pleasant," can function as rewards. Furthermore, their occurrence is accompanied by a surge of the neurotransmitter dopamine. But rather than conclude that the surge of brain dopamine in a rat who receives an unexpected morsel of food reflects the biological basis for reward, scientists could decide that unexpected events, especially those with significance for an animal, evoke a surge of dopamine. This claim is supported by the fact that the dopamine surge does not occur if the food, which retains its desirability, was expected. Cats taught to expect food whenever a light came on showed increased activity in the amygdala and the nearby rhinal cortex as long as the food was unexpected, but this activity disappeared once the cats had learned that delivery of the food was certain. In other words, the brain activity appeared to be caused by the unexpectedness of the food and not by the fact that food is a reward for a hungry animal.[30] An unexpected electric shock is also accompanied by an increased secretion of dopamine, although the number of neurons activated to unexpected shock is smaller than to unexpected food. But these neurons, too, become less active over time as the shock becomes predictable.

Therefore, an unexpected tone followed by the equally unexpected tingling sensation produced by electric shock to a rat's paws can be classified as an incentive for surprise or uncertainty, on one hand, or as the origin of fear, on the other. Most neuroscientists prefer the latter interpretation, despite the evidence summarized that is inconsistent with that decision. It is time to heed Einstein's maxim that a theoretical idea should never contradict a consistent body of facts. Three robust facts require accommodation: animals without an amygdala can show behavioral signs of fear, the amygdalae of animals and humans always react to unexpected and unfamiliar events independent of their aversiveness or potential danger, and this structure shows reduced activation as an unfamiliar event becomes familiar or an unexpected event becomes predictable, even if it still signals danger.

These observations invite a serious alteration in the currently popular claim that activation of the amygdala to an event that might be construed as threatening implies a state of fear. The amygdala, like most brain structures, has many functions, and it seems to be an error to continue to insist that its activation to unexpected signs of danger always reflects a state of fear. To rephrase Bertrand Russell, unreflective certainty about the amygdala should be replaced with reflective hesitation because if one accepts only a single premise that contradicts the evidence it is possible to defend wildly invalid conclusions. Russell offered the following illustration of an argument that, by beginning with one false assumption, concluded that Russell was the pope.

Assume that 3 = 2.
Now subtract 1 from each side of the equation so that 2 = 1.
The Pope and Russell are 2 entities.
But since 2 = 1, the Pope and Russell are one entity.
Therefore, Russell is the Pope.

One reason for ignoring the role of unfamiliarity or unexpectedness is that if the event is assimilated quickly, which occurs often, there is no salient change in feeling and there are no behavioral consequences. Hence, psychologists who restrict the term *emotion* to feelings with consequences are tempted to ignore this quality. I suggest, however, that scientists who rely on measures of brain activity as the primary referents for an emotion would profit from attending to this aspect of experience. The brain's reaction to unfamiliar events is the foundation of uncertainty, or surprise if the emotion is more intense, which, although less salient than fear and possessing a more ambiguous valence, is probably one of the most frequent human emotions. Because the consequences of surprise are usually private cognitive operations, rather than public behaviors, this emotion has suffered an indifference that is retarding a deeper understanding of the relations between incentives and brain patterns and between brain profiles and emotions.

## Biological Features

The enthusiasm for discovering the locations of the brain profiles for psychological phenomena extends to emotions, and many scientists are relying on such measures to classify emotions. Measures of activity in peripheral targets, such as heart, gut, skin, and skeletal muscles, were popular indexes of emotions several decades ago until research revealed that these reactions do not differentiate among most emotional states with sufficient sensitivity. Intense odors, for example, provoke a skin conductance response that is independent of the valence or personal meaning of the odor. Although adolescent delinquents asked to prepare and deliver a speech showed a smaller increase in heart rate than nondelinquents, they displayed no difference in skin conductance, even though both are reactions of the sympathetic nervous system.[31] The insensitivity of these peripheral measures is due, in part, to failure to specify the context in which the reactions occurred. A rise in heart rate and increased muscle tension can accompany the anticipation of meeting a romantic partner as well as the sight of a scorpion. Dilation of the pupil and increased skin conductance can accompany memorizing lists of numbers and viewing erotic films. Furthermore, individuals vary in the responsivity of the targets of their autonomic system; blood phobics, for example, have a more labile parasympathetic system, whereas spider phobics have a more labile sympathetic system.[32] And those who show the greatest autonomic reactivity to an incentive do not always display the most behavioral change or report a more salient emotional experience.

This evidence persuaded most scientists that profiles of brain activity might prove to be more useful signs of emotions and, therefore, a basis for classifying them. But, as I noted earlier, the brain's initial reaction to an event is affected by its expectedness, familiarity, duration, and physical properties in addition to its emotional meaning. Angry or fearful faces activate an area in the posterior part of the right hemisphere (called the fusiform gyrus). However, one cannot conclude that activity in this location is a sign of an emotion because this site is activated when persons simply think about the presence of a neutral face they cannot see, as well as by many stimuli that resemble but are not faces, including a closed, curved contour, resembling a head, containing six small black squares in the upper part of the stimulus that adults do not perceive as a face. The physical features of an event, as contrasted with its psychological meaning, can activate this cortical area.[33]

Some autistic patients viewing photographs of faces look at the nose, mouth, or chin more often than the eyes, whereas most individuals look at the eyes more often than other facial components.[34] A few scientists had interpreted this fact as meaning that autistics have a fear reaction to human eyes. That is why they avoid looking at peoples' faces and are not very sociable. A more reasonable interpretation is that they possess a compromise somewhere in the visual system that either blurs the distinctiveness of the eyes to render them a less prominent facial feature, or makes the mouth and nose especially prominent. The thalamus, a large collection of neurons beneath the cortex that processes all visual information, and the visual cortex, to which the thalamus projects, consist of separate classes of neurons that preferentially process events with low or high spatial frequency. I noted that if the high-frequency components of a face are removed, the eyes lose their perceptual distinctiveness (they appear as blurred dark spots rather than as a dark pupil surrounded by a white sclera), and the nose, mouth, and chin, which are of a lower spatial frequency, become more salient. This fact implies that some autistics might be born with a compromise in the neurons that process higher spatial frequencies. On the other hand, because the amygdala is especially sensitive to lower frequencies, it is possible that some autistics have a more active amygdala that recruits attention to the mouth and nose. In either case, their failure to look at the eyes is probably not a sign of fear. The first interpretation may explain why some autistic patients find it difficult to guess the emotional expression on a face (for example, whether anger, fear, sadness, or joy) from the information contained in the relatively small differences between the diameter of the pupil and the amount of sclera. The eyes are more critical for judgments of fear, anger, and surprise, which involve higher spatial frequencies, than for joy or sadness, which rely more on the shape of the mouth. There is an analogous result in mice. Some mice spontaneously enter a brightly lit area, whereas most mice and rats avoid brightly lit places, presumably because bright light is aversive. Some scientists had concluded from this fact that the avoidant strains of mice were fearful whereas those who entered the lit area were minimally fearful. Later inquiry revealed, however, that the mice that entered the brightly lit areas had an abnormal retina and did not perceive the high level of illumination. They were partially blind rather than fearless.

Furthermore, the emotions of fear and anger are accompanied by changes in the loudness and timbre of the voice characterized by lower sound frequencies. It is of interest, therefore, that the right hemisphere is especially prepared to process the lower frequencies, whereas the left hemisphere is more accurate with higher frequencies. These facts are in accord with the reliable observation that many salient emotions are elaborated more fully in the right hemisphere. However, the frequencies of visual and auditory information produced by a person's face and voice do not specify a specific emotion.

Some scientists insist, nonetheless, that an emotional state is automatically generated when specific brain circuits are activated by a particular class of releasing stimuli. The emotion of fear is nominated as the best example of this position.[35] The releasing events presumed to evoke fear imply danger to the person, with snakes and spiders nominated as prototypes of this class of experience. This biologically deterministic position has three potential problems. First, snakes and spiders possess perceptual features that are extremely deviant from most members of the category of living things. Infants do not know that snakes and spiders have deviant features and have not yet learned that they are dangerous. As a result, most human infants fail to show any signs of fear to realistic toy versions of snakes or spiders and do not orient faster to pictures of snakes than to pictures of frogs. Second, as noted, most components of the circuit activated by snakes and spiders are also activated by the unexpected appearance of events that are perfectly harmless. That is why spider phobics exposed to films of spiders showed greater neuronal activity in the prefrontal cortex than in the amygdala.[36]

A study of graduate students preparing for the oral defense of their doctoral dissertation—an event that usually generates a high level of anxiety over performance failure—reveals not only the extraordinary specificity of biological reactions to threat but also their minimal relation to an individual's subjective emotional state. Self-ratings of the intensity of felt stress, several biological measures, and reports of somatic complaints were gathered on these students, as well as students not preparing for an examination, on three occasions: six to eight weeks before the oral examination, the day of the examination, and several days after the examination. Both the men and women preparing for the examination reported more frequent headaches, sore throats, and fatigue two months before the exam but showed no distinct change in immune function and, surprisingly, did not report feeling more stressed than the students who were not being examined. Further, the women anticipating the oral exam, but not the men, showed increased cortisol secretion on the day of the exam but not six to eight weeks earlier. Last, there were no significant correlations among the several biological measures or between these measures and self-reported stress.[37] This evidence implies that the concept "stress" is meaningless until the investigator specifies the threatening event, the gender of the individual, and the index of stress.

The main point, however, is that it has proven difficult to demonstrate a universal biological reaction that all people show to a particular class of events. Scientists who argue that certain neurochemical or neurophysiological patterns in particular locations regularly accompany fear, joy, or anger, independent of context or the gender, age, class, ethnicity, genome, or cultural background of the person, are going far beyond the evidence.[38] But because the media promote this biological determinism, the public is vulnerable to accepting it as true. An article in the June 20, 1988, issue of *Time* magazine, reporting on a woman who murdered her infant, told readers that the hormonal changes that accompany the birth process create emotional states, especially in women unprepared for the care of children, that can provoke serious aggression that women are unable to control. It is thus not fair, the journalist argued, to hold such mothers responsible for their horrendous actions. This conclusion is a serious distortion of the truth. There is no known hormonal change that can force a woman to kill her infant if she does not want to do so!

The most important point is that although a particular brain profile to an incentive excludes the possibility of a large number of emotions, more than one possible state remains. A brain profile cannot specify a particular emotion, in part because the profile depends on the context and the brain's state just before the incentive, and that brain state is influenced by the person's expectations. That is, the brain pattern induced by the incentive reflects the combination of the state before the incentive and the one induced by it. Because the first state is likely to involve most of the cortex and parts of the subcortex, it is impossible, at least at present, to diagnose the unique psychological state the incentive created in each person. That is, the state that the incentive alone produces is necessarily unknowable. The size and shape of a stone that caused ripples on a pond's surface after being thrown into the water supply an analogy. The ripple pattern is a joint function of the pond's surface before the stone was thrown as well as of the speed and angle with which the stone was thrown. One cannot know the properties of the stone from observing only the pattern of ripples on the surface. Possession of the human genome guarantees that a newborn infant will not become a monkey, mongoose, or mouse, but these genes do not specify the adult profile that an infant will develop because the future environmental experiences are unknown. A child with Down syndrome, born with forty-seven rather than the normal forty-six chromosomes, is unlikely to become an accomplished poet, painter, or physicist, but it is impossible to predict the child's specific traits and talents.

Brain profiles have a limited power to illuminate many human emotions, at least currently, because it is impossible to create the appropriate conditions in the artificial setting of a laboratory. The circuits that accompany most human emotions, as they occur in ecologically natural settings, cannot be quantified in a scanner because the noise, restricted posture, and social context (the participants are aware, for example, that the experimenters sitting in the next room are evaluating them and their performances) can alter a person's psychobiological state in special but unknown ways.[39] More seriously, different measures of brain activity to the same incentive often lead to different conclusions. Not surprisingly, adult men rated images of female nudes as more pleasant than male nudes. However, the event-related potential waveforms and the magnetic fields evoked by these pictures required different inferences. The waveforms were larger to female than to male nudes; the magnetic fields were similar to both types of nudes. A more persuasive example is seen in the reactions to pictures that are symbolic of unpleasant (snakes, bloodied bodies), pleasant (children playing, couples kissing), or neutral (tables, chairs) emotional situations. The unpleasant scenes typically induce the largest eyeblink startle response to a loud sound due to recruitment of the amygdala. However, there is greater blood flow to temporal and parietal areas to the pleasant than to the unpleasant pictures, and, making matters more ambiguous, the amplitudes of the event-related waveform eight-tenths of a second after the appearance of the photographs are equivalent to the pleasant and unpleasant scenes. A scientist who wanted to know whether unpleasant or pleasant scenes were more arousing could arrive at three different conclusions depending on the evidence selected.[40] Every conclusion about the psychological state of a person depends on the measure used!

Nonetheless, most inferences regarding the relations between brain states and emotions are based only on changes in blood flow to varied brain sites, even though scientists remain puzzled as to what these changes mean. One reason for their frustration is that the magnitude of increased blood flow to a site is a function of the amount of input to that site, not its output, and the local neuronal activity the input created. Pictures of snakes usually produce a greater increase in blood flow to the amygdala than pictures of fruits because there is greater input to the amygdala from areas that respond to unexpected events as well as from sites associated with the knowledge that snakes are dangerous. The degree of activation of the amygdala to photographs of snakes is a product of a circuit comprising many interconnected sites. Hence, many different combinations of activity within the distinct sites of the circuit could result in the same level of amygdalar activity, just as different combinations of the weight and velocity of a boulder rolling down a mountain could cause the same degree of damage. The amount of activity in the stomach will be correlated with the amount and quality of the food introduced into the mouth, but hunger is not located in the stomach.

Many investigators assume, incorrectly, that the blood flow changes observed to an emotional incentive, say pictures of spiders or fearful faces, are due primarily to the psychological significance of the stimulus. However, as I noted, blood flow changes can be induced by at least four factors: the physical properties of the stimulus (for example, amount of contour, range of colors, and degree of motion in visual events), the unexpectedness of the stimulus, the amount of mental work the incentive requires, and, finally, its meaning. The first three often produce greater changes in blood flow than the fourth and swamp the effect of the psychological meaning of the incentive, which is what the investigator wants to know. For example, if pictures of men crying produce greater blood flow to the amygdala than photos of crying women, it is likely that this is because the former scenes were unexpected and more surprising. This finding does not necessarily mean that crying men are more "threatening" than crying women.

At the moment, therefore, the hope of finding a well-defined biological pattern that always accompanies a particular emotion has not been realized.[41] However, should future investigators discover such a profile, it will have to be described with biological, not psychological, words. Individuals expecting an electric shock showed the expected increase in neuronal activity in the somatosensory cortex. The scientists who conducted this experiment concluded that this brain profile was the neurobiological foundation of the emotion of *dread*. But the same cortical area is activated by events unrelated to the anticipation of pain. Hence, they should have invented a new term to describe the correlation between the anticipated shock and the neural pattern. The activation of the amygdala and prefrontal cortex by the unexpected presentation of a picture of a rattlesnake might be a necessary feature of a "fear of harm." But excitation of this circuit should not be called fear both because humans do not always experience this emotion when this circuit is active and because harmless events, such as the unexpected photo of a nude figure can activate the same circuit.[42]

Three interconnected structures (amygdala, insular cortex, and anterior cingulate) were activated in adults exposed to an aversive event and in adults experiencing penile erections while watching erotic films. A scientist examining the brain profile in these areas could not know what emotion was being experienced. The brain's reaction is always a function of the person's mental set, expectations, and private interpretation of an event, and these processes recruit activity in neuronal clusters that are not the same across individuals.[43]

We need to use biological names, not psychological ones, for the changes in brain activity produced by an incentive. For example, scientists might write about a medulla-amygdala-striatal circuit evoked by a painful stimulus or a locus ceruleus–medial temporal–prefrontal circuit to an unexpected or unfamiliar one. Biologists do not call a drop in blood sugar "hunger" because this biological state can occur for reasons other than a lack of food.

The currently popular practice of describing brain profiles gathered with magnetic resonance scanners as if they were equivalent to, or proxies for, feeling or emotional states has serious problems. First, these machines reveal the blood flow changes to brain sites several seconds after an incentive, whereas some emotional reactions occur immediately and last less than two seconds. Second, conclusions regarding the activation of a site to an incentive can vary with the field strength of the scanner; areas that are active in a powerful magnetic scanner are not always detected in a less powerful machine. Third, a particular profile of brain activity to an incentive can be accompanied by different feelings when the immediate context and the individual's history and temperament vary. The anxiety evoked by the novelty of lying in a scanner and being evaluated by an examiner usually produces a brief rise in cortisol that can alter a person's brain and psychological state. These problems are one reason why two scientists highly respected for their understanding of this methodology urged more caution among their colleagues. They argued that because the causes of changes in blood flow remain an enigma, the psychological meaning of any alteration in blood flow is, at least at present, necessarily ambiguous.[44]

Equally important, different brain states can be accompanied by similar conscious emotions, as different mutations can result in tumors that appear identical. For example, the first exposure to faces displaying fear or disgust evoked a distinct profile of activation along with a verbal report of high arousal. However, the presentation of the same pictures a week later was accompanied by a dramatic reduction in brain activation but no difference in the participants' descriptions of their level of psychological arousal. Although a single dose of the male sex hormone testosterone administered to women reduced both the magnitude of eyeblink startles and level of tension in the facial muscles to a signal announcing an electric shock to the wrist, the sex hormone had no effect on women's conscious feelings as they watched film clips of smiling and frowning persons.[45] Apparently, male sex hormone inhibits the tension in facial muscles. The more expressive faces of women, compared with men, might be mediated by a lower level of male hormone, even though most men and women are unaware of the expressiveness in their faces. With few exceptions, most phenomena are the product of different underlying conditions. I can think of no class of human or animal behavior that has only one cause. Hence, it is not possible, at least currently, to expect a one-to-one correspondence between a particular brain state and a specific emotion.

One reason for this skepticism is that the person's gender often modulates brain activity. Men and women who reported equivalent levels of sexual arousal to erotic film clips showed different profiles of brain activation, especially in the amygdala and hypothalamus.[46] As with the dissociation between autonomic reactivity to a stressor and self-reported anxiety, there was no consistent relation between the person's conscious emotional state and the biological measures purported to reflect that state. Finally, the consequences of some emotional incentives are not always revealed at the time the brain measurements are being made but occur one, two, or more hours later. Adults who were classified as vulnerable to anxiety over social rejection did not report more intense feelings of ostracism or show more behavioral signs of social anxiety than others until forty-five minutes after the social rejection.[47]

Most twenty-year-olds living in affluent homes in industrialized nations report a stronger feeling of emotional well-being than adults over age sixty-five whose bodies are beginning to show signs of wear. Yet a team of scientists who used only brain activity (created by faces with different expressions) as a measure of well-being arrived at the counterintuitive conclusion that "emotional wellbeing improves over seven decades of the human life span."[48] This example should persuade resistant readers that the meanings of concepts referring to emotional states change seriously when brain states are the sole source of evidence. Emotional well-being is a subjective judgment based on a variety of factors with varied weights in different agents; hence, there cannot, in principle, be a specific brain state that defines a feeling of well-being for all persons.

The relation between the sound spectrograms produced by a spoken utterance and its psychological meaning provides an instructive analogy. The sound spectrograms of one hundred Americans speaking the phrase, "Pass the salt please," with different dialects, intensities, and frequencies would be sufficiently different that it would be impossible to pick any one at random (or to study all hundred) and figure out the meaning of the utterance, even though all who heard the utterance would be able to do so.

The scientists who believe that a well-defined brain state, say greater activation of the prefrontal cortex in the right than in the left hemisphere, implies the presence of a particular emotional state resemble the fourteenth-century Jewish scholars who were convinced that each of the twenty-two consonants in the Hebrew language had a numerical value. The letter *shin*, for example, had a value of three hundred, and one could discern the meaning of a biblical passage by adding up its numbers. If the sum happened to be forty-four hundred, the passage represented the summoning of the angel Samael.[49]

Although it is theoretically useful to know the probabilities (that is, the likelihood) of activation in a large number of neuronal clusters to varied emotional incentives, the table of probabilities does not represent a psychological state. Neuroscientists would be sublimely happy if they were able to predict, 70 or 80 percent of the time, the profiles of activation to a well-defined event. Their inability to do so has forced them to select the much coarser strategy of summing the neuronal activity in a small number of areas over five or six seconds and comparing that value with the activity that existed before the incentive appeared. If the difference is statistically significant, they conclude that the incentive created a distinct brain state, even though their predictions of the profiles would be correct only 30 to 40 percent of the time. Consider a table representing the proportion of cells in the respiratory systems of one hundred persons that contained rhinoviruses in December compared with the number in July. A table with positive values should not be called a cold because all individuals harboring rhinoviruses do not display the sneezing, fatigue, or coughing that define this illness. Similarly, a table representing a greater level of activation of the amygdala to a threatening incentive (for example, a picture of a snake compared with a picture of a snail) does not define an emotion. The probability that an emotion will emerge from a brain state is much less than 1.0 because individual variation in life history affects the tightness of the relation between an incentive and a brain state, between a brain state and a detected feeling, and between a feeling and an appraisal. If we adopt a generous mood and assume that the probability of amygdalar activation to pictures of snakes was 0.9, the probability of a detected bodily feeling following the brain state was 0.8, and the probability of appraising the feeling as fear was 0.7, the probability that the snakes would evoke a judgment of fear is only 0.5. That is, we would expect the pictures to produce a conscious appraisal of fear only 50 percent of the time. This modest value should invite some humility; the probability that a glass will shatter if struck with a hammer is 1.0.

The concept of probability has a second meaning, however. It also refers to a person's a priori belief about the likelihood of a future observation. For example, I have great confidence in the estimate that every one of the next one hundred motorists passing my house will stop at the red light five hundred yards down the hill. The probability that my belief is correct is very high, close to 1.0. But note that the confidence of my belief is restricted to the American drivers in my middle-class neighborhood. The confidence in the correctness of my belief that one hundred motorists in Cairo will stop at a red light is much lower because Cairo drivers have less respect for red lights. Because most emotional phenomena have more than one interpretation, scientists holding different a priori beliefs will use the same evidence to support divergent beliefs. The probability that the unexpected appearance of a picture of a cobra with open jaws will activate the amygdalae of one hundred adults is very high. This observation strengthens the belief that the amygdala mediates fear among those who hold that premise. But among scientists, like myself, who believe that events that generate stimulus or response uncertainty always activate the amygdala, the same observation will strengthen this different assumption. Unfortunately, at the moment, most of the information on the relations between an emotional incentive and brain activity can be used to support different beliefs. Few geologists changed their view about the impossibility of slowly moving continents when Alfred Wegener made that suggestion about a hundred years ago.

## The Significance of Consciousness

The popular assumption that specification of a circuit that regularly accompanies a particular emotion provides a sufficient explanation of the psychological state is vulnerable to critique. The brain state of a pedestrian who, while thinking about an important appointment, sees in peripheral vision a stranger slap a three-year-old harshly would be changed by that perception. But if the brain profile did not pierce consciousness to create a feeling, we should not assume that the emotion of empathy, which might have occurred if the consequences of the brain state were detected, was evoked.

I question the utility of the belief, held by Freud and some contemporary scientists, that there are unconscious versions of the same emotions that are conscious.[50] This position does not deny that brain activity, muscle movements, activations of representations, and autonomic activation can occur without conscious awareness to create psychological states with implications. Although women rated the pheromone androstadienone as equivalent in intensity and valence to androstenone, which is not a pheromone, the former molecule evoked a significantly faster set of waveforms in the electroencephalogram. This fact suggests that the brain responded to the pheromone in a special way, despite no effect on the woman's psychological state. Similarly, women administered a small amount of androstadienone directly into their nostrils showed an immediate increase in vagal activity in their cardiovascular system, even though they did not detect the pheromone and reported no increase in sexual feelings. A nice example of the effects of a biological state on behavior is the tendency of young women to dress more attractively within two days of ovulation, even though they were in a relationship and were unaware of trying to appear sexually inviting.[51] Their feeling tone on those days probably motivated them to select a more alluring dress or display more skin. It is less obvious that calling their state "unconscious sexual arousal" is clarifying. Freud's concept of sublimation, which exploited this semantic preference, implied that creativity in art and science was, in fact, the result of an unconscious state that, if conscious, would have motivated the agent to seek a sexual partner. Biographical data on Pablo Picasso, Paul Gauguin, Albert Einstein, and Ernst Schrödinger suggest that their creativity was not a substitute for their sexual urges. Indeed, Schrödinger's profound insight regarding the wavelike properties of quantum processes, which won him a Nobel Prize, occurred during a week when he was enjoying sex with a mistress in a vacation hideout.

Unconscious biological and psychological states are important, but they represent a special class of phenomena that should not be given the same names we award to conscious states.[52] Cognitive scientists invented the new term *implicit memory*, rather than use the phrase *unconscious memory*, when subjects recognized words they saw in the past but were unaware of having seen those words earlier. The absence of appraisal in unconscious states prevents a judgment of the agent's ability to cope with the feeling or subsequent emotional state.

Some individuals with a "short fuse" will, without obvious provocation, raise their voice or become hypercritical toward others while remaining unaware of feeling angry or being perceived as angry. Although these individuals are in a significant psychological state, I do not believe it is theoretically fruitful to call their state "unconscious anger" because sarcastic, hostile responses to a friend or spouse can be caused by a chronic dissatisfaction with self that is expressed to whoever happens to be present. They are not angry with their friend or spouse but aroused by a previous frustration, loss, or ethical violation and are unaware of the cause of their emotion. By contrast, a consciously hostile comment toward a friend or spouse who has actually frustrated or threatened the self is the product of a different psychological state. Remember, an unconscious smile or eye blink is mediated by a circuit that differs from the circuit that mediates a willful smile or blink. A reflex smile to a passerby need not reflect unconscious happiness. Most Americans are unaware that they possess an association between male gender and first names composed of a single syllables ending with a consonant (Mark, Carl, Frank, John) because more sons than daughters are given such names. It will prove fruitful to invent new conceptual names for states whose origins are not conscious but are accompanied by behaviors that resemble those provoked by conscious states. Not every vaginal engorgement or penile erection is accompanied by sexual excitement. Many Algerian Arabs who rebelled against the French in the late 1950s were motivated consciously for freedom from oppression but less consciously by a desire for greater dignity.

I noted that individuals displayed a specific pattern of brain activation to faces with fearful expressions they did not perceive because the brain was probably responding to the greater amount of black-white contour characteristic of the enlarged eyes of fearful faces.[53] But because they did not perceive a fearful expression and did not report any change in feeling, the brain profile should not be called "unconscious fear." This assertion finds support in the fact that the patterns of connectivity among the amygdala and other sites were distinctly different when adults could perceive a fearful face compared with occasions when they could not. Because the brain profile provoked by a fearful face that was not perceived has special features, the corresponding psychological state should be awarded a special name and should not be called "unconscious fear." I am not suggesting that unconscious states, biological or psychological, are unimportant, only that they require their own vocabulary.[54] Chemists distinguish between the right and left forms of certain molecules because the two forms often have different functions.

The obvious advantage of awarding the properties of conscious emotional states to unconscious processes is that this strategy avoids the need to construct a new vocabulary for unconscious states. Such a vocabulary does not exist. But the brain state accompanying the conscious interpretation of a detected change in feeling must be different from the unconscious form. The activity in the neurons of motor, prefrontal, and cerebellar cortex, along with their projections to the skeletal muscles involved in the planning and execution of a serve that wins a tennis match, are unconscious. But the victor's decision as to where the ball should land in the opponent's court, governed by the desire to win, is conscious. The neuronal profile should not be called "an unconscious desire for victory."

A good reason for advocating this austere position is that there is often a dissociation between brain activity, which necessarily occurs outside of awareness, and conscious processes. Six epileptic patients with microelectrodes placed in many neurons of the hippocampus and amygdala saw a series of twelve different visual stimuli in one of four locations and had to remember both the stimuli and their locations. Their recognition memory was tested thirty minutes and twenty-four hours later when they had to report whether a stimulus had been seen before or was new. The patients accurately recognized the identity of the stimuli (88 percent correct) but were less accurate in recognizing their locations (50 percent correct). Select sets of neurons in the two structures, however, were extremely sensitive to the familiarity or novelty of the stimulus and its location. The activation patterns in clusters of six neurons corresponded to the correct stimulus 93 percent of the time. That is, on many trials when a patient said that a stimulus was new when in fact it was old, their neuronal profile matched the pattern appropriate for old stimuli, indicating a dissociation between brain activity and the conscious psychological state.[55]

Notice that I did not write that the brain "correctly recognized" whether the stimulus was new or old because that predicate is appropriate for conscious individuals, but not for neurons. The brains of sleeping newborns display a distinct change to an unexpected sound, but few scientists call this phenomenon "unconscious surprise." The same restraint should be practiced with other examples of brain profiles that never pierce awareness. When one cell divides to become two entities biologists use the term *mitosis*; when a university department divides to become two units faculty use the word *sepa-*

*rate.* Hence, scientists should invent a vocabulary for states that are believed to resemble conscious ones but lack their critical properties. A failure to do so forces us to treat involuntary smiles as reflections of unconscious happiness and involuntary frowns as unconscious sadness. Spontaneous frowns often appear on the faces of two-month-old infants who have no reason to be sad. The first cohort of psychoanalysts believed that the facial tics of patients with Tourette's syndrome were a sign of an unconscious urge to masturbate. This interpretation, which should evoke a smile in contemporary readers, is an example of the mischief that is possible when unconscious states are given the same names as conscious ones.

This semantic error is especially troublesome when terms intended to describe conscious human states are applied to genes. Two eminent biological scientists believe that it is perfectly acceptable to attribute the predicate *selfish* to a gene if its increased prevalence is correlated with the decreased prevalence of another gene.[56] This claim, however, resembles the metaphor "The moon is an aphrodisiac" because the primary feature of a selfish human is the placement of self's interest above the interests of others, whereas this property is a secondary feature of a gene. I trust they would not call a large boulder selfish if it displaced a smaller one on a smooth, sunny meadow on the side of a mountain. These scholars chose the term *selfish* as a characteristic of genes because this decision rationalized the increase in human self-interest that historical events created over the past few centuries. If medieval scholars had known about genes, one of them might have proposed that they are "damned by their sinful acts." Plato would have declared that genes "strive to do good."

Neurobiologists who taught monkeys over many, many trials to associate one set of visual cues with the delivery of various amounts of one liquid (A) and a different set of visual cues with the delivery of varied amounts of a second liquid (B) made a similar error. The monkeys were shown many pairs of these visual cues and indicated their selection of one member of each pair by moving their eyes to the location of the preferred liquid, after which they received the liquid they had chosen. Select neurons in the orbitofrontal cortex became maximally active, during the brief interval before the animal had moved their eyes, on those trials in which one of the two liquids was clearly preferred over the other. To my surprise, the authors concluded that these active neurons "encoded economic value."[57] It would have been more accurate to write that this neuronal profile represented a brain state, acquired through extensive experience with the tastes of the two liquids, reflecting the learned anticipation of a preferred taste. These two statements do not have the same meaning.

The neurons in the motor cortex of a Red Sox batter preparing to hit the ball speeding toward him would be more active if he anticipated hitting a single that would drive in the winning run and allow him to be hailed as a hero than if he expected to strike out. But I trust that no neurobiologist would conclude that these neurons encoded the "value of getting a base hit" or the "desire to be a hero." The term *love* provides more persuasive support for the request to restrain the impulse to describe activated neural circuits with the terms used for conscious emotions. I have no doubt that particular clusters of neurons are activated in couples engaging in sexual activity on their wedding night, but hope I will never read a paper suggesting that these neurons "encode love" or worse yet "ecstasy."

## Facial Expressions

The interpretation of involuntary facial expressions invites an equally skeptical posture. The notion that facial expressions reflect an emotion, an idea introduced by Darwin and elaborated by Silvan Tomkins ninety years later, provoked a popular strategy for classifying emotions.[58] Tomkins, who took Darwin seriously, offered the bold claim that the sensory feedback from facial muscles to the brain was the source of all emotional states. When a person smiles, Tomkins asserted, activity in the muscles of the eyes and mouth, which is transmitted to the cortex, automatically evokes *joy*. Aware of the new discoveries in the neurosciences, Tomkins suggested that innate neural programs located in subcortical centers and responsive to particular incentives, generated facial expressions representing eight primary emotions called *interest, joy, surprise, distress, fear, shame, disgust,* and *anger*. The problem with this claim is that each is a family of states and not a unitary emotion. The smile that is a conditioned response to a greeting, a biologically prepared reaction to a sweet taste, and the product of anticipating a desired future encounter are mediated by different brain profiles and do not reflect a single state. Thirty years later, Antonio Damasio minimized the significance of the face but retained most of Tomkins's argument. The evidence that has accumulated since the publication of Tomkins's books, however, has not been kind to his speculative but creative thesis.

Although the emotion of disgust is usually accompanied by a reliable change in facial expression, most emotional states are not accompanied by equally specific changes in facial muscles. For example, although adults said that they experienced surprise to an unexpected event, fewer than one in four showed any change in facial expression. The emotional states that accompany an ambivalent intention to deceive another person, an erotic scene, and the tension felt during a six-hour plane trip are usually free of obvious alterations in facial muscles. Adults reported feeling more joy to the sweet taste of chocolate milk after watching a film provocative of this state, compared with their feeling to the same taste before the film, but their facial expression to the sweet taste was unaffected by the film.[59]

Some facial expressions, moreover, are unaccompanied by any change in feeling, heart rate, skin conductance, or attention. A brief, involuntary smile often reflects an unconscious disposition to communicate a friendly posture to another rather than happiness. Soccer fans watching a match, as well as Olympic gold medalists during award ceremonies, reported feeling happy, but they rarely smiled unless they were interacting with another person. That is why the smiles of children engaged in playful teasing belong to a category different from the smiles reflecting a wish to be friendly. Men generally smile less often than women (I noted earlier that this may be the result of a higher level of male hormone that suppresses activity in facial muscles), but men do not report feeling less happy than women. And analyses of the facial expressions of talented actors in four Hollywood films failed to reveal the expected facial profiles when they were simulating the emotions of surprise, fear, anger, disgust, or sadness. The dissociation between facial changes and private emotional states is also revealed by the fact that the facial movements of congenitally blind adults to requests to feel anger, sadness, or concentration resembled the movements of their sighted relatives more than the movements of others.[60] This observation implies a genetic contribution to facial muscle profiles, such as biting the lip, narrowing the eyes, and opening the mouth, that may have little to do with feeling states. People vary in their susceptibility to furrowing the muscles of their forehead, smiling, and grimacing. But this variation, some of which is inherited, is not necessarily related to variation in the frequency or salience of their emotions.

The accumulated evidence has persuaded many scientists, including Paul Ekman and Carroll Izard, that an emotion can occur without any change in facial expression. However, this conclusion does not mean that changes in facial muscles lack significance. The muscles of the right and left sides of the upper portion of the face receive greater input from the hemisphere on the same side than from the hemisphere on the opposite side. Surprisingly, the projections from the right hemisphere to the muscles on the right side of the upper portion of the face, compared with the projections from the left hemisphere to the left side of the face, are stronger in women than in men. Because the right hemisphere contributes more than the left to the elaboration of feedback from the body, including the facial muscles, and, therefore, to the generation of feeling states, it follows that the brain states that are actualized as emotions should produce more observable signs in the upper half of the faces of women compared with men. Perhaps it is not a coincidence that female adolescents watching unpleasant scenes displayed greater activity in the forehead muscles than males. And unusually aggressive preadolescent boys showed less activity in these muscles to faces with angry expressions than minimally aggressive boys.[61]

Although the face is neither the origin of all emotions nor a trustworthy sign of an emotional state, nonetheless, it can on occasion reveal a feeling state or temperamental bias. Almost twenty years ago I saw in my laboratory a two-month-old boy who displayed frequent facial frowns to small toys and recorded speech. The frequency of this facial reaction was uncommon among young infants. A year later this boy presented a rare behavioral profile when he returned to the laboratory. He protested every procedure, fretted without provocation, and displayed prolonged facial expressions suggestive of pain or internal distress. Darwin and Tomkins were not completely wrong. The face can reveal important information about a feeling state. But robust evidence from many laboratories has reined in the overly enthusiastic ambitions of theorists eager for broad, simplifying statements that ignored the inconsistencies. Natural phenomena were designed by an extremely compulsive architect who paid attention to the details.

## Valence

The *valence of a feeling* refers to a judgment of its pleasant or unpleasant sensory quality. This judgment dominated the theorizing of nineteenth-century European psychologists, as well as the experiments of many American psychologists in the early twentieth century, because eighteenth-century Enlightenment commentators trying to free their societies from the premises of Christian philosophy insisted that humans, like animals, were motivated primarily by a desire for sensory "pleasure." However, the dramatic individual variation in the judgments of the pleasant or unpleasant quality of musical chords or colors led the first cohort of behaviorists to question the validity of these subjective declarations of pleasure or displeasure.

The *valence of an emotion* refers to its symbolic classification as a desirable or good state compared with an undesirable or bad one. Every known language has terms for the concepts *good* and *bad*, and these evaluations are often categorical when described with words. A semicircle is classified as "pleasant" and an acute angle with vertices pointing downward as "unpleasant" only after someone requests these judgments.[62]

Some psychologists have suggested that the term *emotion* should apply only to states with either a desirable or an undesirable valence.[63] Surprise, whose valence is ambiguous, is denied membership in this category. The advantage of this austere position is that it restricts emotions to states that individuals try to attain or avoid. A serious disadvantage is that it excludes states characterized by salient feelings that are not consistently sought or avoided (for example, the blend of excitement and uncertainty that accompanies taking responsibility for a difficult assignment, or the blend of vigilance and satisfaction that accompanies walking on a dark street to one's hotel at 1:00 AM after a pleasant evening with friends).

There are two bases for assigning a valence to an emotion. One originates in the sensory qualities of the underlying feelings, including its familiarity and contrast with a prior state; the other resides in each person's ethical values. The warmth of a fire when one is cold evokes a desirable emotion, whereas a pounding headache generates an undesired emotion, because of their respective sensory properties. A more pleasant valence was assigned to odors or photographs of people engaged in various activities if the odors and photos were familiar rather than unfamiliar and if the subjective state contrasted with a less pleasant one.[64] The second glass of water on a warm day is judged as pleasant if it follows the drinking of a glass of warm water but not if it follows the drinking of much cooler water, a fact established in the laboratory almost a century ago but probably appreciated by the first humans.

However, reading that a neighborhood rapist was caught and imprisoned or learning that a sibling was not awarded a needed fellowship evoke pleasant and unpleasant emotions, respectively, because of the relation between these events and the agent's values. Therefore, the valence of an emotion, which is a primary feature in the recall of autobiographical memories, often depends on a culture's values. I noted that events that deviate from normative experience often generate emotions with an undesirable valence. The emotion provoked among ancient Israelites by a person's death was judged unpleasant if it were premature, the result of violence, or unaccompanied by a burial because these conditions were discrepant from the norm. A survey of the attitudes held by residents of four countries toward eight emotions, desirable and undesirable, revealed that Americans and Australians regarded pride as a desirable and guilt as an undesirable emotion, whereas Chinese informants offered the opposite classifications.[65] This cultural difference is in accord with the popular belief that individualistic societies value the emotions that accompany personal achievement and the freedom to do as one wishes. Cultures that celebrate social harmony and group loyalty urge some restraint on the desire to perfect self when this motive exacts the cost of failing to honor these ethical norms.

The uncomfortable feeling that accompanied worry over God's wrath for violating an ethical standard was regarded as a desirable emotion among sixteenth-century Europeans. Americans regard the uncomfortable feeling that accompanies worry over disagreeing with friends who hold very different beliefs as immature and an undesirable emotion. The Romans, however, celebrated the emotion evoked by worry over disagreeing with others, which they called *verecundia*.[66]

The behavioral decision to approach or to avoid a target is occasionally controlled more by the valence of the emotion than by the valence of the feeling. The taste of a martini is aversive to and avoided by infants but judged as pleasant and sought by many adults. A bite of chocolate cake is judged more pleasant by those who are hungry and have no desire to diet than by overweight adults who have eaten a large meal and are trying to restrict their caloric intake. Thus, if a person had not eaten chocolate recently, the anterior portion of the orbitofrontal cortex became active to this taste and the sensation was judged as pleasant. But if the person were sated on chocolate, the same taste would be judged as less pleasant and this brain site would be less active. Thus, the valence of an emotion is not always inherent in, or consistent with, the valence of the sensory-based feeling.[67] The guilt that pierces consciousness minutes after a pleasant but illicit sexual act and the masochist's appraisal of pleasure while being whipped are classic examples.

There is often little or no relation between the judged valence of an event and biological activity in peripheral targets. The valences young men assigned to pleasant, unpleasant, and neutral pictures were not associated with distinct biological profiles. For example, pictures illustrating adventure and judged as pleasant (for example, cliff diving, motorcycle racing) and pictures of combat brutality judged as unpleasant produced similar magnitudes of eyeblink startles when a loud sound occurred as the men studied the pictures. But adventure pictures and erotic scenes, both judged as pleasant, produced different profiles of skin conductance and muscle activity in the mouth region (the muscle is called the zygomaticus major).[68] Although the valence of an emotion can change over the course of development and often varies with historical era and culture, a reliance on valence to categorize emotions remains attractive to scientists who wish to restrict emotions to those feelings that have behavioral consequences. I shall argue later, however, that classifications based on consequences have serious problems.

## Salience

The perceived salience, or intensity, of a feeling or emotion is a potentially useful feature in classifying emotions because salient feelings recruit attention, disrupt ongoing thoughts or behaviors, and are difficult to ignore. Salient feelings are often induced by events that are distinctive because they are physically intense, discrepant, or contain biologically prepared features. Bright streaks of lightning across the night sky are physically intense but need not be discrepant. A rich, pink sunset set against the dark blue of the sky at dusk possesses color patterns that have a privileged influence on the brain, even though the patterns are neither physically intense nor discrepant. Seeing a person with one leg generates a feeling because it is a discrepant experience, although neither intense nor biologically privileged. A sharp pain, the smell of acrid smoke, a very sour taste, a wildly racing heart, sudden dizziness, and the siren of a state trooper's automobile usually produce an autonomic reaction and a salient feeling or emotion. Although the salience of an emotional experience is typically a function of the perceived intensity of the underlying feeling, it can refer to the effort associated with a behavioral component of the emotion.[69] Fear and anger are both salient emotions, but anger has a more active motor component than fear.

The salience of an emotion is always influenced by the unfamiliarity or unexpectedness of the incentive or the feeling it generates. The detection of tachycardia by someone who just missed being hit by a speeding motorist acquires its salience from the intensity of the bodily reaction. The perception of a smaller increase in heart rate while reading about a local sports event in the morning paper is salient because the feeling is unexpected. I noted that unexpected or unfamiliar events or feelings potentiate all emotional states. Individuals overestimate the potential danger of harmful events that occur infrequently. Although domestic airline crashes are far less frequent than equally serious bus or car accidents, people are more likely to avoid flying after learning of a plane crash than to cancel a bus or automobile trip after reading about a fatal accident on these vehicles. I suspect that sexual feelings possessed greater salience during the nineteenth century than they do today because there was greater response uncertainty over their expression. This is one reason why Freud's ideas were popular during the early decades of the last century. A significant node of uncertainty among contemporary Americans centers on the ethical premises that deserve unquestioned loyalty.

Magicians of the ancient world typically performed very unfamiliar actions with familiar objects in order to arouse observers and thereby increase their faith in the power of the ritual to cure an illness or help them obtain a desired resource. In one ancient Egyptian ritual, the magician drowned a falcon (falcons were regarded as divine animals) in a vessel of cow's milk sweetened with honey, wrapped the dead falcon in cloth, and placed it near samples of his fingernails and hair. Many novel medical and psychotherapeutic procedures recruit enthusiasm and hope from both therapists and patients, before there is validation of their effectiveness, simply because they involve unfamiliar requests or actions by the therapist. Eighteenth-century physicians used leeches to bleed sick patients of their "toxic" blood. Psychoanalysts required patients to lie on a couch and free associate. One imaginative analyst placed the feces of a dog under the couch where the patient lay in order to facilitate the recall of childhood memories. Once the novelty of a therapeutic procedure has dissipated, however, its therapeutic power often wanes because it ceases to arouse both therapist and patient. It is unclear how many currently popular therapeutic regimens will suffer this fate.

A scientific procedure that later research revealed to be an insensitive source of evidence for a concept, because the procedure was based on false assumptions, is analogous to a magical ritual. The inkblot test of personality designed by Hermann Rorschach and used by a generation of clinical psychologists during the middle decades of the last century provides an example. Rorschach, who reproduced color photographs of ten inkblots on expensive paper, declared that certain interpretations of the blots revealed personality traits. For example, a man who based his interpretations on small details of the blots, rather than the whole, was diagnosed as obsessive-compulsive. Thousands of psychologists defended the power of this diagnostic ritual with passion. Some of the arcane mathematical equations economists use to predict inflation and recession, which make assumptions about human decision-making that are inconsistent with all we have learned about human nature, are rituals trusted by political leaders. We should not smile condescendingly at the ancient magicians who believed in the power of drowning a falcon in milk. Hope ascends on the wings of every new idea. But because most novel ideas turn out to be mistaken, too many high-flying hopes enjoy only a brief period of flight toward the gleaming sun before descending with a thud to their rendezvous with disappointment.

There is reason to suspect that the right hemisphere is preferentially engaged by intense stimuli, whereas the left hemisphere participates more fully when individuals are trying to understand or classify an unfamiliar event.[70] Four types of emotions are generated by crossing the two bases for valence (sensory quality and relation to self's values) with the two bases for salience (perceptual intensity and unfamiliarity). In this scheme, the emotion that accompanies eating chocolate after six hours without any food is distinguished from the emotion generated in a mother who has just seen her ten-month-old daughter stand up and take her first steps.

The salience of a feeling or an emotion is always affected by its relation to a prior state, as is true for valence. A large increase in heart rate, common in the emotions of fear and anger, and a feeling of nausea accompanying disgust, are more salient than the change in muscle tension that occurs when individuals anticipate a desired event because heart-rate increase and nausea are more discrepant from a person's usual state. Hence, their distinctiveness is exaggerated, and occasions of fear, anger, and disgust are memorable among those who do not experience these states frequently. These emotions would be less salient among refugees in a lawless refugee camp or soldiers in a war zone. Adults undergoing a colonoscopy who experienced peak pain at the termination of the procedure had a more vivid memory of, and greater reluctance to repeat, this examination than those whose peak moment of pain occurred minutes before the probe was withdrawn from their body.[71] This intriguing fact helps explain why the beginnings and ends of long epochs of experience are remembered best. College students have firmer representations of their emotional states their first day on campus and while studying for final examinations at the end of the year than of the many occasions of anxiety, joy, sadness, and anger that occurred during the intervening eight months. The person who happens to be the first source of intense sexual arousal or gratification often retains a unique halo for many years. The first occasions for intense fear or disillusionment possess the same salience and are usually not forgotten.

As with valence, the context in which an incentive occurs influences the appraisal process and enhances or dilutes an emotion's salience. For example, the judged unpleasantness of a painful thermal stimulus was greater when it was administered along with an unpleasant picture rather than alone. The salience of an unhappy or disappointed state among individuals who had just failed a task was greater if they expected to succeed than if they anticipated failure. That is why Olympic athletes who won a silver medal were more unhappy than those who won a bronze medal. More of the silver-medal recipients expected to win a gold medal, whereas more of the bronze-medal recipients did not expect to win any medal at all. The salience of shame or guilt following an ethical violation is greater if the person judges the violation as intentional instead of as an unavoidable accident.[72]

The differential salience of the many potential emotional states in each individual's hierarchy is, of course, influenced by the frequency of relevant experiences. Homeless men and women in urban settings worry about being humiliated or attacked by cruel adolescents; middle-class adults worry about performance failure. In addition, within a particular culture, the salience of an emotion is often due to temperamental biases that favor particular feelings, whereas the frequency of an emotion is more often the result of life conditions. For example, adults who were unusually sensitive to their heartbeats rated emotional pictures as more arousing than those who were less aware of their heart rates.[73]

Less salient emotions are usually, but not always, judged as pleasant; very salient states are more often appraised as unpleasant. The mild feeling of fatigue following exercise, compared with the more intense feeling of muscle strain following ten hours of manual labor, illustrates this dynamic. The seventeenth-century English writer Thomas Wright, who posited eleven basic passions, relied on salience as a defining feature when he classified anger and hatred as separate emotions.[74] Scientists who perform classical conditioning experiments usually use salient unconditioned stimuli (for example, electric shock, a feeling of nausea, or a puff of air to the cornea) because they have learned that the more salient the unconditioned stimulus, the faster the conditioning.

Adults found it easier to discriminate between similar odors when they were standing up than when lying supine, implying that the differences between the stimuli were more salient under the former posture. This fact has implications for the conclusions derived from magnetic resonance procedures that measure changes in blood flow when subjects are lying supine. It is likely that some of these inferences would have to be altered if the participants were scanned in an upright posture, more characteristic of the natural situations in which emotions are evoked, because patterns of blood flow differ in the two postures.[75]

Finally, an often-overlooked perceptual phenomenon has implications for the events that give rise to emotions. The internal elements within bounded objects, or the separate features of a scene, vary with respect to the magnitude of difference in physical properties, such as color, luminance, size, motion, and contour, between adjacent elements. The greater the difference between contiguous elements, the more alerting the event. A pale face with large, dark eyes and eyebrows, for example, is more salient than most faces. Equally important, the brain extracts this property from events originating in different sensory modalities. As a result, the mind treats visual and auditory events characterized by a large difference between adjacent elements in a similar way. To illustrate, most Americans asked to decide whether the nonsense word *queep* means fast or slow chose fast because the adjacent phonemes of *queep* and the concept fast share the feature of rapid change. Similarly, adults asked to assign the most appropriate nonsense syllable to a design with angles versus one with rounded counters selected the word *kiki* as the better name for the former and the word *boubu* for the latter.[76] There is a greater change in the direction of the contour in angles than in curved contours, and a greater change in pitch between the phonemes of *kiki* compared with those of *boubu*.

Painters, composers, and poets rely on this principle to create an aesthetic effect. The pattern of color and luminance on the man about to be shot, compared with the elements in the rest of the scene, in Francisco José de Goya's *The Fifth of May* awards the painting a special aesthetic power. There was a major change in the paintings of European artists after the First World War. Picasso, Georges Braque, and other modernists replaced the smooth, curved contours of the Impressionists with more abrupt lines and angles. Both children and adults shown curved and angular designs regarded the angular forms as less pleasing and more symbolic of tension, anger, and fear. It is reasonable to suggest that the new cohort of artists was responding to their society's frustration over the lost idealism that characterized the end of the nineteenth century and the beginning of the twentieth. The poet e. e. cummings, a master at exploiting phonemic contrasts, described stars as "driving white spikes of silence into joists." Other poets rely on seriously contrasting semantic concepts in the same line to achieve an effect. T. S. Eliot wrote in the *Four Quartets*, "And the fire and the rose are one." Sharp contrasts within an event also affect the judgment of the aesthetic quality of a proverb. Most individuals prefer proverbs that contain contrasting elements, such as "Every uphill has its downhill" or "Half of a truth is still a lie" to those that have no contrast (for example, "A wounded spirit is hard to heal").[77]

An aesthetic emotion is based on more than the perceptual features of an event, however. It also requires agents to possess the notion of an ideal representation. Knowing the origin of the creative product contributes to the judgment that it approaches the ideal. I experienced a less salient aesthetic feeling while viewing a photograph of the Snake River at dusk than while gazing at a painting of the same scene because I appreciated the greater talent and effort required for the painting. Humans assign more value to an outcome that requires more rather than less effort to obtain. There is a good reason why faculty establish a set of difficult hurdles a student must conquer before obtaining a bachelor's or professional degree. It is probably relevant that maintaining sustained effort to achieve a goal—what many call motivation—requires high levels of dopamine in select midbrain sites. It is likely that the psychological state accompanying this neurochemical profile contributes to the value imposed on the desired goal. An aesthetic reaction to art and music is rare in children because they have neither the experience nor the cognitive ability to relate most creative products to an ideal and to understand the effort required for its actualization.

The perceptual properties of events are occasionally ignored by investigators who compare brain reactions to unpleasant scenes, such as bloodied victims, snakes with open jaws, revolvers, and snarling dogs, with neutral objects, such as tables, chairs, and fruits. The unpleasant pictures often possess greater color and contour contrast than those in the neutral category. Hence, differences in brain profiles might be due in part to the special physical characteristics of the unpleasant pictures.

## Consequences

The behavioral or cognitive consequences of a brain state or feeling are the most controversial bases for classifying emotions. Most ancient and medieval commentators considered the origin, valence, and salience of an emotion as more critical than the actions that followed. More important, most psychological processes, including motor and cognitive phenomena, are defined by their intrinsic features rather than by their outcomes. For example, actions are categorized as voluntary or involuntary, involving specific muscle systems, or described with respect to their speed or force. Cognitive processes are parsed in accord with the nature of their activities; for example, detecting sensory events, creating perceptual or semantic representations, recalling or recognizing representations, inferring causes, and deducing conclusions. Although behaviors and cognitive processes are also classified by their consequences (for example, actions that harm another or performances that meet a preselected criterion), these categories are often used by psychologists interested in questions other than the inherent properties of the cascade that produced them. That is, the social scientist who classifies all behaviors that harm others as "aggressive" is not interested in the details of the muscle systems that participated in the action. Thus, a concern with the consequences of an emotion has some value, but it cannot illuminate the brain and psychological processes that define emotional families.

Nonetheless, a fair proportion of contemporary psychologists and philosophers favor restricting the concept "emotion" to states with consequences, whether protective of self, aiding the attainment of personal goals, or influencing asocial acts, social relationships, or beliefs. The mind likes ideas that possess simplicity, have breadth of application, and are concordant with ethical values. The decision to make consequences an important criterion for an emotion has the advantage of eliminating many states, relating to the broad notion of adaptation, and being in accord with a pragmatic ethic that is attractive to North Americans and Europeans. Thus, some psychologists insist that a feeling should be classified as an emotion only if it is linked to a readiness for action; others limit emotions to the realization of motivational states. One definition in a respected handbook states: "We propose a working definition of emotion that emphasizes action, the preparation for action, and appraisal of the significance or relevance to concerns of person-environment transactions."[78] Joseph Campos, one of the authors of this statement, and a distinguished scholar who has brooded on this issue for many years, restricts the meaning of *emotion* to experiences that are personally significant for the agent and motivate attempts to maintain or change the agent's relation to the world.

It is not clear why Western commentators, compared with Chinese and

Indian writers, celebrate the salient emotions that accompany intimate relationships and acts of self-enhancement but are relatively indifferent to the less salient states that accompany listening to a symphony, exercise, walking in a forest, or brooding on the state of the world. In the popular film *My Dinner with Andre* (1981), two men engage in an extended conversation about life over dinner. Andre, reflecting the mood of the young during the 1960s and 1970s in America, tells his companion that a relationship has no meaning unless it is accompanied by strong, honest emotion. A married couple who no longer feel passionate love for each other, Andre implies, are in a flawed relationship and should separate.

The contemporary obsession among Americans with being involved in a sexually arousing, gratifying relationship required a number of historical changes. Among the more important were economic and demographic arrangements that made it harder to honor the demand for feeling engaged by one's work or friendships but easier to gain moments of excitement from temporary sexual liaisons. If a large proportion of the population feels that their daily work is meaningless, their friendships are superficial and unreliable, and their children are neither grateful for their sacrifices nor willing to conform to their requests, and if an egalitarian ethos denies them the opportunity to extract private feelings of pride because of their religion, family pedigree, or ethnicity, at least the arousal of sexual attraction and the pleasures of lovemaking remain attractive possibilities. The fifth-ranked baboon in a troop ascends to the alpha position if the four more dominant animals are killed by predators. It seems we must confront the possibility that Aristotle, Cicero, Confucius, and Kierkegaard, who believed that happiness was found in the feeling of virtue that followed honoring one's obligations, simply did not understand human nature, but Andre did.

I have the intuition that the celebration of salient feelings of arousal by Americans and Europeans is due in part to a trio of factors. The most obvious is a product of the importance attached to each individual's striving to perfect the self. The excitement linked to new experiences—new places, new relationships, and new activities—renders agents more sophisticated, worldlier, more knowledgeable, or more talented. Travel to a new country, learning a new skill, and establishing a new friendship are sought for an excitement that is based, in part, on the anticipation of self-enhancement.

A second, less obvious, factor is the rise of bureaucratic institutions in Western societies. Because most workdays are predictable, boredom is common. By contrast, many citizens in third world countries cannot be certain each morning that they will escape attack, have sufficient food, and be free of illness that day. Life in these settings is sufficiently unpredictable that few have to look for additional sources of arousal.

A third factor might stem from the fact that Christianity values the emotion of faith in a benevolent spiritual force. The seeking of emotional arousal by those who are secular could be a derivative of this religious heritage. Although all three factors could contribute to this cultural difference, the first seems the most likely and the most significant.

The decision to award special status to emotions that affect actions or the quality of interpersonal relationships makes it easier to meet science's demand for constructs with referents that can be measured, an imperative whose authority derives from the heroic stature of Galileo and Isaac Newton and the philosophical positions of Ernst Mach and the members of the Vienna Circle. Actions have a measurable form, velocity, and location in space; feeling states possess none of these characteristics. Western scientists, since Plato's hypothesis of geometric forms and Democritus's image of atoms as the foundation of matter, have been friendly to discrete, bounded entities as the bases for all natural phenomena. The success of this epistemology, compared with the less fruitful consequences of the Chinese commitment to the formless energy of chi, persuaded a majority of natural scientists that material forms—things—are the building blocks of nature. This bias is so pervasive that some advocates of string theory illustrate its constructs as cylinders of varied shapes and lengths so that readers who are not physicists will have a stronger faith in the reality of ideas that are abstract mathematical propositions representing energy states with different resonating frequencies. There is no way to draw the concept of packets of energy oscillating at different frequencies, just as there is no way to illustrate the concepts of imaginary number or imaginary time. The only opposition to the worship of things comes from orthodox advocates of quantum mechanical models of matter who insist that there are no stable objects in the world. My perception of the computer I am using to type this sentence is an illusion.

The decision to restrict emotions to states with consequences is, as I noted, loyal to the program of the American pragmatists who were eager to accommodate to the growing importance of science at the end of the nineteenth century. The significance of emotions, according to the pragmatists, derives from their effects on the world and not because they alter consciousness. Advocates of a consequential definition of emotion appear to be bothered by events that have no useful purpose or outcome, such as a gene with no implications for the phenotype or a sated hawk soaring high above a meadow on a warm, windy afternoon. The early behaviorists also defined the concept of reward in functional terms (remember, it referred to any event that strengthened a stimulus-response connection) because they did not understand its inherent features. Contemporary scientists, recognizing that this definition suffered from circularity, nominated some intrinsic features of this concept. A discrepant change in the perceptual surround following a response and a dopamine surge to an unexpected desired event are two useful, although different, candidates.[79]

Because it is difficult to measure private emotional states, psychologists are forced to assume that particular behaviors (for example, an act of aggression, shyness with others) reflect an emotion, even though these actions are often well-practiced habits unaccompanied by any change in emotional state.[80] Eating lunch because it is noon, smiling on seeing a friend, and kissing a child at bedtime are examples of routine habits that need not be linked to any feeling. Moreover, requiring an emotion to have personal significance for the agent permits psychologists to compete with neuroscientists for control of this scientific territory because the neuroscientists are unable, at least at present, to determine which events or psychological reactions meet the slippery criterion of "personal significance."

It is likely that the attraction to a functional requirement for emotions, especially when the function is adaptive, has the implicit aim of promoting human affects to a position as prominent in the human psychic economy as rational, cognitive processes and awarding them a benevolent, rather than only a disruptive, role in human affairs.[81] An emphasis on psychological states that maintain or alter a person's relationships to others also redresses the current imbalance between the power enjoyed by physical scientists, economists, and computer programmers, who rely on logical operations free of emotion, and the status loss experienced by social scientists after the demise of Freudian theory, the limitations that had to be placed on earlier, broad generalizations from conditioning principles, and the failure to discover profound, experimentally verified insights about human behavior that were indifferent to feelings and emotions.

A fair proportion of psychologists who study humans harbor a secret wish to return to Jonathan Swift's century, when it was understood that passion controlled reason. The popularity of the concept *emotional intelligence*, which altered the traditional meaning of intelligence as seriously as the phrase "cooperative yeast" changed the meaning of cooperation, is one sign of this motivation. The lack of sensitive methods to quantify the subtle complexities of feelings and emotions, what W. V. Quine called "the empirical check-points that are the solace of the scientist," remains a serious source of frustration for those who believe Swift was correct.[82] If the rational deductions of physicists, however, require us to believe that a stream of photons directed at a screen with two slits passes through both openings simultaneously (medieval Christian scholars speculated that an angel could be in two places simultaneously), and a temporal interval too short to imagine was sufficient to allow the marble-size bundle of energy that existed before the big bang to expand to a universe measured in billions of light-years, it may be time to honor the legitimacy of the emotion English calls "confusion," even if this state is hard to measure with the precision Lord Kelvin demanded.

Many emotions do have consequences, and some incentives have enhanced salience when accompanied by an appropriate motor response (for example, actively sniffing an odor increases its perceived intensity).[83] Feelings and emotions have consequences for the effectiveness of cognitive functions, interpersonal behavior, goal-directed actions, self's evaluation of its virtue, and the severity of symptoms of psychopathology. The emotions that enhance attention and concentration, and aid completion of a task, preparation for a rendezvous, and reflection on a change in career are useful, whereas those that interrupt cognitive processes or behaviors directed at a desired goal are not. Feelings and emotions also ensure that the individual will inhibit asocial behaviors that would incur community criticism, provoke anxiety or shame, or lead to actions that engender moments of guilt and mar a person's judgment of his or her virtue. Finally, the events that produce a change in feeling are often remembered best and therefore increase the probability of displaying, or suppressing, the behavior that produced them. These events belong to the category psychologists call "rewards" or "reinforcements."[84] In a later section on basic emotions I shall argue that attention to consequences permits a distinction between the emotions that do or do not contribute to the universal human competences that aid fitness.

Some emotions that seem to have the appearance of legitimacy, however, have no obvious consequences. Consider two people watching the evening news who experience the same brief bout of sadness as they hear about the terrible state of refugees in Sudan. One of them acts on that state by sending a donation to a charitable agency. The other does nothing, but the absence of action does not negate the fact that this individual experienced an emotional state. This hypothetical example implies that it is not possible to declare that a particular state does or does not have consequences. Rather, an emotion does or does not have consequences in particular agents on particular occasions. The emotion induced by seeing a deep pink sunrise, recollecting the death of a friend, or remembering the evening one was impolite to a visitor need not have any consequences or motivate actions that maintain or change the agent's relation to others. Nonetheless, these states are as coherent as an autumn leaf falling from a tree or a spring robin perched on a windowsill. Perhaps that is why Hindu philosophers writing between the third and eleventh centuries nominated *sama* (best translated as a feeling of serenity) as one of nine primary emotions.[85]

A serious problem trailing a functional requirement for emotions is the tendency to ignore the origins or special psychological and biological characteristics of feelings. An object called a "seat" has a clear function, but seats vary in the conditions that produced them as well as in their inherent features. A plastic chair, wooden bench, cement slab, fallen log, and flat rock can all function as a seat. Thus, the claim that the brief feeling of muscle tension provoked by reading about Nazi concentration camps that is interpreted as anger should not be called an emotion if it has no behavioral or cognitive consequences requires a rationale based on richly textured theory or empirical evidence. Neither advantage characterizes the current state of knowledge. Hence, it is not obvious that an emphasis on consequences is a useful strategy to prune the long list of possible feeling or emotional states into those that are or are not legitimate emotions. This strategy is popular when understanding is immature and is cast aside when inquiry has revealed the nature of the phenomena. Modern biologists do not classify diseases by the likelihood that they will cause death or plants by their edibility. A planet is not defined as an object that astronauts might visit; a hole is not something into which children might fall.

Emotions do, on occasion, have consequences that can be observed, but declaring, a priori, that a consequence is a necessary component of an emotion requires arguments more persuasive than those offered thus far. A flowing stream in a remote Alaskan forest is a natural event worthy of study whether or not it sustains life or animals drink from it. If future research reveals that emotions with consequences have a history, biology, and form that differ from the states without consequences, which is possible, scientists will accommodate to those facts and posit two classes of emotions. A similar dichotomy occurred in astrophysics when new evidence required inventing the novel concepts of dark matter and dark energy. We will have to wait for the evidence that verifies the need for two categories of emotions distinguished by the presence or absence of consequences, or perhaps several categories based on the exact nature of those consequences.

# THREE

# Language and Emotions

M any contemporary scientists parse the emotions with abstract semantic concepts, such as "fear," "sad," "angry," and "joy," that contain little
or no information on the brain state, origin, target, expectedness, or consequences for self or others of the underlying feeling. These words resemble
the abstract concept "locomote" rather than the more concrete terms *walk,*
*run, jog, hop, saunter, burrow, swim, fly,* and *slither,* which contain some
clue as to the species and the speed and form of the motion. Humans invent words to name both events perceived and ideas that can organize the
plethora of similar perceptual schemata into a smaller number of conceptual groups. The beagle puppy next door is an object in the world, but the
words *canine, mammal,* and *living thing,* to which the puppy is assigned, are
concepts. Similarly, an unpleasant feeling of nausea on seeing and smelling
a rotting squirrel is a perceived event, whereas the words *disgust, negative
affect,* and *emotion,* to which the feeling belongs, are conceptual ideas. A
yellow, a red, and a purple object on a surface create a perceptual schema;
the statement, "Three pieces of fruit are on a counter," is a conceptual invention. The perceptual experiences are guaranteed a similar instantiation in
human consciousness; the concepts, however, are inventions that are likely
to change with time and culture. That is why philosophers like Alfred North
Whitehead warn us to remain vigilant lest we confuse the two mental forms
and why I chose "Theories come and theories go. The frog remains" as an
epigraph for this book.

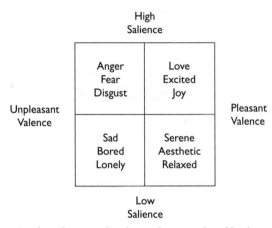

Some of the emotional words assigned to the quadrants produced by the two dimensions of valence and salience

When humans are judging the similarities between emotional words, without additional information from pictures, sounds, feelings, or nature of the setting, they tend to rely on the two dimensions of valence (pleasant to unpleasant) and salience (low to high intensity), which imply a special interest in the person's private feeling tone. Each emotional term can be assigned a position in one of four quadrants created by crossing the valence and salience dimensions. Joy, for example, has a pleasant valence and high salience; serenity has a pleasant valence but low salience. Boredom has an unpleasant valence and low salience, whereas fear has an unpleasant valence and high salience. Most emotional terms in English, Chinese Japanese, Indonesian, and Dutch fit this scheme, even though Asians differ from Americans in the celebration of moods of lower arousal and the ability to control one's emotions.[1]

One problem with this simple, four-cell semantic structure is that it is hard to use with emotional blends. The state of many college seniors as May approaches, which combines a feeling of intense joy with sadness over leaving their beloved campus, is not easily assigned to one of the four quadrants. Furthermore, the two semantic dimensions are not unique to emotions. Individuals from varied cultures use the dimensions good-bad and potent-impotent, which share meaning with valence and salience, to classify names for social roles, animals, foods, and objects that have little or no relation to feelings or emotions.[2] For example, most adults use the dimensions wild/dangerous to domesticated/safe (and by implication bad to good) and large to small (and by implication potent to less potent) to classify words for animals. A chicken is domesticated/harmless and small; a bear is wild/dangerous and large. But no biologist uses these dimensions to classify animals into phyla, families, or species, and no neuroscientist uses valence and salience to classify brain processes because they do not reflect the history or physiology of the animal.

Moreover, the valence and salience dimensions for emotional words are not faithful to the biology or the detected feeling states that give rise to emotions. Even adults who cannot experience any autonomic feedback from body to brain, as well as patients with a lesioned amygdala, rely on valence and salience when they use words to classify emotional events.[3] This fact is surprising, for these patients could have relied on how much the emotion involved other people, led to an action or facial expression, or owed its origin to thoughts or external events. A few cultures do honor these features. Most adults would use the features of gender and age, not valence and salience, to judge the similarities among photographs of human faces; size and purpose for illustrations of buildings; and pitch and loudness for brief sounds. Professional wine tasters choose words describing the color, bouquet, and taste of the wines they are judging.

The main point is that the dimensions that come easily to humans when they judge the similarity between words have special features that are chosen less often when they judge the similarities between scenes, behaviors, or brain states. All conclusions about emotions based only on verbal descriptions, therefore, have distinctive meanings that often do not apply to inferences derived from biological or behavioral data. Remember inferences about the phylogenetic history, and therefore the genetic similarity, of animals based on fossil evidence often disagree with conclusions based on shared DNA segments. Put plainly, the low-level principles about emotions that have been extracted from studying the language people use are restricted to this source of evidence. The words *disgust* and *anger* share the same valence and salience, but neither brain profiles nor behavioral observations indicate that these emotions are similar. Each of these words belongs to a family of related semantic networks. For example, one network for *anger* contains semantic representations for frustration, insult, attack, or coercion by another; a second network contains representations for personal mistakes; and a third has representations for events that violate the person's sense of justice. The networks are accompanied by different feelings, schemata, and brain states, although united by the term *anger*.

The measured strengths of the separate associations among the terms in the collection of networks are determined by the local context. For example, the probability of activating the association between anger and injustice is higher while reading about the refugees in Darfur than after failing to honor an appointment with a friend. Second, some semantic nodes have an association with perceptual schemata (for example, some persons are likely to activate perceptual representations of the sorry refugees at Darfur while reading about conditions at the camp). The variation in the probability of activating perceptual features defines the concrete-abstract continuum. Finally, some semantic nodes have conditioned associations with brain profiles that create bodily feelings and, as a result, an emotion. It is likely, but not proven, that use of a semantic term is more likely to reflect an emotion if it also activated a perceptual schema. The term *terrified* is more likely to be associated with a schema than the word *uncertain*. And, of course, those who have experienced terror (a soldier who fought in Iraq) are more likely to activate a schema than an individual who has never served in the armed forces.

## The Centrality of Evaluation

Wolfgang Koehler, whose William James lectures at Harvard University in 1934 were titled "The Place of Value in a World of Facts," restated the significance of the contrast between good and bad. But the behaviorists, loyal to logical positivism, ignored his message, and Quine, one of the most respected philosophers of the past century, believed that these evaluative terms had no claim to objectivity because their referents were too varied.[4] Nonetheless, the pervasiveness of the good-bad dimension in the semantic categorization of many phenomena implies that it might have a partial foundation in brain function. Newborns show one facial expression to sweet liquids placed on their tongues and a very different expression to sour tastes. It is possible that whenever an individual classifies a feeling as pleasant (or unpleasant), a restricted set of neuronal clusters might share a certain property. If, for example, a sweet taste, gentle stroking, and the smell of roses evoked synchronous firing of a pool of neurons at the same dominant frequency, and sour tastes, the prick of a pin, and the smell of rotting food evoked synchronous firing of a different neuronal pool at a different dominant frequency, each class of events might be bound together to create a foundation for the pleasant and unpleasant semantic categories.[5] Because praise, mastery, and meeting a personal ethical standard are appraised as good as well as pleasant, these more symbolic, less sensory experiences might become associated with the representations of the pleasant sensory states. This claim is not totally unreasonable because tastes activate circuits involving twenty brain sites with different preferred frequencies.

The semantic concepts "good" and "bad," therefore, function like magnets to pull diverse ideas and experiences that share the same semantic evaluation into distinct orbits. But that possibility, albeit speculative, does not mean that all good experiences share the same brain state or that their origins or consequences are similar. Thus, even if a select set of neurons were activated to all events categorized as pleasant, that fact would not mean that these events shared all the features of the complete brain profiles evoked by these events. Sixteenth-century herbalists classified wheat, which is a grass, with buckwheat, which is not a grass, simply because the two plants shared the word *wheat*. A similar error is made when the emotion following mastery, exercise, and orgasm are grouped together as "positive affect," or when anger at self for losing the house keys is treated as similar to anger at a stranger who pushed ahead in a queue.

Because all violations of ethical standards are categorized as bad, the symbolic representations of relevant behaviors are located in the same or linked semantic networks. Adults were first asked to remember either an unethical or an ethical action committed in the past. Each of these two groups was then shown word fragments and asked to guess the intended word. The fragments could be completed by choosing a word that was or was not related to cleanliness (for example, "w——h" could be "wash" or "wish"; "s——p" could be "soap" or "step"). The adults who had earlier recalled an unethical behavior more often chose words related to cleanliness, indicating that disparate events that violate an ethical standard share semantic networks.[6]

As I noted, however, the valence and salience dimensions that dominate semantic concepts for emotions are less applicable to the perceptional representations, or schemata, that represent the events the words are supposed to name. Most adults rely on the sensory qualities of odorants, not the semantic categories good or bad, when they judge the perceived similarity of two olfactory stimuli. When adults reported the first word that came to mind when they saw a picture, they usually thought of a verb, but when the provocative stimulus was a word, they were likely to think of a related noun. Thus, a picture of a dog would provoke the association "bark," but the word *dog* would elicit the response "cat."[7] The distinguishing perceptual features of the study in my home, my office at the university, the rooms in my dentist's suite of offices, and the building where I play indoor tennis are location, total area, types of furniture, usual behaviors, and people usually encountered, rather than judgments of their position on a good-bad or salience dimension. The pleasant, visceral feelings that follow exercise, a gourmet dinner, and a deep night's sleep are distinctive, associated with different brain states, and are easily discriminated from each other. The schemata for this trio of experiences are categorized as good following a symbolic appraisal that ignored their unique sensory properties. The valence of an emotion is a judgment that is not inherent in the underlying sensation. That is why an intense salt solution, which rats usually avoid because it is presumably aversive, is ingested if the animals have been deprived of salt.[8]

Representations of a person's goals, past actions, and decisions are channeled into valence categories that distinguish between gratifying, successful, or ethically correct choices and aversive, unsuccessful, or ethically incorrect ones. However, the perceptual products of the present moment escape, at least momentarily, these symbolic judgments.

## Selecting Features

Because feelings and emotions occur in contexts that contain a number of features, each individual has a choice in the features selected for translation into language. If the context were different, the features with priority, and the emotional label, might be altered, too. Humans probably perceive a ten-beat rise in heart rate in a similar way, but a person wishing to communicate that feeling to another could emphasize its valence, salience, origin, or un-expectedness in the emotional term selected. The English language makes it easier to describe valence and salience than origin or unexpectedness be-cause English vocabulary provides little or no information on the origin of a feeling or the degree to which it was anticipated. As a result, Americans talk about feeling anxious or happy rather than anxious over the unexpected diagnosis of cancer or the happiness felt in a new job. The latter descrip-tions are more accurate; no individual is anxious over all potential threats or happy with every aspect of their lives.

A person describing a bottle with a stopper resting on a table confronts a similar situation. Although there is probably little variation in the visual perception of this scene, the verbal description could refer to the compo-sition of the stopper (a cork or plastic form) or the bottle (glass or plastic), the bottle's contents (wine or olive oil), the tightness of fit of the stopper in the bottle, and/or the bottle's orientation on the table. Languages vary in the availability of semantic forms to describe one or more of these features. For example, English has no single term that allows a speaker to distinguish a bottle with a tight-fitting stopper lying on a table from one with a loose-fitting stopper standing upright. Some languages, however, permit the communi-cation of one or more of these distinctions. For example, the Mayan Indian language Tzeltal has six words for "inside" and six for "on" that specify the kind of stopper, the container in which it is inserted, and the surface on which the container rests.[9] The reply "In front of the chair" to the inquiry "Where is the ball?" fails to convey the fact that a large red plastic ball is on the floor one foot in front of a brown wooden chair at the far end of a living room with an oriental carpet on which rest six small toys.

Analogously, the reply "Sad" to the query "How do you feel?" spoken by a person who has just learned of the death of a close relative cannot capture the intensity or quality of a particular mourner's experience. Because En-glish words for emotions name families of different feelings and fail to specify the specific form these states assume in different contexts, they do not name natural kinds. The terms *full moon, storm cloud, palm tree,* and *pregnant woman* do.[10]

The problem with most emotional words, then, is that each has multiple and thus ambiguous meanings. Americans, for example, use the term *fear* (or *afraid*) to name worry over harm to the body, loss of property, social rejection, task failure, unfamiliar situations, and being alone. Each is accompanied by a different subjective feeling and biological foundation. Some fears are realistic; others are less realistic. College students from seven cultures agreed on the origins and prevalence of realistic fears (for example, dangerous animals, a serious illness), but there were significant cultural and gender differences in the worries nominated as less realistic (for example, encounters with cockroaches, worms, crowds, or being struck by lightning). Further, the heritability of the less realistic fears was considerably higher than the heritability of realistic ones, implying that the two types of fears have distinct biological foundations.[11] Adults would say it was realistic to be fearful while driving in a blizzard on an icy road but unrealistic to be afraid of speaking at a dinner party.

A second reason why most emotional terms have ambiguous meanings is that individuals occasionally use different words to describe feelings that, if measured, might be similar. For example, American social phobics use the words *anxious, worried,* or *apprehensive* to describe how they feel when they interact with strangers. Japanese social phobics choose terms that, in English, are closer in meaning to embarrassment and shame.[12] The origins of the feeling (that is, interacting with a stranger), its unpleasant and salient nature, and the consequences of socially awkward behavior are similar; nonetheless, Americans and Japanese use semantic terms that have different connotations because the Japanese are more concerned than Americans with maintaining harmony in their social relationships. Many Japanese feel obligated to honor two critical imperatives: offend no one and remain sensitive to one's role and status when interacting with others. That is why the Japanese have four verbs for the term *eat* that specify the status of the person eating and the relationship between speaker and listener.[13] The English language is relatively indifferent to these distinctions.

Finally, individuals who have actually experienced an emotion possess a meaning of the term that differs from the meaning held by those who have not. The meaning of "fear of harm" for those who have been victims of violence differs from the meaning held by those who have never experienced a direct physical attack on their body. That is why young children's replies to questions about emotions, which require the experiences and cognitive abilities of adults, have a special meaning.

## The Static Quality of Language

Feelings are dynamic, fleeting experiences; semantic concepts freeze-frame these states into static categories with core properties resembling Plato's geometric forms. Adults can easily discriminate between a pair of faces displaying variation in fear, anger, or sadness but will name all the faces belonging to a semantic category similarly when asked to label a facial expression; that is, they award the same term to all faces with a fearful expression.[14]

A similar phenomenon holds for the perception of color. All humans appear to judge the visible color spectrum categorically (red, yellow, green, blue) rather than as a continuum of wavelengths. Hence, most individuals usually choose the same word to name all the hues that fall within the range of wavelengths for green but use different terms when an equivalent range of wavelengths crosses the color boundary between green and blue. This observation is so robust some scientists have suggested that the categorical perception of color must be biologically determined. However, baboons, whose visual physiology is very similar to that of humans, do not show categorical perception of color.[15] This surprising discovery suggests that although biology clearly constrains the semantic terms for the visible spectrum, the vocabulary of a culture has some influence on the terms used to label colors.

A similar mechanism operates when individuals select an emotional label for their feeling. A mother who knew that her adolescent daughter had lost her boyfriend to another girl and noticed that her daughter had been unusually morose for several days would be apt to describe the daughter as "sad" or "angry" and unlikely to use a phrase that represented a blend of these two states. Languages, which invite an either/or categorization of experience, have difficulty classifying animals like the platypus, which has the bill and webbed feat of a bird but nurses its young and has a layer of hair characteristic of mammals. Languages throw away information in order to construct a tidy package.

Although emotions vary in duration, few words capture this property.

One-third of a group of young German women who reported extreme levels of social anxiety at one point in time (7 percent of a large sample) denied feeling anxious eighteen months later.[16] From their perspective, their anxiety is a dynamic rather than a static event. But from the perspective of an investigator asking informants to describe their emotions, in order to estimate the lifetime prevalence of social anxiety, the verbal replies are treated as categories. Niels Bohr's concept of complementarity between waves and particles may be useful. An emotion is a dynamic event (that is, like a wave) in the subjective frame of the agent but a category (that is, a particle) in the objective frame of the scientist.

The words that describe the changing brain states that accompany feelings and emotions are also summarized with categorical terms (for example, activation of the left frontal lobe or the amygdala), even though the brain's reaction varies over time.[17] Neuroscientists try to deal with this problem by presenting pictures illustrating the variation in the amount of blood flow to the areas of interest so that readers can appreciate the range of activity across the brain. Scientists who gather event-related potentials also present illustrations of the latencies and magnitudes of the beginning, peak, and end of the waveform. Meaningless words with the orthographic features of words (for example, *waagun, jinp*) evoke larger and later waveforms than meaningful words, such as *wagon* and *jump*, but do not produce distinctive waveforms. That is, meaningful words produce a waveform that is quantitatively, not qualitatively, different from the one produced by the meaningless words. The same is true for photos of faces with neutral, distressed, or angry expressions that vary in intensity. Words for emotions, like a photograph of a dancer, transform an inherently dynamic event into one frozen in time and space. The moment a woman announces that she is happy after reading a letter informing her of a promotion, her emotional state has already begun to change.

## Do Words Reflect Feelings?

Research on emotion would be easier if the frequent use of emotional words, in speech or in writing, accurately reflected the frequency of the states to which the words refer. Sadly, the correspondence between the two is minimal. Adolescents with an internalizing disorder characterized by frequent states of anxiety and guilt did not use more words referring to these emotions than other adolescents when both groups described the emotions of characters in a story or when administered a challenge that evoked uncertainty. Nor was there any relation between the frequency of emotional words in eight autobiographical essays and the writers' judgments of the salience of the feelings associated with the experiences described in their memoirs.[18]

Because most individuals are understandably reluctant to reveal emotions they regard as socially undesirable, psychologists have tried to invent indirect ways to measure these states. One popular method, called the implicit association test, assumes that individuals who hold a prejudicial attitude toward a class of people should possess a semantically closer association between the concept for the disliked class and the category "bad," compared with those who are less prejudiced. It is implied, often implicitly, that the prejudiced persons also experience the emotions of contempt, anger, or condescension toward the disliked other. The third assumption behind the method, which has the most support, is that the stronger the semantic link between two concepts, the less time required to decide that the two belong to the same category.

Consider one group of adults who did not like Mexican immigrants and a second group who favored their immigration. The two groups are first shown a stimulus intended to prime the semantic network for the concept "immigrant"; for example, they might see the word *immigrant* or a picture of an immigrant arriving at an official border crossing between Mexico and the United States. A second later they are presented with the words *poison* and *cake* and told to select, as fast as possible, the word most closely associated with the prime (that is, the picture or the word). The adults who opposed immigration should be faster in selecting the word *poison* compared with the word *cake*, whereas those who favored immigration should be faster in selecting the word *cake* compared with *poison* or slower in selecting *poison*.

Unfortunately, this method of evaluating the emotions that are linked to cognitive categories is vulnerable because one can possess a close semantic association between two undesirable semantic concepts without any accompanying change in feeling or emotion. Women who reported a fear of spiders and were reluctant to approach them in a laboratory setting did not show a stronger implicit semantic association between spiders and an undesirable semantic concept than women who had no fear of spiders, although some have found evidence for a modest effect of a fear of spiders using the indirect procedure. Finally, although more American women than men report feeling stigmatized by their gender, ratings of the desirability of more than seventeen hundred English words for personality traits revealed that the words most closely associated with femaleness were classified by both women and men as more desirable than the traits linked to maleness.[19] In French, more words naming undesirable events (for example, canker sore, bacteria, feces, and vomit) are in fact marked with a masculine morpheme.

The corpus of evidence, therefore, does not support the assumption that a tight semantic link between two undesirable (or two desirable) concepts, a verbal report of an emotion, or the detection of emotional words or faces presented for durations too brief to permit conscious awareness is usually accompanied by a feeling or emotion, although this conclusion is not consensual.[20]

The problem with the assumption that the implicit procedures can measure an emotionally based attitude is that unconscious cognitive processes can influence semantic judgments through the automatic activation of firmly established associations. That is why patients with an affliction preventing any feedback from bodily targets to brain and, therefore, an inability to experience bodily sensations make accurate semantic judgments of the emotions displayed on various faces and use the correct words to infer emotions in others.[21] Put plainly, a declaration containing an emotional term does not necessarily imply any change in feeling or emotion. Although poets and novelists rely on the power of words to arouse emotions, semantic networks can, on occasion, retain a degree of autonomy that floats free of both affect and action. That is why political speeches leave many listeners unmoved.

## The Influence of Culture on Emotional Terms

Emotional words and the sentences in which they occur are often embedded in distinct semantic networks among members of varied cultures because of different life experiences and ideologies. The semantic concept in the center of the network—called the prototype—is related, through an extensive set of semantic and schematic links, to actual events at the edge of the web of related symbolic representations. A robin is the prototype for the concept "bird" for North Americans but not for Indonesians. The prototype for an emotional term can refer to a personality trait or the feelings, origins, or consequences of an emotion. An analysis of more than a hundred Chinese words related to *shame* revealed terms for a shy personality, the act of blushing, acts that violated community norms, anger toward those responsible for the emotion, and individuals who are shameless.[22]

The term *apathy* is the prototype for the English term *depressed*, whereas *hopeless* is the prototype for Indians, *disappointment* for Sri Lankans, and *sad* for Indonesians. Today's North American college students regard a mother's love, not love of God, as the prototype for the concept *love*; medieval monks and nuns would have reversed this profile. Seneca, the Roman philosopher and dramatist who wrote as the modern era began, regarded the desirable state of serene tranquillity as the prototype for the Latin concept *apathy*, whereas the prototype for apathy among modern writers is an undesirable state of depression. The German term *angst* refers to an uncomfortable emotion that accompanies the inability to know the future. Because all future events are unknowable, only a culture that found this psychological state unusually distressing would have invented a concept that separated this form of uncertainty from others.[23]

The following ideas are likely to be the prototypes for some popular emotional terms used by Americans: the death of a friend or relative or the loss of a personal friendship for *sad*; imminent physical harm for *fear*; anticipation of task or social failure for *anxiety*; an insult, coercion, or domination for *anger*; receipt of a gift, praise, or task success for *happy*; anticipation of a novel experience for *excitement*; committing an act that hurt another for *guilt*; and accidental violation of a community norm for *shame*. Individuals who react emotionally to incentives that deviate from the prototypical cause are likely to be labeled as deviant. A feeling of anxiety over rising to speak at a town meeting fits the American prototype, but anxiety over the thoughts of a dead ancestor does not. The prototypes for emotional terms among Americans often differ from the prototypes found in other cultures.

When American and Japanese college students reported their emotional state the moment a signal occurred, Japanese students were more likely than their American counterparts to report feeling happy when they were with a friend. The American students were more often happy following receipt of a gift or success at an assigned task.[24] The prototype for the Greek term *philia* is a mutuality of affection between two people, whereas the prototype for the English term referring to the affectionate feeling for a friend does not include a reciprocal emotion on the part of the other. Americans treated the words *happy* and *excited* as more similar in meaning than the Japanese; Chinese informants regarded *shame* and *fear* as closer in meaning than the Japanese; *shame* and *fear* had a more similar meaning for Indonesians than for residents of the Netherlands.[25]

Both the culture and its unique vocabulary influence the features of a feeling or emotion that will be the prototype and awarded privileged status in a description. Although most languages emphasize the valence and salience of a person's private psychological states, the members of a small number of cultures promote the bodily origins of the feeling to the position of prototype (dizzy, headache, racing heart). A few languages award priority to the origin or consequences of the emotion. The Chinese have five distinct terms for shame or guilt that specify its origin and whether an agent's action injured another.[26] The English terms *shame* and *guilt*, which emphasize only the agent's mental state, do not provide this extra information. Two factors contributing to this cultural variation might be the celebration of the individual rather than the social contexts in which the agent acts and the attractiveness of the premise that a small set of fundamental units, the atoms of mental life, can account for the extraordinary variety of emotional phenomena.

The extensiveness, or complexity, of the semantic network for an emotional term is a joint function of the number of its semantic features and the degree to which they distinguish one word from terms with a related meaning. Some psychologists call this dimension *semantic relevance*. Slang words referring to sexuality have more semantic relevance for American men than women; *tenderness* has greater semantic relevance for women. The words *fear, anxiety, anger,* and *disgust* probably have a more extensive network than *serene, uncertain, empathic,* and *bored.* Hence, pictures or words suggestive of the former quartet will evoke a richer semantic network than members of the latter quartet and, as a result, should be accompanied by more brain activity.[27] Enhanced neuronal activation accompanying the reading of the words *fear* or *anger* on a screen therefore could be a function of a richer semantic network rather than a more intense emotional reaction to the words. I rarely detect a change in feeling on seeing a gun, a snake, or men fighting on a television screen, but I am aware of a rush of semantic associations to such scenes.

The cultural variation in semantic networks implies that investigators cannot assume that a word or sentence has the same meaning across speakers from different societies. The phrase "I love you" provides a nice example. Americans use this phrase far more often than members of most societies, but it lacks the salience that it has for others. Bilingual adults who know both English and their native language find it much easier to say, "I love you," in English than in their native tongue because this phrase implies a deeper emotional relationship in the native language. The same phenomenon holds for obscenities. Cursing in one's native language has emotional overtones that are missing when the same meaning is expressed in a language acquired later. The brain's reaction to varied sounds is often a function of their personal significance for the listener rather than the sounds' objective properties.[28]

These stubborn facts mean that it is probably impossible to translate all known emotional words from one language into another and assume that they have the same intended meaning. When the fourth-century Christian philosopher Augustine reflected on the differences between his feelings and the states he believed God wished him to have, he used several words to describe his emotion: "How foul I was and how crooked and sordid, bespotted and ulcerous." Most contemporary Europeans or Americans could not have experienced Augustine's state because it required strong beliefs in God, the devil, and absolutely sinful acts that condemned a soul to purgatory. The emotion felt by medieval men during coitus may have differed from the experiences of moderns making love because medieval Europeans believed that semen originated in the brain. Therefore, every orgasm depleted the brain's reservoir of vital energy.[29]

The emotional state of a Palestinian suicide bomber who believes he is going to paradise the moment before he blows himself up on a bus is difficult to create in an American college student. The feeling of surprise that occurs when a friend behaves in a way inconsistent with their usual personality is stronger among Americans than among Koreans because Koreans regard an act in a context as the significant unit. Because contexts vary, Koreans are less likely to be surprised when someone behaves in different ways across settings. The Ifaluk of Micronesia use the word *fago* to describe not only the emotion evoked when a friend dies but also the state of a person in the presence of one who is admired. There is no English term that comes close in meaning to the concept *fago*.[30]

The main implication of these facts is that investigators writing about emotion should use full sentences that specify: (1) the event and its presumed origin (for example, a criticism from a father, a tornado caused by natural forces, a headache caused by the wish of a dead ancestor); (2) the target of any emotional reaction (self, another person, an animal); and (3) the context in which the event occurs (the agent is alone, with others, in a familiar or an unfamiliar place). If, as is likely, some emotions are restricted to particular cultural settings, it will be impossible to map all the emotions experienced by the members of one society on to those from another culture.

## The Contrast between West and East

A critical but unsolved puzzle is why ancient Greek and Chinese societies developed different conceptions of humans, objects, and animals and their relations to their natural or social settings. It is worth noting that among the major ancient civilizations—China, Mesopotamia, Egypt, and India— China was unique both in its assumption that children were born with a bias for compassion and good acts and in its relative lack of concern with a god or gods that humans were to please and to fear. The contrasting assumptions about the foundation of natural phenomena held by the Greek and Chinese may be one basis for the different linguistic descriptions of humans and their emotional capacities.[31] The Greeks, and later the Europeans, assumed that atoms were the fundamental bases of all material things. But atoms do not change their properties when the setting changes. The Chinese placed their bet on energy—ch'i—as the basic substance, but the form that ch'i assumed did vary with the context, including the seasons of the year. The observed form that ch'i assumes in anger differs from its form in sexual arousal.[32]

The European emphasis on the inherently stable properties of atoms across settings was the foundation for the twentieth-century version of atomic theory and the search for the fundamental units of matter. The Darwinian idea of natural selection, which became the foundation of modern evolutionary theory, was more likely to have been invented by a European than an Asian because Europeans assumed that the individual, not the family or group, was the primary unit, and each individual strove for dominance and reproductive fecundity by competing, not cooperating, with others. The Chinese choice of energy as basic led to the view that natural phenomena reflected a balance between the forces of *yang* and *yin*. As one force waxed, the other waned, and each made a unique contribution to every phenomenon. In sexual activity, for example, the man received the health-giving benefit of the woman's yin. It was not until the twentieth century that Western neuroscientists began to write about the balance between the excitation and inhibition of a neuron or circuit. For the Chinese, dryness is a temporary state due to a lack of moisture and not a permanent quality. It may not be a coincidence that Japanese scientists, not Americans, investigated the therapeutic effects of a regular regimen of walking on level of anger and cardiovascular function in young women.[33] The disciplined practice of walking, which occurs in a unique setting, reduced both the salience of anger and the walker's heart rate. The ancient Chinese and Japanese took the changing quality of natural phenomena as they appeared to a perceptive mind as the events to understand. The Greeks assumed that these surface phenomena were deceptive and, therefore, tried to imagine the unchanging, invisible elements that were their foundation. Immanuel Kant was thinking like a quintessential European when he brooded on the essence of space and time. Contemporary scientists looking for the defining biological features of fear, anxiety, and anger are carrying on this tradition. But if anxiety over meeting strangers is treated as the temporary absence of a serene state of certainty, scientists should try to measure the balance between them.

The concepts "frame" and "attribute" are basic ideas in Japanese social life. Every personal attribute, especially one's role or position, is linked to a frame or social setting. An individual is a professor of a specialty at a particular university, not just a professor. There is no single word for "leader" in Japanese, for one is always a leader of a particular group. Leadership is not a personal property that an individual carries from one setting or group to another.[34] American and European faculty who offer courses on "leadership" assume that a particular set of personal attributes, say Napoleon's boldness and confidence, are required for leading any group of followers. Only a Japanese filmmaker would have made the movie *Maborosi* in which the settings of the actors and actresses were rendered distinctive through frequent long shots that portrayed just-discernable individuals in the distant background of a larger scene in the foreground.

These contrasting worldviews can be seen in how the members of two cultures describe people. There are two complementary ways to describe a person. One can list his or her distinctive features or describe their behaviors and moods in different settings or when assuming distinctive social roles. The former set presumably transcends settings, whereas the latter provides information on the specific behaviors one expects to see. A woman can be described as extroverted, tireless, conscientious, and amiable, on one hand, or as a hard-working trial lawyer, caring mother of two young children, and member of the local town meeting and hiking club, on the other. Americans prefer the former strategy, which emphasizes the traits preserved across time and situation, even though it fails to specify the specific behaviors most likely to occur in a particular situation. The Japanese and Chinese prefer the latter verbal style. This difference is captured by the contrast between the following descriptions of the famous painting of George Washington crossing the Delaware during the Revolutionary War: (1) Washington and his troops crossing the Delaware; (2) the crossing of the ice-filled Delaware River at night by American troops under the leadership of General George Washington.

Chinese informants asked to describe a person who is affectionate or charitable are likely to say, "Fei hugs her friends at parties" or "Jing gives money to beggars on the street." Americans are more likely to report that "Mary is loving" or "Bill is generous." The former sentences are more informative than the latter. The term *affectionate* emphasizes the stable features of a person; the verb phrase "hugs her friend at parties" points to the restricted nature of the trait. The more frequent use of verb phrases by the Chinese allows them to specify the settings in which an individual displays a behavior or emotion.

Compare the following two sentences: (1) obese adolescents eat too many carbohydrates at parties; (2) eating too many carbohydrates at parties will make adolescents obese. The first sentence implies a stable personal disposition; the second implies that eating habits at parties might differ from those at other times and, therefore, might be altered. Speakers who habitually think of each individual's characteristics, actions, roles, and social relationships in terms of the settings in which they behave should be biased to select verb phrases. The preference for using nouns and adjectives to describe individuals invites a stereotyped conception, whereas verb phrases imply a more malleable view of the individual.[35] The Big Five personality dimensions, an American invention, are adjectives that are free of a context (extroverted, conscientious, neurotic, open-minded, and agreeable). No Asian psychologist would have invented the Big Five.

There are fewer classes of distinct verbs than nouns. As a result verbs usually require specification of a context in order to resolve meaning ambiguity. The intended referents for the nouns *water, dog,* and *child* are less ambiguous than those for the verbs *fall* and *run* because water, dogs, and children fall and run in different ways. Thus, many verbs require the addition of a noun referring to an agent or a target to disambiguate meaning. This may be one reason why the reading of single verbs on a screen is accompanied by greater cortical activation than the reading of nouns.[36] They require more mental work. The English verbs *murder, impeach,* and *hire,* which imply a human agent and target as well as an intention, are exceptions. It is worth noting that this issue is irrelevant for perceptual schemata or brain states. Every brain state is necessarily contextualized, and the origin of every schema is an event in a context.

The speech exchanges between people are affected by the agent's wish to influence his or her relationship with the other, either to preserve an affiliation or to impress, dominate, hurt, or seduce the other. American psychologists usually ignore this motive when they ask informants to fill out questionnaires. They assume that only the content of the questions and the truth of the replies are worth worrying about and expect most informants to provide honest, accurate answers to their questions. This premise is naive. Because the power relation between the psychologist and the informant is usually unequal, the informant tries to avoid presenting an unflattering impression of self. The Japanese experience more salient anxiety than Americans over leaving a message on an answering machine because they worry about how the recipient will interpret the verbal communication.[37] Two Japanese business executives or scientists meeting for the first time exchange cards immediately so that each will know the relative social rank of the other and therefore how to behave. Americans would regard this practice as rude.

Put a bit too starkly, members of Western societies are primarily interested in empirically validated ideas that transcend settings. Members of Asian cultures care about truth, but they are also concerned with the subtle aspects of interactions that affect the mood and quality of relationship with the other. I recall asking a Japanese friend for an example of *tatemae* (this word refers to the persona one adopts with a non-intimate). He asked me to imagine sitting in a plane next to a Japanese writing on a pad of paper and asking, "What is that you are writing with?" The tatemae reply would be, "It's a pen, isn't it?" American and European readers of poetry automatically try to discern the ideas the poet was attempting to convey; Asian readers strive to imagine the feelings the poet had when the lines were being composed. An admitted caricature of these two psychological frames is contained in the presumed ruminations of a hypothetical American and Asian reading, "The darkness arrived and the birds have vanished." The American is likely to infer that the artist was trying to communicate a deep truth about human aging, the Asian apt to imagine the poet's momentary state of sadness.

An emphasis on a salient foreground object with features preserved across settings, on one hand, compared with an intimate blending of object and background, on the other, represents a critical distinction between West and East. One speculative argument that might aid understanding of this cultural variation relies on differences in climate, economy, and social structure. Ancient China was primarily an agricultural society composed of small hamlets and villages in which frequent weather extremes, such as drought and flood, forced the population to recognize their interdependence with nature. There are more popular fairy tales involving collaborative relationships between humans and animals in Chinese literature than in European folklore.[38] When animals do appear in European fantasies, as in "Little Red Riding-Hood," they are often dangerous threats to avoid.

The Greeks, by contrast, were a commercial society that enjoyed a more benign environment and celebrated the few who were unusually brave or talented. There are few ancient Chinese plays, poems, or novels comparable to Homer's *Odyssey* in which the courage and abilities of a single person, preserved across settings, were the central theme of the story. Chinese literature honors wise emperors and caring magistrates who serve and minister to those for whom they are responsible and loyal, obedient children. I suspect that the Chinese media would not have awarded prime coverage to a person who swam a mile in thirty-two-degree water from a boat to the Antarctic coast. American television celebrated this thirty-minute feat by a woman whose only motive was to achieve a uniquely human goal that was of no help to anyone. Finally, the Greeks' awareness of the heterogeneous appearances, languages, mores, and institutions of their trading partners in the Mediterranean and Aegean, compared with the greater homogeneity of Chinese society, might have led the Greeks to emphasize the stable differences among people. These contrasts between the cultures in economy, ecology, and premises about nature have derivatives, three thousand years later, in how language is used to describe humans and their emotions.[39]

## Discrete Emotions or Variation in Salience

A second unresolved issue is whether the use of different words to name emotions that scientists assume belong to the same family reflects variation on a continuum of salience or represents qualitatively discrete states? This question is related, of course, to the debate over whether conscious and unconscious processes lie on a continuum or are distinct phenomena, or whether the term *autistic spectrum* refers to one disease with symptoms varying in severity or different symptom profiles reflect diseases with separate causes. Consider, as an example, the semantic trio *happy, joyful,* and *exuberant,* which each of three individuals used to describe their imminent wedding day. If both brain and behavioral evidence revealed different profiles among the trio, we can ask whether the three individuals are experiencing different emotional states or variations on the same state? The same issue applies to the terms *sad, grieving,* and *depressed.*[40]

We can ask the same question when the origin of an emotion varies. Does a fear of being bewitched represent variation on the state that occurs when one is driving in a blinding snowstorm, or are these emotions qualitatively distinct? Furthermore, different origins can evoke distinctive emotional blends. The state of a fifteenth-century resident of Martin Luther's town of Wittenberg who was anxious over the possibility of going to purgatory might be qualitatively different from the state of a contemporary resident of the same city who was anxious over going to parties with better-educated guests because the former state combined anxiety with guilt over a life of moral errors, whereas the latter state combined anxiety with embarrassment. Vietnam veterans with post-traumatic stress disorder blend anxiety with guilt over having participated in, or witnessing, an act of atrocity on an innocent civilian. The state of an older person who locked herself out of the house combines anger with anxiety over possible loss of mental competence. The emotion felt toward a neighbor whose lawn is an eyesore blends anger with anxiety over the threat posed by her neighbor's indifference to the ethical standards she relies on to guide her daily behavior. The sadness that follows a mother's death is often combined with guilt over a past failure to be sufficiently affectionate to the parent when she was alive. By contrast, the sadness provoked by losing one's job is often combined with anxiety over one's financial future.

This issue is not an instance of "nit-picking" because the intensity and origin of a feeling can affect the appraisal of its valence and subsequent behaviors. A slight rise in heart rate and muscle tension felt before boarding a roller coaster is usually interpreted as excitement, whereas a large increase in the magnitude of these two reactions is likely to be interpreted as fear. An electric shock of mild intensity activates the ventral portion of the central gray of animals to release one set of responses. A more intense shock excites the dorsal portion of this structure and provokes different behaviors.

Psychiatrists were wise to invent distinct anxiety disorder categories, but they should have invented a unique term for patients who combined anxiety over encountering strangers and crowds with a depressive mood instead of concluding that these patients had "social anxiety comorbid with depression" simply because the patients reported that their anxiety was more salient and compromising than the depression. A sore throat and fatigue are more salient than muscle strain in patients with the flu. But physicians do not describe this syndrome as "a sore throat and fatigue comorbid with muscular discomfort" because the combination of all three defines the category "influenza."

It is not possible, at least at present, to point to evidence that could provide a definitive answer to our original question. The decision to treat the states happy, joyful, and exuberant as varying in intensity or as qualitatively different depends on the investigator's assumptions regarding the relations among the biological, cognitive, and behavioral features of the state. Fevers of 99, 101, and 103 degrees can be accompanied by distinct physiological patterns. The physician who knows that the same bacteria caused the three fevers is likely to regard them as falling on a continuum; the physician who knows that the three fevers were the result of different causes is likely to treat the patients as belonging to discrete categories.

When psychologists gain a deeper understanding of the relations among incentives and the brain patterns, feelings, and interpretations that follow, they will be in a better position to decide whether the semantic descriptions *happy*, *joyful*, and *exuberant* should be regarded as qualitatively different emotions. I suspect that the latter is closer to the truth, but at the moment either position is defensible. Water and ice vary quantitatively on a continuum of temperature but have qualitatively distinct structures and properties. Bohr's notion of complementarity is helpful again. The decision to regard electrons as wavelike or particlelike depends on the explanation that best fits the observations produced by a specific experimental procedure. The descriptions given by three individuals anticipating their wedding day that contained the words *happy*, *joyful*, or *exuberant* imply a continuum of salience. However, measurement of the amount of dopamine secreted by their brains might imply qualitatively different states if only the exuberant adult showed a large concentration of this neurotransmitter in the frontal lobes.

## Subjective and Objective Frames

A fair proportion of contemporary psychologists assume that individuals from the same culture who use a particular term to describe a present or past emotion probably have, or had, a similar feeling. Unfortunately, the evidence implies a flaw in this assumption. If a man participating in a group discussion with six other people cannot recall thirty minutes later how often he interrupted someone else, it is unlikely that most individuals are able to recall and/or describe accurately emotional experiences that occurred days, months, or years earlier.[41] This problem raises the historical distinction between subjective and objective frames.

Scientists who study human psychological states recognize the need to distinguish between the terms individuals use to describe their emotions and the theoretical terms that are intended to explain covariation between events, on one hand, and behavioral or biological outcomes, on the other. This distinction shares features with the anthropological contrast between emic and etic descriptions. A person's subjective judgment of their social class position is a somewhat better predictor of their health than the sociologists' objective indexes of social class. Trained raters judging the emotional quality and intensity of the dreams of participants awarded a less salient and less pleasant valence to the dreams than the dreamers did.[42] The Nobel poet Czeslaw Milosz wrote a letter to Thomas Merton when Milosz was teaching Polish literature at the University of California. One sentence read, "Ten years ago I just escaped from America, being afraid of a life without purpose and of acedia."[43] "Acedia," for Milosz, referred to a feeling of terror in the face of spiritual emptiness. Acedia is absent from every psychologist's list of emotions. This quotation is intended, not as an argument for relying on concepts originating in the subjective frame, but to indicate how difficult it is to invent scientific constructs for the extraordinary variety in subjective emotional states.

Many scientists use the term *fear* as a construct to explain a correlation between an aversive event and a reliable biological or behavioral reaction, and not always as a description of a human or an animal psychological state. For example, one team of investigators attributed fear to healthy human participants because they showed a conditioned rise in heart rate to a signal that announced the presentation of an aversively loud noise as the unconditioned stimulus. I suspect that if the individuals who showed a conditioned rise in heart rate were asked about their emotional state, they would have said that they were annoyed, irritated, or even angry, and few would have reported feeling afraid.[44] After all, the brief bursts of loud noise, which became predictable over trials, posed no threat of harm, status, loss, or rejection. Hence, their subjective state did not match the one implied by the construct "fear."

Perhaps the most serious problem in writings on emotion is that the variation in the salience of self-reports of emotions to a cognitive or social challenge is not highly correlated with variation in the biological or behavioral measures believed to be signs of those states. An examination of twenty-seven studies that gathered both verbal reports on extroversion, neuroticism, and emotional expressiveness and relevant behavioral observations revealed that the two sources of evidence were not equivalent.[45]

Recall that women given testosterone reported similar levels of fear to a signal for electric shock as those given a placebo, but the first group displayed smaller startles to the signal. Adults told to suppress all external signs of emotion while watching two short films of medical procedures designed to evoke disgust displayed significant changes in both behavior and peripheral physiology but, surprisingly, did not differ in ratings of their emotional states from those who simply watched the films and did not suppress emotion. Similarly, Caucasian American college-age couples discussing their relationship smiled more and expressed fewer comments referring to shame or sadness than Chinese-American couples, but the two groups reported similar emotional states and displayed equivalent changes in heart rate and skin conductance. Preadolescents who reported feeling intense anxiety failed to display more behavioral signs of anxiety when they had to speak in front of a camera than youth who reported less intense anxiety. Moreover, the parents and teachers of the former youths did not describe them as highly anxious. There were dissociations among behavior, biology, and self-reported emotion in all of these studies. Even a person's subjective estimate of her or his sensitivity to smells bears little relation to objective measures of that person's olfactory thresholds.[46]

One reason for the modest, often negligible, relation between self-descriptions of feelings and emotions, on one hand, and biological or behavioral measures, on the other, is that humans vary in their usual level of stimulus or response uncertainty. Among those who are relaxed most of the time, a feeling of uncertainty is unexpected, and therefore it is salient and better remembered. Among those who usually maintain a mood of uncertainty, moments of relaxed serenity are discrepant and better remembered. Hence, when psychologists ask these two types of persons to describe their usual feeling before examinations, a fair proportion of the former group say they are anxious, whereas more members of the latter group say they are relaxed.

A second problem with verbal reports of emotions is that the questions must accommodate to the language repertoire of the respondents. For example, psychologists cannot ask parents if they hold ambivalent attitudes toward their children or ask high school students if they feel acedia. Although most individuals can recognize the facial expression characteristic of individuals who are condescending toward those they regard as less worthy, they are unlikely to use the term *contempt* to name this distinct facial expression because this word is used infrequently.[47]

Third, individuals hold implicit beliefs regarding the quality and intensity of the emotions they believe they ought to experience as a function of their gender, age, religion, or ethnicity. That is one reason why American women usually report more intense emotions than men to the same incentive and why African-American college students who say they are closely identified with their ethnic group deny worrying about anything.[48]

For all of these reasons, a person's semantic reports cannot provide all the evidence needed for a more complete understanding of feelings and emotions. How many more demonstrations of this robust fact are necessary before investigators acknowledge that people's verbal descriptions of their emotional states are not sensitive indexes of theoretically relevant behavior or biology, especially in nonclinical populations? This class of evidence has some value and should not be ignored, but it has a unique set of determinants, a special structure, and does not possess a transparent meaning. The author of an extensive review of research on personality suggested that verbal self-reports have limited value because "psychologists want and need to know what people actually do, think, and feel in the various contexts of their lives."[49]

The validity of conclusions pertaining to emotions or their variation based only on questionnaires or interviews is necessarily restricted to that source of evidence. No student of primates would construct a theory of the psychology of chimpanzees based only on recordings of their vocalizations without behavioral or biological information and descriptions of the contexts in which the vocal calls occurred. Remember, medieval biblical scholars spent hundreds of hours performing hermeneutic analyses of sacred texts certain that, with persistence, they could discern the *true* meaning of each sentence. Those who have read Jonathan Swift's *Gulliver's Travels* may recall that he satirized those who argued that language was potentially capable of describing nature accurately. Swift described two philosophers scheduled for a debate who arrived in the hall with large sacks filled with objects that they planned to pull out in order to make their communications unambiguous. This cumbersome strategy may work well for conveying the meanings of bricks, broccoli, and balloons, but it fails for emotions.

## *The Significance of the Investigator's Interests*

The evidence reviewed points to the potential utility of combining origin (external event, thought, or spontaneous brain activity), brain state, subjective judgments of the valence and salience of a feeling (which are influenced by expectedness and familiarity), and semantic labels when classifying emotions. A change in any one of the above features could represent a distinct emotion. For example, an unexpected criticism from a parent in the context of the home that evoked a particular brain profile, a salient, unpleasant perception of a rise in heart rate, furrowing of the forehead muscles, and an interpretation that the criticism was motivated by the parent's wish to help the adolescent develop better character habits would represent a state different from the one evoked if four of the above features were the same but the adolescent interpreted the comment as unjust and motivated by parental hostility. A third emotion would be realized if the origin were an episodic memory of the above incident. And a fourth state would emerge if the criticism were expected. Remember, an outcome as biologically significant as the sex ratio in many egg-laying vertebrates can be influenced by a slight change in the temperature of the environment in which the fertilized eggs are developing. The reluctance to acknowledge the extreme specificity of emotional phenomena is retarding theoretical progress. Scientists bothered by this suggestion should examine any recent text describing the extraordinary complexity of the biochemistry of cancer cells.

The perception of color provides an analogy. Although the 1,269 color chips in the Munsell system can be derived from combinations of the three dimensions of value, hue, and chroma, humans can discriminate among all 1,269 surfaces.[50] It is unlikely that one particular classification of the 1,269 surfaces will be the most fruitful. Sometimes it will be useful to treat all red surfaces as similar; on other occasions theory will be better served by distinguishing crimson from pink or the short wavelength colors of violet and blue from the long wavelength hues of red and orange. The same principle holds for emotions.

Some scientists are convinced of the theoretical advantages of regarding all instances of amygdalar activation to unpleasant pictures as an index of the same emotional state, even though the biological and behavioral signs of emotion evoked by a photograph of a bloodied soldier are different from the signs generated by a picture of a cobra with exposed fangs.[51] I can discriminate among the feelings and emotions engendered by a Bach cello sonata, a Monet painting, a glass of wine, an hour of tennis, an elegant argument, and a walk in an autumn forest, even though I would describe all six states as familiar, pleasing, and low in salience and would try to reexperience them on many occasions. Hence, the question the scientist poses will determine the criteria awarded primacy.

Put plainly, the features that define an emotional state cannot be fixed because they depend on the investigator's interests. Cows are classified with soybeans for the commodities investor, with alligators for the shoe manufacturer, with bison for evolutionary biologists, with fish for the grocer arranging foods, and with gods for practicing Hindus. A stretch of DNA can be classified with respect to its nucleotide sequences, the proteins its transcription and translation produce, the tissues in which it is active, the species in which it appears, or the diseases, if any, it can cause. Feelings and emotions are no exception. Emotions, like motor habits, are such a pervasive component of daily life that a single definition or theoretical argument is unlikely to serve the interests of all investigators.

Clinicians award special weight to the consequences of emotions because their central concern is with the influence of a patient's emotions on their adaptive functioning and the therapeutic effects of drugs and psychotherapy on those states. Although both outcomes might vary with the origins of the emotion, the current assumption that a drug's effectiveness in reducing anxiety or depression is relatively independent of the reasons for the patient's emotional state turns clinicians' interests away from origins, whether past experiences or temperamental biases. This indifference to origins is unwarranted. Patients with post-traumatic stress disorder who reported chronic feelings of shame due to their history or temperament failed to show improvement on the drug risperidone, whereas those free of this chronic mood improved. Similarly, depressed patients who failed to respond to a popular serotonin antidepressant were more likely to show right frontal activation in the electroencephalogram, a modest sign of chronic uncertainty, whereas those with left frontal activation were helped by the drug. Adults who displayed greater right rather than left activation in frontal areas were more likely than others to report high levels of anxiety one year later. Thus, clinicians might prescribe more effective treatment regimens if they attended more seriously to the origins of their patients' states and gathered biological information.[52]

Neuroscientists eager to pinpoint the circuits that make each emotion possible select the biological features of the feelings and emotions provoked by specific incentives. They should also be interested, however, in the salience of an emotion, which is always influenced by the unexpectedness or unfamiliarity of the incentive or the change in feeling, because of the relation between perceptual salience and brain activity.[53] Neuroscientists should also be concerned with origins because the brain profile produced by an external provocation, like a painful fall, is different from the one evoked later by thinking about the pain during the fall. And individuals with different life histories display distinct profiles to the same incentive.

Unfortunately, neuroscientists are limited in the range of emotions they can study, at least at the present time. It is difficult to generate guilt, terror, rage, serenity, and many other states that require direct interaction with another in individuals told to remain immobile and indifferent to the noise as they lie supine in a scanner. A change in blood flow in the amygdala produced by a photograph of a face with a fearful expression should not be equated with the brain state provoked by encountering a masked adult with a revolver demanding money. Biologists often arrive at different conclusions when the evidence is based on in vitro compared with in vivo preparations.

Investigators committed to evolutionary theory emphasize the consequences of emotions that have implications for inclusive fitness; hence, they award significance to fear of physical harm, sexual arousal, and anxiety over threats to kin. Psychologists concerned with personality or its development have to be interested in the historical conditions that produced emotions. The vicarious feeling of shame harbored by an adolescent whose father was arrested years earlier for selling illicit drugs to children is not equivalent to the shame that was the result of direct participation in an incestuous relationship during childhood. Philosophers have traditionally focused on the valence of an emotion because of its implication for morality. Anthropologists are concerned with the words members of different cultures use to name emotional states, but their inquiries would profit from attention to the unfamiliarity of the feeling and the incentive.

The features scholars select for categorizing emotions depend on the questions they wish to answer and the premises they bring to the evidence. Scientists trying to understand the bases for the anger felt by thousands of Iraqis toward American soldiers need psychological information on the degree of identification with their national and religious categories and will not be helped by measuring brain reactions to pictures of the American president. But investigators wishing to know why one particular Iraqi volunteered to be a suicide bomber and another did not are likely to be aided by biological data. Attempts to understand why guilt over striking another always emerges later in development than shame over spilling food require measurements of brain growth. However, explaining why one eight-year-old is guilty over striking another but not over lying to a parent and another has the opposite predispositions requires psychological information on the children's histories.

The immaturity of our current understanding implies that scientists should resist a premature temptation to announce that they know what an emotion is or to insist on one particular way to categorize emotions. Chemists classify matter into categories of atoms and molecules, whereas physicists rely on the heady constructs of quarks, leptons, and gluons. Evolutionary biologists debate the best way to classify animal groups, geneticists argue over the most fruitful categories for DNA strings, and astrophysicists are not certain how many types of energy exist in the cosmos. Some reduction in the current level of frustration will occur when we have gained a deeper insight into the relations among incentives, brain states, feelings, and their appraisals.

# FOUR

# Variation in Emotional Experience

I ndividuals vary in the frequency and salience of the emotions most often provoked in their society. Two critical but very different determinants of this variation are the social categories individuals accept as self-defining and their temperamental biases. The social categories influence the appraisals imposed on feelings and, therefore, the susceptibility to particular emotions. Temperaments affect a person's vulnerability to specific feeling states. I deal first with the effects of social categories.

The categories of gender, ethnicity, social class, nationality, religion, and stage of life are acquired by adolescence. Most individuals regard the first two as fixed and the latter four as subject to change, although the significance of all the categories varies across historical eras and cultures. Class and nationality had particular salience in nineteenth-century Europe, but ethnicity ascended in the hierarchy during the next century. The categories for spouse, parent, friend, lover, and vocation are acquired during the adolescent and adult years. But each of the categories is linked to a hierarchy of appropriate characteristics its members are supposed to possess. Individuals automatically evaluate the degree to which their physical features, actions, beliefs, feelings, motives, and values are in accord with, or deviate from, the set appropriate for the categories to which they belong. These categories are part of the definition of who one is and clarify what one is supposed to do. Some readers might prefer the concept "identity" to represent the qualities and obligations implied by each category. The striving to be loyal to the features that define the category and a perception of deviation from them are separate incentives for emotional states.

Each category can be likened to a psychological filter that mutes or enhances an emotional profile. For example, the Presbyterian farmers who emigrated first from Scotland to northern Ireland and later to the United States in the early nineteenth century felt uneasy when they were not working, spent money frivolously, or were excessively emotional with others. Andrew Mellon, the wealthy Pittsburgh banker who in his ninth decade donated his extensive art collection to the public, was a grandson of one such farmer. Some individuals acquire a chronic feeling tone as a function of experiences during the first two decades of life. If this feeling is evaluated as good or pleasant because it is associated with the gaining of prized goals, the person tries to maintain it and feels uneasy when it is temporarily muted. Ambitious youth, for example, who work exceptionally hard from the first grade through a graduate degree in a profession are likely to be in a chronic state of arousal. If they judge this feeling as a necessary feature of the pleasures that accompany their later life success, they often feel tense or nervous in the middle-age years when they detect a lower level of arousal. As a result they look for some additional responsibility in order to restore the mood of higher arousal. Andrew Mellon may have been a member of this category.

Consider some frequent examples of the effects of a social category. A comment criticizing one's inability to endure physical hardship will evoke more intense anger in American males than females because this property is a more essential feature of the category *male*. Unskilled workers who did not complete high school are more easily angered by a comment implying that they are lazy and incompetent than are professionals who enjoyed sixteen to twenty years of education. Disputes are more common between individuals of similar status than between pairs with very different statuses because humans regard the former comparison as more self-defining. Religious Israeli adolescents reported less stress to terrorist attacks than less religious youths because their religious commitment protected them from excessive anxiety. Students who sensed that they enjoyed a position of respect among their peers had a larger rise in cortisol to a social stressor than those who believed they had a less admirable status.[1]

An emotional identification with any one of the social categories renders a person vulnerable to a vicarious emotion when a relevant incentive occurs to another member of the same category. Many Swiss adults who have never played tennis enjoy a moment of pride when Roger Federer wins another championship; some scientists feel a twinge of shame when they read about an investigator who had to resign from a university because of a fraudulent claim based on invented evidence. German youth born during the first decade of the twentieth century who were identified with their national category felt extreme humiliation following Germany's defeat in the First World War and became enthusiastic supporters of Hitler when he promised to restore Germany's reputation. Perfectly happy adults become suddenly vulnerable to an unexpected bout of doubt when they learn that a parent or grandparent had been imprisoned for a crime, was a drug addict, had been hospitalized for a psychosis, or was a Nazi storm trooper. Simply possessing the name of a well-known person can, under some conditions, create an identification with emotional implications. My former colleague David McClelland told me he often felt surges of confidence as a child after learning that he had the same first name as the biblical hero who killed Goliath. Fritz Stern, a historian born in Germany in 1926 to Jewish parents, was named after Fritz Haber, an acclaimed German chemist who was the first to synthesize a nitrogen fertilizer. But Haber was also responsible for synthesizing the ingredients for gunpowder and a poison gas that killed many thousands during the First World War. As a result, Stern recalls experiencing a blend of vicarious affect that combined pride with shame.

The vicarious emotion that accompanies an identification, which can last for many years, has a different quality than the state experienced when the agent is the direct target of the same provocation. The intensity and quality of the shame felt by many Americans when they learned about American soldiers killing Vietnamese peasants, and experienced today by some who read about our troops murdering innocent Iraqi citizens, differ from the shame experienced by a person caught shoplifting or by an airline passenger whose coffee has spilled on the stranger in the adjoining seat. The vicarious guilt felt by some contemporary German adolescents reading about the Nazi era is less corrosive than the guilt that accompanies an act of serious disloyalty to a close friend, in part because it is easier to rationalize the former as an event that was not under self's control.[2] Nonetheless, a vicarious emotion can be salient when the social category happens to be central to the person's identity. For example, some adults born in the United States whose parent was a victim of the Nazi Holocaust live with continuous anxiety and depression. Of course, an identification can have adaptive consequences. George Homans, an eminent Harvard sociologist, noted in a memoir that he coped with his intense childhood anxiety over poor school grades and unpopularity with peers by silently rehearsing the fact that he could trace his family pedigree to John Adams.[3] The confident leadership displayed by Franklin Roosevelt and Winston Churchill during the Second World War owed some of its potency to their childhood identifications with their elite families.

The suggestion that a social category can prepare a person for a salient emotion is analogous to the responsivity of select neurons in the monkey's brain (in the hypothalamus and orbitofrontal cortex) to the sweet taste of a glucose solution. These neurons responded to the sweet liquid when the animals were hungry and became silent when they had been sated on the sugar solution, but they became responsive again when a different food was presented.[4] This result has two important implications for emotions.

The first is that the neuronal circuits that are the foundations of feelings are selectively tuned to very specific incentives. A stranger's insult, a cool greeting from a close friend, seeing a stranger throw garbage on a neighbor's flowers, or accidentally leaving one's car keys in a locked automobile provoke different members of the anger family. Recall that the Romans invented separate terms for anger that specified its origin. An individual is angry at a particular person or anxious over a particular situation. The concepts "anxiety" and "anger," free of any target, may have a sense meaning but, like goblins, have no instantiation in nature because the validity of a concept requires specifying the events to which the word refers. Psychologists and psychiatrists should not write about abstract emotional states that fail to specify origin, target, and source of evidence.

The second implication is that an individual, like the hungry monkey, must be psychologically or biologically prepared for an emotional state. The occurrence of anger following a stranger's mild insult is far more likely if the agent was in a state of frustration before the rude comment and less likely if she or he was feeling exuberant or serene. Parents show a larger cortical response to a photo of a crying infant than adults who have no children. Scientists must know the individual's state when an incentive occurs in order to predict the most probable emotion. Membership in one or more of the social categories contributes to the state that will be realized. I now consider the implications of three self-defining social categories that most find difficult to ignore: social class, gender, and ethnicity or cultural heritage.

## Social Class

Each individual's conception of their relative status, or rank, within a society affects their expectations of the privileges, opportunities, and respect they are likely to enjoy. In many communities with minimal variation in religion and ethnicity, such as colonial New England during the seventeenth century, a person's social status was defined primarily by property and education and, by implication, the size of one's income and how it was earned. Because both features were subject to change, colonial Americans in less advantaged positions may have experienced less intense anger or depression than contemporary Americans in the same position for whom these features are correlated with membership in an ethnic minority. That is why poor Pakistani youth living in Texas, who feel marginalized, were at a high risk for a suicide attempt.[5]

Some Americans are puzzled by the fact that many children of the poor, often illiterate, European immigrants who arrived in the United States a century earlier became upwardly mobile, whereas many adults who grew up in families of more recent immigrants have not achieved middle-class status. However, the ethnic identifications of the children of recent immigrants from Mexico, Guatemala, Puerto Rico, Jamaica, Pakistan, Cambodia, and Vietnam might be so strong that a large number may find it hard to reject the imperative for placing family loyalty, a defining feature of their ethnic group, over personal achievement.

The social class of the family can override the influences of neighborhood, peers, and school. Warsaw, which was destroyed by bombs during the Second World War, rebuilt its homes and schools in accord with a Soviet policy requiring families of different classes to live in the same apartment buildings and to send their children to the same schools. Nonetheless, the children of parents who had a college education had higher IQ scores and obtained better grades than the children of parents who had less education.[6] The young children of highly educated, upper-middle-class Jewish émigrés to America from Nazi Germany in the 1930s did remarkably well in school and achieved eminence in their professions, despite the trauma of settling in a new country with little money and no friends, because their parents, often professional too, had socialized them to value personal achievement, a respected status, a willingness to compete, and financial security.

Then, as well as now, the social class in which a person was reared over the first dozen years can protect against or create a preparedness for academic failure, post-traumatic stress disorder, depression, suicide attempts, delinquency, criminal behavior, divorce, or distinct physiological reactions to challenges. North Carolina youth living in poverty were overrepresented in the small number of adolescents who had suicidal thoughts or made a suicide attempt. Class can even compete with, or take precedence over, an abusive childhood. Although about 25 percent of adults who had been seriously abused or neglected as children were depressed, 21 percent of adults who grew up in the same social class but had not been abused received the same diagnosis.[7] This fact does not mean that abuse is unimportant; rather, it means that class has a powerful effect on mood.

Adults from egalitarian democracies raised in socially disadvantaged homes are vulnerable to shame over their relative lack of educational achievements and material possessions, anxiety over their economic future, and bouts of depression because their teachers and the media inform them that all citizens willing to invest the effort have the opportunity to attend college and attain greater economic security and dignity. Perhaps that is why many lower-class African-American adults have greater sympathetic tone in their cardiovascular system (indexed by lower heart-rate variability) than Caucasians, whereas most African-American infants have the high heart-rate variability indicative of low sympathetic tone.[8] Several centuries earlier, when the proportion of poor was far greater than 20 percent, adults from less privileged class categories blamed the social structure of their society for their plight and were more likely to feel anger, rather than the more corrosive emotion of shame, because the smaller number of privileged regarded the poor with far less empathy than they do today. The undergraduates attending my university are extremely tolerant of differences in religion, ethnicity, sexual orientation, and class. Nonetheless, a graduating Caucasian woman with excellent grades confessed that she felt continually ashamed during her four years because the parents of all her friends were college graduates but neither of her parents had attended college.

Social class is a far better predictor than genes of the development of some form of anxiety, depression, delinquency, or criminality in most populations, as well as the likelihood of remission of symptoms following treatment. The symptoms of an anxiety disorder are more resistant to a therapeutic regimen in impoverished than in middle-class patients. These facts are not restricted to industrialized nations. The degree of income inequality in each of thirteen ethnically similar, foraging-farming villages in the Bolivian Amazon predicted the frequency of reports of sadness, anger, and fear—the greater the inequality, the more frequent these emotions. David Hume, the eighteenth-century Scottish philosopher, recognized the power of class to shape a person's identity when he noted in his *Treatise on Human Nature* that "the different stations of life influence the whole fabric" of emotional preparedness. The emotional consequences of social disadvantage are a bit stronger in America than in Germany because of the greater disparity in income between those in the top and bottom 25 percent of the distribution and the stronger association between income and ethnicity in the United States. Recall that Larry King's voice varied as a function of the difference in status between King and his guests. The effect of class of rearing on values, emotions, and social behaviors resembles the influence of geographical isolation on the shape and size of the beaks on the finch species living on the islands of the Galápagos chain.[9]

When, however, the status differential is modest and ethnic prejudice is muted, members of a group who are only modestly disadvantaged often strive for unusual levels of accomplishment in order to repair their sense of compromised legitimacy. Most seventeenth-century Quakers living in England were merchants and craftsmen who regarded themselves as marginal members of their society because of their religion. This feeling of separateness freed them from the pressure to conform to the antiscientific prejudices of the upper middle class, and as a result, many became scientists, including John Dalton, the architect of atomic theory. This dynamic is present today.

There is always a small proportion of poor or minority adolescents who try to cope with their feeling of relative impotence by striving for, and often attaining, high levels of achievement. However, even if successful, a small number retain remnants of their childhood emotions. John Updike, who grew up in a working-class family in Pennsylvania, confessed in a memoir that he feels nervous and occasionally stutters when in the presence of a Boston Brahmin. The celebrated British literary critic Frank Kermode, born to extremely poor parents, admitted to always feeling like an outsider: "Looking the part while not being quite equal to it seems to me something I do rather well." Robert Nozick, a distinguished Harvard philosopher from a poor, immigrant Jewish background, questioned his right to address profound intellectual themes: "Isn't it ludicrous for someone just one generation from the shtetl, a pisher from Brownsville and east Flatbush in Brooklyn, even to touch on the topics of the monumental thinkers?" Neither Bertrand Russell nor A. N. Whitehead, who spent their childhood years in more privileged homes, would have harbored these doubts.[10] A vulnerability to feelings of response uncertainty when challenges occur can be due to temperamental biases (which I deal with in a later section), chronic guilt over serious transgressions, earlier trauma, or membership in a class group that the person perceives as disadvantaged and less potent.

Excessive privilege is not without some dangers, however. A childhood and youth spent in a wealthy, educated, nurturant family can create a sense of entitlement and an unrealistic self-confidence that is not based on actual ability or achievements. This combination can lead to extraordinary accomplishments, as was true for Charles Darwin and Franklin Roosevelt, or to such an exaggerated sense of potency it blunts the self-critical attitude necessary to avoid serious error. Egon Moniz, a Portuguese neurologist who grew up in an aristocratic family, had the hunch that cutting the connections between the frontal lobes and the rest of the brain might cure hospitalized mental patients who had been resistant to all treatments. Moniz performed the first operation on a sixty-three-year-old woman in 1935 and, with insufficient evidence, announced to the world that the surgical lobotomy had cured her illness. After performing additional operations that he described in papers as successful, he was awarded the Nobel Prize in medicine for this so-called

miracle cure. Neurosurgeons around the world began to apply this tech-
nique to many hundreds of patients for the next twenty years. But Moniz's
self-assurance proved to be excessive. This operation does not cure psychosis,
and a little more self-doubt would have protected the hapless victims of this
surgery from additional suffering. If the arrogant actor John Wilkes Booth
had not been raised in a famous family of celebrated actors, he might not
have decided he had the right to murder Abraham Lincoln on Good Friday
in 1865 only a week after his beloved Confederate armies surrendered. The
illusion of enhanced virtue and potency that a childhood of privilege occasionally creates can be exploited for benevolent or malevolent ends.

A compromised expectation of the respect others will display, a vulnerability to doubt, shame, guilt, or anger, and a feeling of not being in complete control of one's life, which can accompany disadvantaged status, can
lead to chronic changes in hormones and brain chemistry and contribute to
the inverse relation in industrialized nations between level of education and
occupational status, on one hand, and number of illnesses and life span, on
the other. Working adults in Great Britain who had many supervisors, and
therefore less psychological control over decisions in their jobs, had higher
blood pressures than those in more demanding vocations who had fewer
supervisors and greater freedom to decide on their actions each workday.
Lawyers, doctors, and scientists have fewer diseases and die at a later age than
bank clerks, sales representatives, and secretaries, and bank clerks, sales representatives, and secretaries have fewer illnesses and die later than unskilled
construction workers, janitors, and restaurant employees.[11]

A comment implying that self is less worthy than others—called "dissing"
by adolescents—is a reliable way to provoke immediate anger. The accusa-
tion that a man had the soul of a woman was one of the most serious insults
a male citizen of ancient Rome could receive because gender was linked
to status. The intense emotions that fueled both the French and Bolshevik
revolutions required a serious imbalance in status between the privileged
few and the rest of the population. On the eve of the French Revolution over
90 percent of the citizens belonged to the third estate, and the total burden
of taxation fell on them rather than on the much smaller estates reserved
for the elite clergy and nobility. Maximilien de Robespierre, the despot who
ordered the guillotining of hundreds of Parisians during the revolution, was

a member of the third estate who lived with the continuous shame of being the son of an irresponsible father who had abandoned his young family.

A critical change in Western conceptions of some emotions occurred in the nineteenth century following industrialization and the dissemination of Darwinian theory. These historical events sharpened what had been a subtle contrast between the urban poor and the rest of society. This fact, which could no longer be denied, required an explanation. Evolutionary ideas answered this social need by suggesting that many of the disadvantaged who lived in squalor were biologically less fit. This interpretation freed some emotions from their traditional semantic link to ethical concepts and implied a biological basis for variation in emotional propensities. The middle class, it was presumed, possessed an inherently superior ability to control intense anger, carnal desire, and temptations to drink excessively, as well as an enhanced capacity for joy while working toward a future goal, pride following accomplishment, and guilt over violating ethical norms. The distinct emotional patinas of the uneducated poor were viewed as biologically inevitable phenomena rather than the products of unpredictable historical events. A wealthy lawyer complaining of fatigue and insomnia a century ago was told that because he was working too hard he had temporarily depleted his store of bodily energy. Lenin received such a diagnosis. An illiterate dockworker with the same symptoms would be advised that he had a constitutional defect. George Bernard Shaw's play *Pygmalion*, which was the basis for the film *My Fair Lady*, challenged the elitism inherent in that dogma.

Alcoholism, crime, unemployment, and homelessness continue to be more prevalent among the urban poor than the middle class in modern societies. But a more robust egalitarianism that emerged between the two world wars competes with the earlier biological perspective that assumed that genetic polymorphisms rendered individuals vulnerable to these emotional disabilities. Thus, the current debate in the U.S. Congress over restricting immigration is motivated by a concern over indigenous Americans losing their jobs to newcomers, whereas the same debate a hundred years earlier was fueled by worry over polluting the gene pool of the twentieth-century descendants of the *Mayflower* voyage. Many would like to remove some of the blame now attributed to a patient's genes or lifestyle and place it on a particular past experience. As a result, some patients who have insomnia or worry excessively are given a diagnosis of post-traumatic stress disorder if they can remember just one event that could be considered traumatic, such as an automobile accident or an unwanted sexual advance.

Class distinctions are inevitable because members of every society necessarily differ in possession of the features their community celebrates as signs of virtue. Much of the modern world values wealth because, being potentially achievable by everyone, it is in accord with an egalitarian ethos. But the light-skinned Indo-Europeans who invaded the Indus Valley of what is now India four thousand years ago made skin color a sign of status. A person's occupation and gender were far more important than wealth in determining class position in ancient China, and membership in a religious category, which awarded privilege to Catholics in medieval Europe, remains a sign of status in many contemporary societies. No society is free of status distinctions. What has changed over time, especially in industrialized cultures, is the replacement of fixed features defining what a person was with attainable ones representing what one was able to do as the result of an unpredictable historical sequence that most would applaud.

## Gender

Gender, too, generates a preparedness for particular hierarchies of emotions. But in this case, the preparedness is due to both cultural norms and subtle, biological differences between males and females. Unlike the category for social class, which is acquired in later childhood and can change with time, children learn their gender category early, usually by age three, and regard its biological features as fixed. As a result, serious deviation from the culturally approved standards for one's gender has a greater potential to generate guilt rather than anger.

Although both males and females worry about their relative status, acceptability to peers, and the quality of their friendships, boys and men are concerned more with differences in status and relative power with peers than with the acceptance and affection derived from their social relationships. Hence, they are more easily threatened by any challenge to their potency, whether this quality is defined by the ability to dominate an interaction, strength, intellectual talent, athletic skill, sexual prowess, the control of fear, or the ability to defend self against coercion. By contrast, girls and women are more vulnerable to feelings of uncertainty over the quality and loyalty of their personal relationships than over their ability to dominate age-mates. For example, members of same-sex college crew teams displayed different reactions to an upcoming competition. Although both men and women showed the expected rise in cortisol in anticipation of the event, the men with large increases in this hormone reported an intense desire to win in order to feel more potent with their friends. The women with equally large increases in cortisol wanted to win in order to strengthen their emotional bonds with their teammates. For women, loss of a close, gratifying relationship is more likely than a loss in status to create sadness. This may be one reason why serious depression is more prevalent in females than in males across varied cultures. It is of interest that female bonobo chimpanzees are also more affiliative than males in social play.[12] Young men from several cultures say they would be threatened by an act of sexual infidelity in their partner because of its implications for their potency as lovers. Women are more often bothered by the emotional estrangement their partner's infidelity implies because it means that they have become less attractive and less acceptable to their lover.

The fact that gentleness with friends is a more obligatory standard among females may explain why more adolescent girls who were very shy as two year olds were far less timid than adolescent boys who had been equally shy as toddlers. Adolescent girls are kinder to and more understanding of socially anxious girls and, as a result, help them overcome their uncertainty. Adolescent boys, by contrast, are harsh with timid peers who violate the sex-role stereotype of a tough, fearless persona and, in so doing, exacerbate the shy boy's doubts and uncertainty.

The most consistent sex differences involve a greater vulnerability among females to fear of physical harm, anxiety over social rejection, bouts of depression, panic attacks, and somatic distress. American women, compared with men, judged unpleasant odors as more aversive, reported in daily diaries more frequent days marked by feelings of distress, admitted to more frequent bouts of anxiety or fear, and were more likely to come down with an illness following the death of a close relative.[13] Similar differences existed in seventeenth-century England and are present in a majority of Islamic countries.

Although sex differences in physiological profiles probably contribute to the differential susceptibility to particular emotions, the biology only creates an initial bias for an emotional state. The social environment must support these tendencies, and a majority of cultures have done so. Medieval Europeans loyal to Galen's categories of hot-dry and cold-moist assumed that cold and moist fit most women. Because this combination also characterized winter, when people are apathetic and sluggish, women were believed to be biologically prepared for moods of depression. The ancient Greeks regarded iron, a hard metal, as symbolic of maleness and phosphorous, a softer metal, as symbolic of women. Nineteenth-century Chinese regarded women as objects that could be sold or bartered in times of need. During a serious famine in northern China in the 1870s men sold their wives and daughters to traders who forced the women into prostitution or to butchers who prepared their bodies for cooking.

## The Influence of Biology

The sex hormones contribute to gender differences in emotions because estrogen potentiates the perception of pain and women experience pain with greater intensity than men. Women in the follicular phase of their menstrual cycle may experience slightly less pain than at other times of the month because estrogen also increases the availability of opioid receptors.[14] If the higher estrogen levels of females contribute to an enhanced susceptibility to distress, anxiety, or depression (it can not be the only cause), girls and women should be more prone than boys and men to report episodes of anxiety over future harm or rejection and acquire an avoidant behavioral style to potential threats. Most societies guarantee this outcome by promoting the stereotyped notion that females are especially prone to fear. Medieval commentators remained loyal to Galen's second-century declaration that females were vulnerable to fear because they had an excess of black bile and therefore less internal body heat. Indeed, the medieval explanation of the sex difference in genital anatomy was that the females' insufficient heat reserve prevented their genitals from being pushed from the inside to the outside of the body. Nineteenth-century writers, who replaced sex differences in heat with differences in energy, argued that because women required a great deal of bodily energy for reproductive activities, especially pregnancy, lactation, and infant care, they necessarily had less energy available for intellectual work. This bizarre notion was used as a rationale for not sending young women to college. Thus, the powerful hand of culture sculpts the subtle biological differences between the sexes to create exaggerated stereotypes of the emotional lives of men and women, even though history continually alters the forms these stereotypes assume. Compare Gustave Flaubert's description in 1857 of Emma Bovary's highly controlled sexual feelings with James Joyce's description, only seventy-six years later, of the unrestrained sensuality of Molly Bloom.

Young children of both sexes have already acquired some components of these stereotypes, albeit implicitly, for they, too, believe that females are more fearful and weaker than males. Young children asked to indicate whether a frightened or a fearless animal, or a thin or thick plank of wood, was more appropriate for their mother or for their father assigned the fearful animal and the thin plank to the mother and the fearless animal and the thick plank to the father. And four- to six-year-old American children of both sexes from varying class backgrounds and family structures agreed that girls cried and became frightened more often than boys, whereas boys were regarded as stronger, faster, and braver than girls. The ancient Chinese held a similar stereotype: yin, the female force, is characterized by softness and passivity, whereas yang, the male element, is hard and active.[15]

These observations may help explain why boys and men are more concerned with their position in a status hierarchy of peers, whereas girls and women worry more about establishing and maintaining harmonious relationships. One speculative interpretation begins with the assumption that initially, say at two or three years of age, there are no sex differences in the salience of these two motives. But, as noted, by age three to six children have learned that most men are physically larger and stronger than most women, and boys are more aggressive and can run faster than girls. The recognition of these apparent facts persuades many girls that it is unlikely they will be able to dominate most males. (This conclusion is, of course, premature and

incorrect since many women assume a dominant role with their lovers, hus-
bands, and male colleagues.) As a result, girls subordinate a desire to dominate others to the other major form of social interaction—namely, maintaining friendly, supportive relationships.

Although this argument attributes the sex difference solely to girls' interpretations of their childhood experiences, there is the strong possibility that
inherited neurobiological differences between the sexes contribute. Accepting the influence of biology, however, requires the reader to be less skeptical
of the relevance of animal functioning for human emotions than I implied in
Chapter 1. The hypothalamus in animals and humans of both sexes secretes
the molecules oxytocin and vasopressin, which have different bodily functions and different consequences in males and females, in part because they
bind to different brain structures. Oxytocin and vasopressin are released during sexual behavior and facilitate pair-bonding in many species. But oxytocin
contributes to a stable relationship with a partner in female prairie voles (a
small rodent species), whereas vasopressin does so in males. The more critical fact is that the level of oxytocin activity, which is enhanced by estrogen,
is usually greater in female brains, whereas vasopressin activity, enhanced by
androgen, is usually greater in males. Oxytocin facilitates maternal behavior,
social contacts, and parasympathetic activity; vasopressin mutes fear, raises
pain thresholds, facilitates aggression, and enhances sympathetic activity in
animals and humans.[16]

Men and women respond to the administration of vasopressin in different
ways. While viewing faces with angry, happy, or neutral expressions, men
showed increased furrowing of the muscles of the forehead to the neutral
faces, a response often associated with the emotions of puzzlement or anger.
Women, however, showed increased activity in the mouth muscles that produced smiles to happy and angry faces, a reaction associated with affiliation.[17]
There are two interpretations of this intriguing, and surprising, result. On
one hand, it could imply that male and female brains are "wired" to react in
different ways to a surge of vasopressin. On the other hand, this observation
could mean that the vasopressin created a temporary brain state that evoked
the behaviors that had become habitual over time. In either case, this discovery suggests that males and females react in distinct ways to the same
neurochemical intervention.

The behavioral consequences of variation in oxytocin among animal species is in accord with this expectation. A species of monkeys called bonnet macaques is socially gregarious, whereas the species called pigtail macaques is decidedly nongregarious, volatile, and aggressive. Bonnet macaques have higher levels of oxytocin in their cerebrospinal fluid than the less social pigtail monkeys. And infant rat pups who received a great deal of maternal licking and grooming became adults with a high density of receptors for oxytocin, but only if they were female, and not if they were male.[18] These observations imply, but certainly do not prove, that nurturant care of infants enhances oxytocin function to a greater degree in girls than in boys.

Because oxytocin contributes to the establishment of close, emotional relationships in humans and animals, and oxytocin activity is much greater in females, it is possible that the heightened concern among girls and women with preserving close friendships is due, in part, to the enhanced activity of oxytocin. Put a bit too plainly, the sex difference among humans in the importance of maintaining harmonious social bonds might be influenced, in part, by the enhanced oxytocin-mediated functions in females. Shelley Taylor and her colleagues at the University of California agree. They suggest that the distinct biology of females biases girls and women to seek affiliative relationships when they feel stressed, whereas the biology of males tempts boys and men to display dominating or aggressive reactions to perceived stress.[19]

Even though inherited biological processes probably contribute to the sex difference in the relative importance of maintaining social bonds, compared with preserving or enhancing self's status, a presumption that some might challenge, the experiential contributions, based on perceiving the different psychological and physical properties of males and females and the norms promoted by the society, are not without significance. A similar phenomenon occurs in animals. Young male elephants, for example, are prone to periodic, often prolonged, displays of aggressive behavior. The volatile displays are shortened dramatically, however, if an older, dominant male is introduced into the group of young males. Perhaps the most persuasive illustration of the influence of other members of one's species living in the same social space is seen in a species of fish (wrasse) found in the coral reefs off the islands of Hawaii. A female who becomes the largest fish in the area because the male or a larger female dies, undergoes an anatomical change, stops producing eggs, and begins to make sperm.[20] Both animals and humans are profoundly affected by the features and behaviors of those in their immediate social setting. The mass murders that occurred in Rwanda, Bosnia, and Nazi Germany were made possible by the attitudes and actions of the local group.

One more factor deserves mention. The ancient Greeks held the implicit belief that females were closer to nature than males, in part, because conceiving, carrying, birthing, and nursing infants are prototypically natural acts restricted to females. The paintings intended to depict nature in Renaissance and Enlightenment Europe typically illustrated a woman with two, four, or six exposed breasts. When tuberculosis and syphilis rose dramatically in prerevolutionary France, many citizens blamed these scourges on the increasing tendency of women to refuse to honor what was regarded as their natural obligation to nurse their infants.

Modern children share this presumption. A psychologist first sensitized seven-year-old children to the contrast between natural and manufactured objects by asking them to guess which of two nonsense words (*gip* or *lum*) was the best name for each of a series of pictures that contained both categories. The children solved this problem quickly and applied the words correctly to natural versus manufactured objects or scenes. The psychologist returned one week later and told the same children they would play the same game, but this time with different pictures and different nonsense words (*dep* and *tas*). Initially the pictures illustrated obvious male or female objects (for example, a man's suit, a woman' shoe). When each child had figured out that one of the words was correct for the female objects and the other for the male objects, the psychologist presented the children with a new set of natural and manufactured objects. Both boys and girls applied the nonsense word symbolic of female things to the pictures of natural objects (plant, cloud, lake) and the word symbolic of maleness to the manufactured objects (for example, street sign, television set, clock).[21] Perhaps one reason the Pythagoreans regarded the number 2 as female and the number 3 as male is that more natural events occur in pairs.

Renaissance scholars believed that jealousy was more characteristic of and more intense in women than in men because, unlike anger, it was a "colder" emotion. Jealousy was called the "green monster" because green is regarded as a cool color.[22] Because women were presumed to have less body heat than men, it followed that jealousy should come more easily to them. No male figure in Western literature approaches the prototype of intense jealousy than Medea, the mythical Greek wife who killed her children in a jealous rage. Indeed, this belief may have made a small contribution to the fact that older widows of modest means were most often accused of being witches during the late fifteenth and early sixteenth century when an increased population, unusually cold winters, a strained food supply, and the zealotry of the Counterreformation combined to generate high levels of uncertainty in the European populace. The average adult would find it easy to believe that older widows envied the greater economic security, and especially the sexual intimacy, enjoyed by most couples and therefore might be motivated to commit malevolent acts against the more fortunate. Men were less often accused of witchcraft because they were supposed to be less jealous and were a less attractive sexual target for the devil.

The qualities a culture believes are inherent in human nature are attributed more often to women than to men. The Greeks, who regarded eros as a natural force, awarded greater carnal desire to women than to men. Contemporary Western culture regards the ability to love another, as contrasted to lusting after another, as an essential human quality, and most movies, novels, and plays depict women as having a greater capacity than men to love their children, parents, and partners. By contrast, Americans regard apprehension of and anger toward out-groups with different customs or appearances as a learned attitude rather than a natural disposition (a song in the popular musical South Pacific declared that hate has to be carefully taught). And females are not regarded as more prone to anger or prejudice than males. Because both love and hate come easily to humans, a culture's untutored premises regarding the emotions and actions inherent in human biology provide a clue to the traits that will be associated with the concept "female." Some contemporary societies accept the evolutionary premise that self-interest is a biological imperative. As a result, females, who have traditionally been regarded as passive pawns in marital arrangements, are now depicted in movies and plays as self-interested agents looking for the fittest mating partner. Engaging in a constructive activity is also an inherently human quality, but nineteenth-century Americans classified the world of work as an artifact (a rat race) that was symbolically linked to maleness.

The greater secretion of androgen by male fetuses during months two to six of gestation and the secretion of estradiol by female infants during the first postnatal year prepare men and women for slightly different feelings that later experience sculpts into different emotional profiles. The ratio of the lengths of the second and fourth finger (the length of the index finger divided by the length of the ring finger) is called the 2D:4D ratio. This ratio, which usually ranges between 0.91 and 1.00 and is clearly heritable (at a level similar to that of intelligence test scores), is a rough measure of the amount of androgen to which the fetus was exposed. Most females from varied ethnic groups have slightly higher ratios than males (range of 0.97 to 1.0 versus 0.91 to 0.96) because the prenatal secretion of the male sex hormone in male fetuses lengthens the distal section of the ring finger, resulting in a slightly longer ring than index finger and a lower ratio in boys and men. A similar sex difference is observed in many but not all animals. A female member of a twin pair lying next to her male sibling during fetal growth, and therefore exposed to androgen, has a smaller, more masculine ratio.[23]

The magnitude of the relation between the finger ratio and psychological traits is always small, even when statistically significant, and not consistent across studies. Nonetheless, a sufficient body of evidence suggests that this ratio reflects something important. For example, preschool girls with a more masculine ratio were more active than other girls, and young boys with more feminine ratios were more anxious than other boys. Boys who were interested in female activities (less than 5 percent of most populations) and young men who sought surgical interventions to become females because of the inconsistency between their feelings and their assigned gender, had larger ratios more typical of females. College-age men with smaller ratios, implying greater prenatal exposure to androgen, had greater grip strength and more sexual partners than men with larger, more feminine ratios and were more likely to possess a broad face with a prominent jaw and large chin (androgen contributes to the growth of the jaw). Although European and American women judge men with broader faces and prominent jaws as more dominant and masculine (Bill Clinton and George Bush have this facial shape, but John McCain and Jimmy Carter do not), most do not rate them as more attractive marital partners. Women with smaller ratios reported more masculine interests, had high levels of talent in running ability, and were more likely to be gay. The corpus of information implies that variation in the amount of prenatal exposure to male hormone can have a small but real influence on select aspects of psychological development, especially in boys and men raised in typical settings. In light of the debate over sex differences in careers in mathematics and physics, it is interesting that a more masculine ratio predicted quality of performance on a spatial reasoning task requiring the detection of a shape embedded in a noisy background. However, the composition of the family does have some influence on the sexual attitudes of boys. For example, adolescent boys who have a twin sister or have one or more older sisters but no older brothers are more likely than others to report a sexual attraction to other boys.[24]

Sex differences in other brain molecules could bias males and females for different emotional hierarchies. One example involves the neurotransmitter dopamine, which, among its many different functions, contributes to the salience of the state experienced by someone preparing or working for an uncertain but highly desired event. I noted earlier that animals display a surge of dopamine to the unexpected delivery of food, but not to food that was anticipated. Although men and women received exactly the same dose of a drug that increases brain dopamine levels, the men had a larger increase in dopamine in subcortical sites and reported a more intense feeling of excitement than the women. The sex difference in felt excitement might be due in part to the fact that the female brain binds dopamine to one class of its receptors (called $D_2$) more effectively than the male brain. Hence, the female brain is normally at a higher tonic level of dopamine activity. This condition is also due to the fact that estrogen stimulates the secretion of dopamine and inhibits its absorption from the synapse by acting on a molecule, called the dopamine transporter, in ways that lead dopamine to remain longer in the synapse.[25]

If the tonic level of brain dopamine activity is usually lower in males, more receptors for dopamine will be available for activation in males compared with females. As a result, a thought or experience that normally produces a surge in dopamine should create, temporarily, greater dopamine-related activity in males. One important implication of these facts is that the special feeling of pleasure that occurs when a wished-for but highly uncertain event occurs may be greater in men than in women because the surge in dopamine driven activity is imposed on a lower baseline level. Among a special breed of pigs, the boars who explored a novel object for a longer time had brains with more dopamine receptors available for activation by this neurotransmitter. There was no comparable relation for the sows.[26]

Several more facts support the possibility of gender differences in dopamine activity. Patients with Parkinson's disease, owing to an insufficiency in brain dopamine, show abnormal retinal activity to blue light. Because dopamine is present in the retina, this observation implies that dopamine is required for the normal processing of blue light. Retinal activity is sent to the primary visual cortex (incidentally, dopamine in the cortex affects activity in the retina), so the level of neuronal activity in the visual cortex to blue light might provide an indirect index of dopamine function in this and other parts of the brain. Exposure to two hours of blue light in the evening produces a larger increase in heart rate, core body temperature, and alertness than exposure to red light. The critical observation, however, is that men show greater activation of the visual cortex to flashes of blue light than women, implying a more substantial increase in dopamine-related activity in males than in females.[27] Nature is full of surprises.

Eating a piece of chocolate is far more pleasant if one has not eaten chocolate for weeks than if this treat is enjoyed every day. Perhaps more men than women engage in novel activities that have uncertain outcomes, such as high-stakes gambling, sport parachuting, climbing glacier-covered mountains, and drag racing, because these activities are accompanied by a greater phasic increase in dopamine activity, compared with the usual level, in neurons responsive to dopamine surges. As a result, they experience a more salient feeling of excitement that is appraised as pleasant. Although these biological differences between the sexes are not determining, they do represent initial biases for particular emotions. That is, the variation in estrogen, androgen, oxytocin, vasopressin, and dopamine establishes different brain states in males and females that raise or lower the probability of particular feelings. But they do not guarantee one particular emotion because the person's history, age, current life setting, and culture select specific emotions from the large envelope of possibilities inherent in the brain states. Recruiting an army to conquer the ancient world, trying to prove Fermat's theorem, and sailing solo around the world are all high-risk activities that are preceded by and generate slightly different emotions.

Faculty and students at American universities are debating the reasons why many more men than women pursue academic careers in physics and mathematics, despite no sex difference in the choice of biology, psychology, sociology, anthropology, or the humanities. Some argue that masculine prejudice excluding women from professorships in the physical sciences and mathematics discourages college-age women from selecting these fields. These advocates cite evidence indicating minimal differences between males and females in average scores on tests of the intellectual abilities required for competent work in these areas. Furthermore, if women believed they were less talented in mathematics, they would try less hard and obtain poorer scores. This argument has merit. College-age women did perform less well on mathematics problems after reading an essay stating that sex differences in mathematical ability were genetic in origin than after reading that experience was the culprit. Nonetheless, whenever a scientist does discover a cognitive ability required for math or physics in which males outperform females, the talent usually involves a form of spatial reasoning, which, it will be recalled, is enhanced in males who experienced a greater surge of male sex hormone during the fetal period.[28]

The exclusive focus on intellectual capacities, however, ignores the possibility that men and women differ in their desire to pursue a career in these domains, the emotional satisfaction that accompanies a major discovery in these disciplines following years of effort, and the level of sustained motivation required for success in these fields. There are two possible bases for the muted motivation in women and the greater enthusiasm in men for these academic specialties.

First, most discoveries in mathematics and physics, compared with biology and the social sciences, do not have obvious implications for improving human lives. Because women generally derive more satisfaction than men from activities that might have a benevolent effect on others, these fields are less appealing. Many of my female graduate students who were doing outstanding developmental research told me in their final year that they had decided to become clinical psychologists because the satisfaction they derived from their scientific labors could not compete with a more urgent wish to be of use to others.

A second, quite different reason for the imbalance is considerably more speculative. There is a status hierarchy in the sciences based on the presumed difficulty of mastering its content. Mathematics and physics have always been regarded as the most challenging disciplines, the alpha domains in the academy, whereas the social sciences occupy the bottom ranks because they are perceived as easier to master and productive of less certain principles. I noted that uncertainty over self's potency with peers is a more salient concern for males than for females. Hence, among youth interested in science, males will be more concerned than females with proving their superior mental capacities in order to dominate peers who chose easier disciplines. Put differently, more young men than women are drawn to the intellectually most difficult fields because mastering them permits the satisfaction that accompanies a feeling of psychological superiority. The molecular biologist François Jacob confessed to a nagging anxiety early in his career: "The fear of having no talent; of being good for nothing."[29] It is also relevant that research in physics, compared with the social sciences, is more likely to lead to an unexpected discovery with extraordinary implications for our understanding of matter or for the practical world. The discovery of the uniform temperature of the cosmos, which affirmed the speculative notion of the Big Bang origin of the universe, was made by two men. The men who constructed the first transistor were surprised by the profound effects this device eventually had on every citizen.

If more males than females have an intense desire to prove their brilliance, as distinguished from a wish for fame, to help society, or to add to the corpus of knowledge, their greater preparedness for a phasic surge in dopamine activity should permit a more salient feeling of excitement when an unexpected discovery, whether an observation or a formal argument, satisfies that motive after a prolonged effort. This feeling is usually interpreted as "pleasant." This mechanism could contribute to the gender difference in professorial positions in physics and mathematics without requiring the claim that women are not intellectually capable of great achievements in these disciplines. Marie Curie, who discovered radium, and Margaret Geller, an astrophysicist who made important discoveries about the cosmos, are examples of women who had the cognitive talents necessary for significant research in the physical sciences. The Curies and Gellers are not more common because most college-age women do not feel the "high" their male peers enjoy when they master the technical content of these domains. Over the past forty years I have had frequent lunches with many of the sons and daughters of friends who were Harvard undergraduates. Four women from this group had chosen physics or mathematics as concentrations when they were sophomores. Although they received "A" grades in their science courses and were confident of their understanding, all four decided in their junior or senior year not to pursue a career in these fields because they failed to extract sufficient pleasure from solving the difficult problems these disciplines posed. One woman majoring in physics said that the content was arcane and too far removed from people and the problems of society. Another reported that she could not generate the intense passion the men in her mathematics courses brought to their work. Although the evidence suggests that most women interested in a scientific career possess the intellectual competences necessary for outstanding achievement in mathematics and the physical sciences, the anticipated emotional satisfaction these disciplines promise is an equally relevant consideration when twenty-one-year-olds are trying to decide how they want to spend their lives. I suspect that the variation in the choice of occupations is more often attributable to motivation than to cognitive abilities. It is odd, therefore, that American scientists, but not necessarily the citizenry, assume the opposite because intellectual skills are more easily measured than emotions. This bias resembles that of a man looking for his car keys under a streetlight rather than in the dark field where he dropped them.

Of course, culture and historical era affect the interpretation imposed on the local norms for gender categories. Medieval Europeans believed that women possessed more carnal desire than men; modern Europeans hold the opposite premise. Punjabis believe that a chaste woman possesses magical powers. Nineteenth-century American physicians believed that sexual frustration could lead to insomnia, depression, and panic attacks, symptoms that recently widowed women often reported. Because doctors assumed that widows with these complaints were deprived of the joys of sexual activity, some were massaging their patient's genitals with battery-powered vibrators until the women had therapeutic orgasms. Galen had to use his fingers to deliver the same health-giving experience to his female patients. The belief that deprivation of sexual pleasures could lead to feelings of suffocation, melancholy, and anxiety in women is traceable to the ideology of the ancient Mediterranean cultures of Egypt and Greece. Experts in these societies attributed these symptoms to a shriveled uterus that began to wander through the body, hence the term *hysteria* for these complaints. Therapies included insertion into the vagina of substances that might attract the uterus back to its normal position. Before the synthesis of estrogen, about forty years ago, menopause was regarded by all societies as a natural developmental event along with gray hair and sagging skin. But during the 1980s, when synthetic estrogen could be purchased and self-appointed experts were telling the public that orgasms were necessary for mental health throughout the life span, menopause was reclassified as a "disease" requiring hormone replacement.[30] The availability of Viagra and Cialis is making some sixty-year-old men unnecessarily anxious over the natural loss of their libido.

The Industrial Revolution altered the nature of work in Western democracies by replacing an economy of individual entrepreneurs who were continually competitive with large bureaucratic institutions that required cooperativeness and a willingness to suppress urges for constant dominance. These changes have been accompanied by a growing celebration of women because of their concern with group vitality, the need for someone to hold a fraying social fabric together, and a harsher view of men as selfish, narcissistic, cruel, and uncertain over their responsibilities. Compare the heroic, confident stature of Odysseus or Gilgamesh with the confused tramps in Samuel Beckett's *Waiting for Godot* or the wild rage of Medea with the marital loyalty of Ingrid Bergman in *Casablanca*. Males fare somewhat better in hierarchical social structures; females tend to thrive in more horizontal settings. History changes the scenery in the human drama on an irregular schedule so that each gender has a chance to play the lead role.

# Culture

A cultural category, defined by a pattern of values, actions, and beliefs held by a population, also prepares its members for different emotional profiles. The Puritans, who believed that God was a real entity rather than the mind's invention, could experience an emotion denied to those contemporary New Englanders who do not share the Puritan conception. The Puritan's state of self-abasement and humiliation with respect to God was often followed by a satisfying feeling of grace and therefore was not identical to the state of a contemporary Bostonian who feels humility in the presence of someone who is wiser, richer, or more charitable. The premises that define a cultural category permit unique emotions to be realized.

The contemporary world is sharply divided on four correlated ethical values. Each person, therefore, has to balance their loyalties to a quartet of opposing obligations: (1) perfecting self and preserving its freedom balanced by loyalty to the integrity of self's family, clan, or community; (2) honoring an egalitarian ethic demanding equal dignity for all balanced by a defense of a hierarchical society in which each person's pedigree and achievements have implications for his or her moral authority; (3) believing in a materialistic world governed only by principles in accord with empirical research balanced by some faith in the contribution, however small, of a metaphysical force to natural events; and (4) treating the accumulation of wealth and the presumed sensory pleasures it brings as a primary goal balanced by honoring the obligations to others inherent in each person's social categories.

When the first member of these four contrasts was combined with the replacement of coal for wood as a source of energy, less frequent floods and droughts, and a smaller population to feed, Europe, which in the seventeenth century was at the same level of development as China, surged ahead in economic growth and scientific achievement. These advances persuaded many citizens that the purpose of their lives was to satisfy desires for enhanced status, greater wealth, unchecked autonomy, and personal happiness.

One of Freud's central assumptions was that the unconscious contained only desires; very few Asian intellectuals have offered this diagnosis of human nature. Indeed, Buddhist philosophy declares that the absence of desire, which the West regards as nihilism, represents the ideal state of nirvana. Because all human lives are punctuated with disappointment and loss, a mood of pessimism bordering on anger began to permeate the broodings of nineteenth-century European scholars who presumed that humans were entitled to continuous satisfaction. When history failed to keep this ingenuous promise, "expect nothing" became the cynical mantra. Far Eastern cultures (such as China, Japan, and Korea), by contrast, adopted a mood of resignation, rather than resentment, to the same state of affairs because they saw disappointment, disease, and distress as part of nature's plan. The impermanence of all things, houses as well as happiness, is a central theme in Japanese art and poetry. Few Japanese poems treat the permanence of spades, plows, and boulders with the reverence they receive in Seamus Heaney's verse.

Although many factors have contributed to this cultural variation, the differential celebration of the individual versus the groups to which each person belongs has been, and continues to be, critical. Contemporary Chinese, compared with Canadian, preadolescents asked to choose between (1) telling a lie that would benefit self but harm the children in their classroom and (2) lying in order to help the class while frustrating self's desires were likely to choose the second course of action. The reintroduction of a market economy in China after Mao's death, however, has begun to persuade youth of the current generation that entrepreneurial self-interest is an attractive imperative. Thus, history continues to rearrange the priorities that each community must consider when a choice must be made. Few cultural values are permanent.

The extraordinary material progress in Europe, which persuaded the middle class to expect continued gratification of their needs through individual perseverance, is a second reason for the cultural differences. The much larger proportion of peasants in Asian societies, combined with the unpredictability of natural disasters such as drought and flood, may have checked the growth of excessive confidence in the future. Last, the conceptualization of change in nature and society as cyclical or as linear may have been influential. Agricultural societies that lacked a narrative dating the beginning of the world or life to a particular moment were apt to favor a cyclical interpretation. The commercial cultures of Europe with a myth that posited an originating moment were more likely to favor a linear view. Members of the former communities should be less often angered by daily frustrations than those in the latter societies. Darwin supported both sides in this debate. He suggested that natural selection would lead to the survival of those who were reproductively most fit and therefore that steady improvement was to be expected. But his ideas also required acceptance of the cyclical burgeoning and extinction of a species due to changing ecological conditions as an essential process in nature. The implication that humans are not a special, or permanent, animal bothers the creationists.

The different values of Europeans and Far Eastern Asians almost guaranteed that European intellectuals would hypothesize stages of human development characterized by gradual improvement in the level of attainment of desired competences, as did Freud, Erik Erikson, and Jean Piaget. However, it is not obvious that the adult capacities for guilt, shame, anxiety, hatred, violence, and suicidal depression are preferable to the gentle innocence of infants. The probability that a nineteenth-century English scientist would invent the idea of evolution by natural selection acting on individuals of varying fitness was far greater than the probability that a Chinese scholar would arrive at this insight, because both Charles Darwin and Alfred Wallace saw the individual as the primary unit and were aware of the dramatic differences in health, longevity, and vitality between the large number of urban poor created by industrialization and the smaller number of privileged gentry.

These cultural differences still exist, albeit in muted form. Many North American psychotherapists believe that the client's personal autonomy should take precedence over obligations to spouse, children, or extended family members, and they subtly move their patients in that direction. Because the clients assume that their therapists are wise, rather than products of their culture, the patients try to adopt the therapists' values and when they are successful treat their new ideas as a sign of personal improvement. Put too plainly, American and European therapists regard the emotion that accompanies an urge to honor one's obligations to others as more toxic than a mood of loneliness.

American and European geneticists, who believe in the power of biology to affect behavior, are trying to discover the genes that interfere with adaptation independent of social conditions. The Japanese, however, believe in the power of the social setting to affect behavior and in the sharp contrast between the actions and emotions appropriate for the inside (*uchi* and *honne*) and those more fitting for the outside (*soto* and *tatemae*). It may not be a coincidence, therefore, that a Japanese geneticist, not an American, is credited with the discovery of so-called neutral genes that have no effect on the phenotype. Anne Harrington has suggested that one reason German physicists made many major contributions to the initial formulation of quantum mechanics during the early decades of the twentieth century was that German scholars felt humiliated by their defeat in the First World War and wanted to announce to the world some sign of German intellectual potency. The indeterminacy that is central to quantum theory was inconsistent with the belief among English physicists in a strict determinism.

The early history of psychology in Germany, England, and the United States provides a persuasive argument for the influence of a culture's values on the ideology of its intellectuals. The Germans, for whom Kant and Goethe were unchallenged heroes, celebrated an idealistic conception of the mind. It is not surprising, therefore, that their first psychologists, Wilhelm Wundt for example, tried to find the universal properties of consciousness by asking informants to report their perceptions of simple stimuli. The nineteenth-century British honored their kings more than their philosophers because societal distinctions by family pedigree generated more passion than the universal nature of consciousness. Hence, Francis Galton won English admiration for studying the heritable bases for differences in intellectual ability and accomplishment. Americans, who were the most pragmatic and egalitarian of the three communities, were more receptive than the others to Darwin's ideas because they implied that the most able, rather than those lost in deep thought or the fortunate few born to the proper family line, deserved the greatest rewards. American psychologists were interested in actions and the environmental conditions that might allow the largest number of children to actualize their potential. Culture does matter.

The single-minded worship of a happy, autonomous individual, a materialistic foundation for all natural events, and certainty in scientific conclusions, which have been central premises in Western ideology, has resulted in an extreme imbalance in the amount of public funds allocated for research designed to diagnose and cure a small number of relatively infrequent mental diseases, such as Alzheimer's, autism, and bipolar disorder. The amount of money given to social scientists trying to understand and alleviate the ills that plague current society, many without obvious materialistic causes or cures and offering less certain conclusions, is tiny by comparison.

This asymmetry is especially odd for several reasons. Modern quantum theory rejects the nineteenth century's belief in the certainty of a strict determinism, the individual in industrialized, bureaucratic states is becoming increasingly anonymous, and the information technologies are promoting symbolic meanings to a position that competes with the materialism of neurons and molecules. There is no known chemical substance capable of generating the level of anger that was induced in hundreds of thousands of Muslims around the world when they learned of the cartoon in a Danish newspaper portraying their sacred religious figure Muhammad with an explosive in his head covering. Nonetheless, like the Mesmerists of the 1840s who believed that a few privileged people possessed a magnetic force that could cure distress, many modern citizens place their faith in the material power of chemical substances to exorcize their angst and replace it with a blessed serenity.

The faith in both biological determinism and the ability to measure its consequences is so profound that federal and state legislators who had resisted approving funds for psychological interventions in early childhood that might reduce the risk of future pathology were ready to support the legislation when a respected authority told them that early abuse or neglect produces material alterations in children's brains that could be quantified. Simply altering the rationale from "abuse of children affects their beliefs and emotions" to "abuse of children affects their brains" melted their reluctance to allocate public funds for benevolent interventions. This disheartening fact implies that many well-educated Americans still regard mental processes as mysterious, fluid, impermanent phenomena—wispy clouds changing shape over the course of the day. Biological processes, by contrast, are like scratches on the surface of a table whose depth and length could be measured. René Descartes's sixteenth-century separation of soul and body is alive and well in the twenty-first century. The U.S. Congress and private philanthropies are willing to spend millions of dollars to develop drugs that might help children failing in school but are unwilling to spend a tenth of that to improve the personal strategies a teacher might use to motivate an indifferent student.

Americans are frustrated over the failure of political and professional leaders to improve their society because those in power are unable to violate the twin imperatives that demand a materialistic cause and cure for social problems and a quantitative evaluation of any intervention that might have benevolent consequences. We are like desperately hungry vegetarians who refuse to eat a hamburger because that action would violate our ethical values. Although a sustained educational program with young children at high risk for a criminal career would result in fewer robberies and murders fifteen years later and, therefore, reduce psychological distress in a proportion of potential criminals and their victims, it would not eliminate all crime, and it is difficult to measure "psychological distress." Hence, one cannot prove that the intervention is less expensive than the cost of imprisoning those who violate the law. Americans want less crime, but their values prevent them from satisfying this desire. A theoretical physicist wrote, "The move from certainty to uncertainty that characterized the twentieth century has brought with it a great responsibility. Each of us today realizes our connection to the society in which we live. . . . Each of us helps to generate and sustain the meaning by which that society functions."[31]

A second reason for the imbalance in funding is that Americans have always wanted the products of intellectual work to have pragmatic dividends for the majority. Knowledge should be useful, Benjamin Franklin insisted. The fact that more money is spent on projects that help a minority of the population than on investigations that might repair the torn fabric of our society and in so doing help millions implies that the American romance with individualism, materialistic causes, and certainty continues to trump a pragmatic stance as a strategy to heal the wounded social settings in which each person tries to survive. The eminence of American social scientists who tried to understand society, such as Talcott Parsons, George Murdock, and Clifford Geertz, pales alongside the celebrity of Francis Crick, James Watson, and Jonas Salk.

The extreme individualism of industrialized, capitalist democracies increases the likelihood of select emotions; loneliness is one example. These cultures force adolescents to compete with peers for better grades and adults to compete with others for vocational advances. Many individuals therefore harbor the private wish that strangers or colleagues will fare less well. The pervasiveness of this malevolent thought among those caught in the odd-shaped cage that history has constructed renders some people vulnerable to a guilt that can erode the vitality required for a sanguine or serene mood. Hunter-gatherers, and most members of ancient agricultural civilizations, were more protected from this state because cooperation, not competition, was usually more adaptive. Americans who experience occupational or social failure usually blame inadequate talent, genes, social conditions, or bad luck, but not the actions of neighbors, witches, or deceased grandparents. Citizens of the Shang dynasty in China, a thousand years before the present era, who believed it was possible to contact dead ancestors were prepared for an emotion that residents of contemporary Beijing or Buffalo would find hard to attain. Citizens of Plato's Athens were vulnerable to guilt if they acted or intended to act in ways that implied disloyalty to their city. Residents of the Indus Valley during the same century were advised to minimize their emotional attachments to people, objects, and communities and probably felt less guilt over the same behavior or intention. This imperative remains strong among contemporary Hindus. A schoolmaster told an English visitor, "Great Indian souls, they ignore the things of this world . . . if some close relation dies, even if a wife or son, he is not too much distressed, because he knows that this is the rule of the world. He lives in the world like a pearly drop of water on a lotus leaf—it moves about on the leaf but it is not absorbed."[32]

The prevalence of a bout of depression in a mother following the birth of her child (called postpartum depression) varies dramatically across national groups. For example, the prevalence of this diagnosis is less than 1 percent in Singapore and Malta but greater than 30 percent in Costa Rica, Chile, Korea, and Taiwan.[33] Films often reflect the beliefs, worries, and values of a culture. Suicide is regarded as a more heroic act by Japanese than by Americans, and therefore the thought of suicide evokes less shame in Japan. No Hollywood executive would have produced a movie in which fifty young adolescent girls, holding hands and smiling, jump simultaneously in front of an oncoming train. Yet this event was the opening scene in the Japanese film *The Suicide Club* (2002), which received rave reviews in the Japanese press. The fifty-year span from 1950, when India won independence from Britain, to 2000 was marked by major political and economic changes that are reflected in Hindi films. For example, during the first decade following independence, when the society was idealistic, mentally ill adults were portrayed with compassion and gentleness. But by 1980, when inflation and corruption had become rampant, many more films dealt with angry, psychopathic males. And by 1990, following economic reforms, sexually assertive, angry women became central figures in popular movies.[34]

A distinct origin in place and time, which are fixed and defining features of a cultural category, are less relevant for one's class category. As a result, membership in a cultural category is more likely to prepare individuals for vicarious emotions when other members of the category, alive or dead, are noted for a praiseworthy or distasteful action or characteristic. A Hispanic is likely to feel proud when a Mexican American is elected to high office or is celebrated for an unusual talent. A middle-class woman is far less likely to feel proud when another middle-class woman enjoys a moment of celebrity. Joe Louis was an African-American heavyweight boxer who grew up in a poor family. When Louis defeated the German Max Schmeling for the heavyweight championship of the world in 1938, as Hitler was threatening Europe, newspaper reports reveal that the intensity of vicarious pride was greatest among African Americans of both sexes and all social classes. Poor white American males did not experience the same level of pride, even though they shared Louis's class and gender. Karl Marx did not appreciate that ethnicity usually has priority over class when there is variation in both. Marx's Europe varied more substantially in class than in ethnicity. Most political leaders trying to ignite passion in order to unite a group for a reform movement or a massacre understand this fact. Charismatic leaders in the Middle East appeal to the cultural category of the many poor Arabs in the area rather than to their economically compromised status. The most horrendous acts of mass killing have occurred when appeals to both cultural category and class have been combined. Some obvious examples include the violence between the Hutus and Tutsis, the northern and southern Irish, and the Serbs and Bosnians. Thus, class, gender, and cultural categories have different emotional consequences for those identified with these self-defining ideas. And it is not uncommon for combinations of gender, class, and culture to prepare individuals for certain emotions. Fetuses of Israeli mothers, for example, who were conceived during the Six Day War in 1967 were at higher risk for schizophrenia as adults, but only if they were females born to mothers with little education and marginal incomes.[35]

A dramatic difference between the characteristics a person presumes to be part of their character and the ideal features that define their social categories can provoke an emotion that has various forms and names across cultures. Contemporary Americans and Europeans are apt to call this state *inauthentic, insufficient, insecure,* or in extreme cases *degraded.* The Turkish writer Orhan Pamuk, a 2006 Nobel laureate, noted in his address accepting the prize that he felt a lack of authenticity because he identified with a society that had no interest in serious literature. Sherwin Nuland, a prominent surgeon and writer, described a profound self-doubt that owed its origin to his being the son of a poor, illiterate, physically compromised Jewish immigrant father who often exploded in rage against the young boy. If individuals who live with these beliefs happen to achieve the culture's definition of success, a feeling of inappropriateness often casts a shadow on their victory. Humans are sensitive to notions of fairness and justice, which imply that only the virtuous and talented are entitled to happiness. Thus, those with childhood feelings of taint often regard their achievements as ill deserved, fraudulent, or inauthentic.

Because identification with a social category that has undesirable features evokes shame, guilt, or anxiety, we must ask why many individuals retain their identification with these burdensome categories. One reason is that humans are disposed to believe that names for kinds of people imply stable, immutable qualities. Hindus who belonged to the untouchable caste understood that this category was permanent. Second, denial of one's category is a moral failing for it implies disloyalty to one's family, religious, or ethnic group. A third reason is that the identification provides a guide to action when alternative decisions are possible. Acceptance of self's cultural categories mutes some of the response uncertainty surrounding vocational and marital choices. Very few African Americans become geneticists, whereas many American Jews study psychiatry. Minority-group adolescents growing up in poverty with unemployed, alcoholic fathers who identify with the category "disadvantaged" often accept their semantic assignment because it protects them from the pain of disappointment should efforts to better their condition fail. Humans find uncertainty so unpleasant that they are willing to live with an undesirable conception of self if it absorbs some of the tension generated by not knowing what they should do.

## Temperamental Variation

Variation in class, gender, ethnicity, and culture prepare individuals for different emotional hierarchies. Temperamental biases, by contrast, affect variation in the frequency and salience of feelings. I suspect that most, but not all, of the large number of human temperaments are the result of genetic factors that contribute to the profiles of molecules and receptor densities that influence brain function. These temperamental biases produce variation in the reactivity of, or sensitivity to, a change in heart rate, breathing, gastric motility, skin temperature, or bitter tastes. Among adults who have panic attacks, some experience a sudden feeling of suffocation, whereas others are vulnerable to sharp rises in heart rate or blood pressure. Children who like very sour tastes also prefer bright colors and foods with unfamiliar flavors. Adults who are unusually accurate in detecting their heartbeats report emotional experiences different from those who are less accurate. Individuals who are apprehensive over an unexpected change in bodily feeling, which they interpret as anxiety (a trait called anxiety sensitivity), belong to a distinct temperamental category. Both Alice James, the younger sister of William and Henry James, and the poet Sylvia Plath were members of this group. Some adults who find it difficult to divert their attention from a painful event possess a compromised prefrontal cortex that does not allow them to suppress unwanted sensations.[36]

Temperamental biases resulting from heritable profiles of brain chemistry are the bases for variation in the frequency and salience of the feelings that give rise to acute emotions and moods.[37] Experiences act on these biases to create personality types, such as agreeable with peers or impulsively aggressive following frustration. A small number of individuals, for example, inherit a temperament that makes it difficult for them to experience shame or guilt. A journalist interviewed a number of imprisoned adults who had admitted to a homicide. One woman, who had shot a lover who threatened to tell her husband about their casual affair, confessed: "I was born a Catholic . . . we all went every Sunday to mass. I always felt different from them somehow though . . . I never had a strong sense of sin . . . somewhere along the line I missed out on guilt."[38]

The exact number of human temperaments, although very large, is unknown. It is estimated that any two randomly selected individuals differ from each other in about ten million bases (about 0.3 percent of the roughly three billion bases in the human genome), some of which affect the brain circuits that contribute to temperamental biases.[39] It is unlikely that any temperament is due to a single allele; even the amount of skin pigmentation is affected by more than 150 alleles in more than ninety chromosomal locations.

One source of genetic variation is a small section of the promoter region of the gene for the serotonin transporter molecule. The promoter region, usually next to the gene that is the source of a protein (called an exon), determines its rate of transcription and therefore how much of the protein the cell's machinery will produce. Each person inherits two alleles, one from each parent, in a specific location on the chromosome. Adults who possess two short alleles in the promoter region for the serotonin transporter differ from those with two long alleles. The differences in emotion and behavior between the two groups, however, depend on many factors, including gender, ethnicity, class, season of conception, and perhaps culture.

Although most studies of American or European middle-class white adults find that those with two short alleles are at a greater risk for an anxiety disorder, Asians with the same genetic feature are at a higher risk for an attempted suicide, some adolescent girls, but not boys, are at risk for depression, some youth are at a higher risk for conduct disorder, and some college students with this allele drink more alcohol. To complicate matters, adults with two short alleles who remembered having a benign, supportive home environment during childhood were *less* depressed than those who had the long alleles. And males with the two short alleles were at risk for a suicide attempt only if they had been conceived during the months May, June, or July. The obvious implication of these findings is that possession of the two short, or two long, alleles appears to bias a person for a special profile of brain states, but the specific emotions, symptoms, or behaviors that result from these brain states depend on many psychological factors that include gender, class, culture, and the nature of the individual's past and present life setting.

There is no fixed consequent of this genetic feature. Furthermore, the presence of the short or long alleles rarely accounts for more than 10 percent of the variation in a behavior or symptom, whereas gender, class, and culture account for far more variation in traits.[40]

Because the short and long alleles determine differences in the rate of absorption of serotonin from the synapse (short alleles are associated with less rapid absorption), possession of one or the other genome might be components of distinct brain states. Healthy adults who possessed one or both of the short alleles, compared with those with two long alleles, showed less functional connectivity between the amygdala and a small region in the anterior cingulate cortex that regulates the amygdala while they performed a perceptual task with fearful and angry faces. A subgroup of these adults who admitted to avoiding objects or places that might be harmful had less connectivity between these two regions than others, implying the absence of the normal modulation of the amygdala by the cingulate cortex. Either a more excitable amygdala or compromised modulation of the amygdala could render a person susceptible to feelings that might be appraised as anxiety, depression, or anger, or lead to obsessive-compulsive traits or excessive drinking, depending on the individual's gender, age, ethnicity, past history, and current life conditions.[41]

Under some environmental conditions, however, the same biology could have adaptive consequences. Individuals who inherited the short alleles might be able to use their heightened arousal for constructive ends if they had the benefit of benevolent childhood homes and schools that helped them develop talents and coping defenses to stressful conditions. Thus, only some adults with the two short alleles will resemble Galen's melancholic type who exaggerate the threat inherent in the loss of a job, termination of a relationship, or death of a relative and are chronically pessimistic and vulnerable to bouts of depression following a stress. The confessions of John Calvin, the sixteenth-century Protestant reformer, suggest that he was a member of this temperamental category, for he believed that freedom from fear and anxiety was the most desirable state anyone could imagine.[42]

Galen's sanguine temperamental type, by contrast, is more likely to have inherited the two long alleles and therefore biased to be optimistic and cheerful. This mood, which psychologists call *subjective well-being*, has an estimated heritability of about 38 percent. The adolescents who posed with smiles for their yearbook photographs reported greater subjective well-being thirty years later than those who had a serious expression. Twenty-two-year-old nuns who used sentences referring to frequent bouts of happiness in their autobiographies lived longer than their religious sisters who less often described a happy mood, perhaps because a sanguine temperament is associated with better immune function. Young adults who reported a typical mood of serenity and joy had a more vigorous antibody reaction to a hepatitis B vaccination than less sanguine persons. Signs of the future development of the melancholic and sanguine personalities can be detected in early infancy in the behaviors regarding unfamiliar events.[43]

## High- and Low-Reactive Infants

Two-year-olds who were especially vulnerable to behavioral signs of uncertainty when they anticipated or encountered unfamiliar events had displayed unusually vigorous motor activity and frequent crying to unfamiliar sights, smells, and sounds when they were only four months old. These children, called temperamentally high-reactive, reacted to the unexpected appearance of a clown with an immediate scream and a rapid retreat to the mother. The same clown evoked no signs of fear in most of the two-year-olds who had been classified as low-reactive infants because they displayed minimal motor activity and little crying to the same stimuli when they were four months old. The low-reactive two-year-olds smiled when the clown entered the room and approached the unfamiliar figure within a few seconds. The small proportion of newborns who were unable to regulate their distress once they began to cry, which suggests a compromise in the brain systems that prevent distress from spinning out of control, resembled high-reactive infants when they were four months old.[44]

The first day at school is a novel experience for most five- and six-year-olds, and children with a temperamental bias to become vigilant in unfamiliar settings should have a more salient emotional reaction. It is not surprising, therefore, that the children of mothers who had reported a highly stressful pregnancy associated with high levels of cortisol at sixteen weeks of gestation displayed the highest cortisol levels on their first day of school.

By contrast, five adolescent boys who had been described by their parent as rarely showing empathy to the distress of others or shame or guilt over their asocial behavior had unusually low levels of morning cortisol.[45]

Adolescents who had been high-reactive infants confessed to more frequent bouts of sadness, combined reports of frequent heart-rate changes, sweating of palms, muscle tension, facial flushing, and breathing difficulty with a high systolic blood pressure, and displayed distinct behavioral and biological profiles when they were eleven and fifteen years old. Bodily activity is preferentially elaborated by the right, rather than the left, prefrontal cortex. It is of interest, therefore, that the most introverted college student (among a group of twenty-eight students) had the greatest cortical thickness in the right inferior prefrontal cortex, whereas the least introverted student had the thinnest value.[46]

One important biological property of high-reactive adolescents is a more sustained period of cortical arousal to unfamiliar events. This fact implies that the brain state, and subsequent feeling, of high-reactives to an event that evokes uncertainty, say entering a party of strangers or boarding a plane during a snowstorm, is different from the states induced in others. Among a group of adults who confessed to a fear of flying, those with greater parasympathetic, rather than sympathetic, activity in the cardiovascular system were less fearful to pictures and sounds of airplanes than those with greater sympathetic tone. The greater parasympathetic tone implies an orienting rather than a defensive reaction.[47]

It is possible that among the 15 percent of combat soldiers in Iraq who developed post-traumatic stress disorder, characterized by insomnia, apathy, and nightmares, a large proportion had been high-reactive infants. The conditions of war create both continuous worry over bodily harm and a threat to self's sense of virtue generated by the need to kill or to witness or be an accomplice to terrible atrocities on innocent civilians. Individuals who are temperamentally vulnerable to a more salient form of this emotional blend are apt to develop post-traumatic stress disorder.

High-reactives are also more susceptible to the allergic sensitivities that result in hay fever, asthma, or hives. One factor contributing to these allergies is a chronically higher level of cortisol. Newborns with a parent who had one of these allergies showed a larger increase in cortisol to the brief pain of a sharp instrument inserted into their heel to obtain a blood sample compared with newborns born to parents free of all allergies.[48]

The adolescents who had been temperamentally high- or low-reactive at four months held a different understanding of the self-descriptive statement, "I'm happy most of the time." Most high-reactives who claimed they were happy described themselves as serious and thinking too much, whereas the low-reactives who said they were usually happy described themselves as easygoing and not very serious. The low-reactives were probably relying on their feeling tone when they decided on their happy mood, whereas more high-reactives probably relied on an appraisal of the degree to which their psychological qualities matched their ego ideal. The latter state shares features with the Greek notion of eudaimonia.[49] Identical reports of a "feeling of well-being" can be the product of different genomes and life histories and reflect different states of brain and of consciousness. Adolescents who had been high-reactive infants were more religious than low-reactives and confessed that they felt *purer* and *cleansed* after attending a religious ceremony. The choice of these words implies that their spiritual commitment muted the unpleasant emotions provoked by thinking of the moral errors they had committed or the possibility of a future task failure. However, high-reactives do not violate their ethical code more often than low-reactives; rather, they interpret their unpredictable changes in feeling tone as implying that they have done so.

High-reactives are also a little more likely to possess a thin, frail build, a narrow face, and a smaller body mass. It is interesting, therefore, that adult Finnish men with a genetic polymorphism in the gene for MAO-A that resulted in faster degradation of dopamine in the synapse, which should interfere with the duration of a sanguine mood, had a smaller body mass than others.[50] Film directors are likely to cast actors with a tall, thin body build and a narrow face in roles portraying tense, anxious, treacherous, or suspicious characters and rarely ask them to play the part of a cheerful, sociable optimist. Compare the body and face of the witch in *The Wizard of Oz* with the chubby build and full face of the Wizard or Santa Claus.

One of every four adolescent boys who had been a low-reactive infant fifteen years earlier displayed the strong, silent persona of the film star Clint Eastwood, had low levels of cortical and autonomic arousal, and reported being easygoing. Members of this temperamental category who are raised in affectionate homes that encourage accomplishment and attend good schools are likely to become adults who enjoy high-risk vocations, such as politics, investment, and trial law. But they are at risk for a criminal career if they grow up in deprived homes in which aggressive behavior is not socialized and their neighborhoods contain temptations for asocial acts. Under these conditions they may resemble the woman with no sense of sin who committed a premeditated murder. Thus, the same temperamental bias can lead to very different personalities when development proceeds in distinctive environments.

High-reactive youth ruminate excessively about their feelings and, like middle-aged, middle-class American women who brood about their emotions, are slightly more vulnerable to the traits psychiatrists call obsessive-compulsive. Because high-reactives are vulnerable to uncertainty, they try to adopt habits that will protect them from this uncomfortable emotion. A mistake is the most common cause of this state in modern societies. These adults try to avoid errors and, as a result, appear to friends as super-responsible. When this lifestyle is carried to an extreme, it can result in washing all foods to avoid an infection, double-checking all doors, and saving old string in case it is needed in the future. These are the symptoms of obsessive-compulsive disorder.

High-reactives are also at a slightly higher risk for bouts of depression. Depressed adults were more likely than others to remember being shy and timid as children and to report, contemporaneously, salient social anxiety. However, a high-reactive temperament has the advantage of protecting a person from excessively risky behavior and therefore lowers the probability that the person will have an accident, either while driving a car or racing down a ski slope.[51] High-reactive adults are careful, cautious, and concerned with the possibility of catastrophe.

The high-reactive youth described above were vulnerable to anxiety over encountering unfamiliar people, situations, or challenges for which they were unprepared. They worried excessively about tomorrow and their ability to deal with the unpredictable surprises it might bring. They kept lists of what they were supposed to do and acquired other compulsive habits. But because these adolescents grew up in American society they were biased to interpret the intrusive feelings produced by frequent visceral feedback as implying they were worried about novel encounters or challenges. Ten percent of American adults with both anxiety and depression had distinct arrhythmias of the heart.[52] It is likely that the perception of the sensory feedback from their heart provoked these patients to exaggerate the seriousness of the worries that preoccupied them. Adolescents or adults with the same temperament living in other cultures might impose a different interpretation on the same feeling. Cambodian refugees living in the United States interpret a sudden tachycardia as implying a weak heart caused by a loss of energy due to lack of sleep or a diminished appetite.[53] Two high-reactive infants born with the same temperamental bias, therefore, will acquire different personalities if one grows up in a culture, like America, that presents unfamiliar challenges frequently and promotes the idea that perception of autonomic activity signifies anxiety and the other lives in a rural Indonesian village with few unfamiliar experiences who interprets a change in bodily activity as a sign of fatigue.

Although temperamental biases do render children and adults vulnerable to certain traits, more of the variation in contemporary measures of personality and psychopathology is due to variation in social class, gender, ethnicity, and culture than to the genes that are the foundation for the temperament. This claim does not mean that genes make no contribution to these outcomes. The movement patterns of tiny pollen grains in an outside swimming pool provide an analogy. Under natural conditions the movements of the grains are due primarily to the velocity of the wind above the pool. However, in a still, indoor pool, protected from outside forces, the movements are due primarily to the random contacts of the pollen grains with water molecules. Einstein used this argument in 1905 as proof of the existence of atoms. Therefore, in order to evaluate the contributions of genes to psychological qualities investigators must control for the effects of class, gender, ethnicity, and culture and appreciate that a genetic influence might be restricted to the members of one of these categories, a strategy that most do not follow.

Future research will discover other temperamental biases that render children especially prepared for such traits as restlessness, high energy level, dizziness, listlessness, frequent intrusive feelings of genital arousal, or muted sensory pleasures.[54] The emotional hierarchies that develop from these temperamental characteristics will vary with culture, history, gender, age, and perhaps ethnic pedigree.

## Ethnicity and Temperament

Human populations that have been reproductively isolated for thousands of years across long distances, and therefore for many hundreds of generations, are likely to possess unique genomes with implications for temperaments that influence emotions. Although only 0.02 percent of all bases in the human genome distinguish reproductively separated human populations from each other, this small proportion represents about six hundred thousand bases. This number is large enough to create temperamental variations among populations, even though the genetic variation within a population is usually greater than the variation between two isolated groups. For example, Caucasian infants and young children smile more often than children born to Chinese parents, whether the Chinese infants were born in the United States or the People's Republic of China. College-age American couples of Caucasian descent discussing their relationship smile more often than Chinese-American couples, and Caucasian American adolescents describe themselves as more cheerful and extroverted than Chinese Americans living in the same Midwestern city. Caucasian infants are also more easily provoked to high levels of excitement, characterized by vigorous motor activity and frequent crying (like high-reactives), compared with Chinese infants. More than twenty-five years ago my colleagues and I studied Chinese-American and Caucasian infants, either raised completely at home or attending the same day-care center in Boston, from three to twenty-nine months of age. The Chinese infants were less vocal, less active, less likely to smile, and more reserved in unfamiliar situations. And the mothers of the twenty-nine-month-old Chinese children described them as less talkative, less likely to laugh, and less disobedient than did the mothers of the Caucasian children. In the autumn of 1973 I joined a group of scholars visiting the People's Republic of China to learn about education and child rearing in Mao's radical society. We were all impressed with the ability of five- and six-year-old children to sit calmly for long periods without any movement or giggling. They "seemed to have an ability to attend with laserlike focus to what adults were saying to them . . . or sit almost half an hour separating good and bad pea beans into separate bowls."[55] Chinese infants display this same quality.

Recall that most Asian societies celebrate a low level of arousal as an ideal state. Buddhist philosophy, which did not appeal to most Europeans, regards a serene feeling in which the individual desires nothing and has no intense emotional attachments as the perfect state of nirvana all should try to attain. By contrast, Americans and Europeans with a Caucasian background regard the excitement that accompanies sexual affairs, visiting new places, and engagement in new activities as the ideal states to command. It is possible that temperamental differences between Asians and Caucasians make a small contribution to these cultural preferences.

Far Eastern and European populations, which have been reproductively separated for almost a thousand generations, differ in many alleles. Dogs and wolves, which have been separated for about the same number of generations, differ in alleles that affect brain states related to emotion. Far Eastern Asians and Caucasians differ in one-fourth of the alleles in the regulatory regions that control gene expression. One of these alleles modulates the enzyme that converts inactive estrogen into the active form. Recall that estrogen enhances the activity of oxytocin, which facilitates social attachments and the more relaxed states of the autonomic nervous system. The two groups also differ in alleles modulating the serotonin transporter molecule and an enzyme that degrades dopamine in the synapse. If Europeans were biologically prepared for more arousing emotions, because of a higher prevalence of certain alleles, a philosophy that promoted calm serenity as the ideal would appear to be both less possible and less valid than it would seem to Asians, who more often possessed the alleles linked to a lower state of arousal. It is possible, but difficult, to persuade a person to work toward a goal they do not believe they can attain. It may not be a coincidence that Chinese-Australian patients who suffered from depression required a lower dose of a drug affecting serotonin function than depressed Caucasian Australians in order to achieve the same degree of remission of their depressed mood.[56]

The suggestion that the Chinese and Japanese, as populations, differ temperamentally from Europeans and Americans with a Caucasian genome

finds support in studies of the serotonin transporter molecule during embryological development. During the first two months after conception, a
necklace of cells, called the neural crest, migrates to become the bones of
the face, the autonomic nervous system, the adrenal medulla, part of the
aortic arch emanating from the heart, and the pigment cells of the iris, hair,
and skin. The serotonin transporter molecule influences the differentiation
of these neural crest cells. (Of course, many other molecules affect the neural crest.) Hence, alleles of the gene for the serotonin transporter molecule
could influence the chemistry of the crest cells and, by inference, the nature
of the tissues they become later in development. Asians are more likely than
Caucasians to inherit the two short alleles of this gene, which, it will be recalled, slow the rate of absorption of serotonin from the synapse.[57]

Human groups differ in the shape of the head and the prominence of the
forehead, nose, and chin. Recall that some neural crest cells become the
facial bones. One consequence of the domestication of mammals to render
them easier to manage (such as horse, pigs, and cattle) is a shortening of
the facial snout; that is, a flatter face. Silver fox bred for tameness, for example, had both shorter snouts and higher levels of serotonin than wild, un-
tamed silver fox after only several dozen generations of selective mating.[58]
The fact that more Chinese, Japanese, and Koreans have flatter faces than
Caucasians, especially less prominent noses and chins, and round rather
than long, narrow faces, implies that the genetic differences in the serotonin
transporter gene may have affected the chemistry of the neural crest cells
that become the facial bones. Recall that four-month-old Chinese infants
showed significantly lower levels of motor activity and crying to unfamiliar
events than Caucasians, as well as a less variable heart rate, implying a lower
level of limbic arousal. Chinese adults, too, have a less labile heart rate than
Caucasians to stressors. Both the behavioral and cardiovascular properties
can be affected by variation in serotonin, which influences the excitability
of the amygdala.[59] These scattered pieces of evidence suggest, but cannot
prove, that the subtle psychological differences between Far Eastern Asian
and European Caucasian populations might have a small temperamental
component that traces part of its origin to differences in many genes, including the alleles for the serotonin transporter and neural crest differentiation
within the first months of embryological growth.

Obviously, a person's biology cannot determine a particular personality type, but it can limit how easily certain emotions and moods can be acquired and sustained. That is why few high-reactive infants became consistently spontaneous, sociable, high-risk takers, and few low-reactives became hypervigilant, shy, risk-averse adolescents. I noted earlier that the power of genes rests with their capacity to limit the realization of particular outcomes while not guaranteeing any particular profile. An infant girl born with two short alleles in the serotonin transporter gene could develop any one of a number of personalities. But the probability that she will be an extremely sociable, spontaneous, bold woman who rarely felt anxious or tense is lower than it would be for an infant girl born with two long alleles. That is the limit of what we can conclude, at least at present. The influences of the small number of genetic differences between Caucasians and Asians related to emotion, created by almost a thousand generations of reproductive isolation, have to be shared with the more powerful contributions of culture. Yet it remains possible that biology and culture, acting together, made some philosophical orientations and styles of social interaction more attractive to each of these two populations.

## Emotions and Psychopathology

The distinction between acute emotions and chronic moods assumes special significance for the psychological features of those with anxiety or depressive disorders, on one hand, and character disorders (failure to conform to community standards on honesty, responsibility, and civility), on the other. These two categories were recognized by the ancients in the melancholic and choleric temperamental types and are represented by the terms *internalizing* and *externalizing* in the most widely used questionnaire for psychopathology in children (called the Child Behavior Checklist). Clinicians typically place a patient in one of the psychiatric categories if their emotions are preserved for a relatively long period and interfere with the implementation of their role assignments. It is generally assumed that many but not all anxious or depressed patients possess a temperamental bias that rendered them susceptible to these emotions. There is less agreement, however, regarding the degree of similarity in subjective feelings between patients and nonpatients reporting similar emotions. For example, the acute anxiety felt by a driver caught on a steep hill in a blizzard may not be biologically or psychologically identical to the state of a patient with a phobia of flying waiting to board a transatlantic flight. It remains a possibility that the driver's state is due to activation of the amygdala, whereas the phobic's state is a result of both amygdalar excitability and compromised function of the prefrontal sites that modulate the amygdala. Should this speculation prove valid, it will prove useful to invent distinct sets of terms for the acute emotions of those without psychiatric illness and the more frequent states of patients. The small number of adolescents who report salient anxiety over meeting strangers may differ in important ways from the larger group whose anxiety is limited to worry over an inadequate public performance.[60]

The salience of a symptom affects the diagnostic category the clinician assigns to a patient. When the fundamental cause of an illness is known, the clinician is less likely to award causal significance to a symptom that happens to be salient in the patient's consciousness. For example, fatigue is a distinctive complaint of patients with malaria, but physicians do not award it a privileged causal force because they know the etiology of the illness. Many Parkinson's patients report both tremors and absence of feelings of pleasure, called anhedonia. Because the tremors are more salient to the patients, the anhedonia is treated as less informative. However, a lower level of brain dopamine contributes to both the tremors and the absence of pleasure, and future research might reveal that the anhedonia is a more critical feature of the disease than the tremors.

When the significant cause of a disease is unknown, however, which is true for most mental illnesses, the clinical categories are influenced unduly by the characteristics the patient emphasizes. For example, a majority of Americans and Europeans who report moods of depression are also less well educated, have less proficient verbal skills, have a disadvantaged social status, and hold less challenging jobs with lower salaries. But because the patients regard their apathy and absence of pleasure, rather than their verbal skills, social class, or form of work, as salient, the psychiatric category is called depressive disorder. It is not unreasonable, however, to propose that, for some individuals with these complaints, this syndrome should be called *social disadvantage disorder* because one of its fundamental causes is the patient's social status. This decision would permit a distinction with *melan-cholia*, characterized by apathy, an absence of pleasure, insomnia, and poor appetite, which is not especially linked to social disadvantage. Furthermore, this distinction would alert therapists to the potential value of tutoring language skills along with the usual therapeutic regimens. A group of depressed patients who were poorly educated and had compromised verbal abilities received literacy training along with the standard treatment for depression. These patients improved more than those who received only the standard medical treatment.[61]

The history of discoveries in the physical and biological sciences suggests that, on many occasions, the most salient feature of a phenomenon turned out to be a poor guide to its more fundamental nature or the causal mechanisms that produced it. Paracelsus thought that the distinct smell of sulfur meant that it was a unique metal. Modern chemists use atomic structure, not smell, to categorize metals. The Sun appears to move through the sky; the intensity of the light striking a surface would seem to be more important than its frequency in determining the release of electrons from the surface; and the dramatic differences in form between flies and humans imply that these two species should share very few genes in common. All three assumptions have proven to be wrong. The early Greek and Indian philosophers were right: the surface features of an event are usually poor guides to its structure and function.

# A Pair of Problems

Two final issues require our attention. The first deals with the relations among the three sources of evidence for an emotion and the degree to which they reflect the same or very similar processes and have the same theoretical meaning. If this were true, the varied sources of information could be combined. The technical name for this theoretical equivalence is *commensurability*. The physical concepts "mass" and "energy" are commensurable because scientists know how to translate the mass of an atom or log into the energy it can create. The commensurability of brain activity, behaviors, and verbal reports for emotions is unknown. The utility of nominating a small, select set of emotions as basic states (the atoms of human affect), to be contrasted with a much larger number deemed as less fundamental, is the second issue. I deal with the commensurability problem first.

## Metrics and Structures

I have noted many times that the meaning of every conclusion about emotions depends on the evidence. This issue is especially relevant for the variation among individuals in their emotional reactions to an event. There is far greater variation in brain profiles to scenes of war, infants, or lovemaking than in the feelings, facial expressions, actions, or semantic appraisals evoked by these scenes. Hence, a discussion of the three primary sources of evidence for emotional states (semantic descriptions, behaviors, and biological activity) should be useful. Each class of evidence is described with special metrics, has a distinctive structure (structure refers to the pattern of relations among the measures), and provides unique information on the separate aspects of the cascade that defines an emotion. It may prove impossible to translate all the inferences derived from one source of evidence into those derived from another, as physicists do when they translate the mass of a kilogram of uranium into the energy it would yield if it were fissioned.

## Semantic Reports

The semantic terms for emotions can be rated on the dimensions pleasant to unpleasant and high to low salience as well as semantic distance, or strength of association, between words. However, the semantic distances among a family of words are not correlated with the degree of similarity among pictures of scenes illustrating the objects the words name. The unique properties of words were revealed when adults judged the degree of similarity among twenty-one words for anger and twenty-one photographs of angry faces. The patterns of similarity among the words did not match the patterns found for the photos. Moreover, words with an unpleasant semantic connotation, like *poison* or *kill*, evoked brain states that differed from those evoked by words spoken with an unpleasant voice.[1] Last, a semantic proposition can only be judged as true or false or as consistent or inconsistent with the larger set of statements in which it appears. Verbal descriptions of emotions provide clues to the personal constructions people impose on feelings. These constructions reflect a balance among the person's ego ideal, available vocabulary, and beliefs about the origins of the feeling. But semantic descriptions cannot provide a complete understanding of all aspects of emotion because they have a weak relation to behavioral and biological information. That is, the metrics for words or sentences (valence, salience, semantic distance, truth value, and consistency) are not easily applied to behaviors or brain patterns; hence, it is not obvious that all the inferences about emotions based on questionnaires or interviews also apply to the inferences based on measurements of actions or neural activity. Although the words *terror* and *rage* have a similar valence and salience, these two emotions evoke different behaviors and brain profiles and have different origins. No one would confuse the state

induced by confrontation with a cobra poised to strike with the emotion created by discovering that one's house has been desecrated.[2]

## Behaviors

The relations among behaviors reflecting emotional states are less clear because there are few cross-cultural studies of the usual behavioral reactions to
a variety of emotional incentives. Further, an emotion need not be accompanied by any behavior; that is why the concept of "emotional regulation" was
invented. The metrics for behaviors include frequency of response, success
or failure in attaining a goal, the effect of a behavior on objects, people, or
the enhancement of self's virtue, and the degree to which the acts are voluntary. But actions do not reflect intensity of feeling or nature of the appraisal
and are seriously influenced by the immediate context. Laboratory settings,
whether interview rooms or scanners, do not permit most of the behaviors
that accompany emotions.

The differences between acts that represent approach compared with
avoidance of a target are also critical, but scientists should resist the temptation to equate the semantically based valence categories with those for approach versus avoidance. Most adults wish to avoid states of sadness. Nonetheless, people voluntarily listen to music that induces a sad mood, and such
music activates the left frontal lobe, which often accompanies the pleasant
states that humans prefer to approach.[3] Some individuals who say they wish
to make new friends usually avoid meeting strangers, and economically disadvantaged youth who admit that anger is a dangerous emotion that should
be controlled behave as if anger at rival gang members is sufficient justification for expression of violence toward them.

Some individuals who could not tolerate the distress of waiting for a mild
electric shock preferred to receive a more intense shock immediately rather
than endure a delay they knew would be followed by a less intense shock
later. That is, they approached an unwanted experience. The poems of poets
who later committed suicide, compared with the verse of most poets, contained a larger proportion of words referring to the unwanted state of death,
but also more words related to sexuality, which is a goal that is ordinarily
approached.[4]

Because the determinants and metrics for actions and verbal descriptions are qualitatively different, each provides distinct information. The behaviors displayed to a stranger who insulted one's family would differ, in all cultures, from the actions observed when one encountered a stranger holding a dagger in a threatening pose. Thus, the behavioral evidence would place rage and terror in different categories.

## Brain Activity

Measures of brain activity rely on still another set of metrics. Frequency of discharge, and variation in frequency over time, apply to single neurons. Degree of synchronization of discharge (for various frequency ranges) among neuronal clusters is a metric for networks of interconnected neurons, which is called coherence when distant clusters are synchronized at the same dominant frequency.

Event-related potentials in the electroencephalogram and profiles of blood flow (assessed with magnetic resonance scanners) quantify brain activity to emotional incentives. The metrics for event-related waveforms are latency (in milliseconds) and magnitude (in microvolts) of a cascade of peak responses in specific sites. The brain profile that appears first is determined by the physical features of the incentive; the one seen a little later is influenced by its expectancy and familiarity; and the profile measured still later is shaped by the psychological meaning of the event and any preparation for a response. However, the brain pattern reflecting meaning is influenced by the prior two states and is confounded with them. These constraints are less serious for verbal reports or actions. Arachnophobes would say that they were anxious and would be reluctant to touch a tarantula whether its appearance was expected or was a surprise.

The metric for blood flow, gathered with scanning procedures, is a difference score reflecting the blood flow to varied brain sites, compared with a baseline value, over intervals of two to ten seconds. This measure is highly correlated with the input to clusters of neurons and their synchronous firing at higher frequencies (usually greater than 40Hz and restricted to smaller areas) but less closely related to synchronous activity at lower frequencies, which typically represent coherent activity across larger areas of the cortex that might reflect a mental set or level of alertness. Therefore, the relation between blood flow and neuronal spike rates across the full range of frequencies is less than 0.60.[5] More important, the magnitude of blood flow to particular sites is more often correlated with the amount of mental work provoked by an incentive or its unexpectedness than with the valence or salience of the induced emotion. The memorization of long strings of numbers produces a greater change in blood flow than an intrusive thought that evoked sadness over the realization that one has no close friends. One reason why event-related waveforms and blood flow are often uncorrelated is that the magnitudes of the waveforms during the initial half-second are mainly a reflection of the degree to which an event was unexpected, whereas the blood flow evidence, reflecting later activity, is more closely correlated with the amount of mental work the person implemented. Profiles of blood flow can provide information on a person's susceptibility to particular feelings but are less sensitive indexes of the specific actions that are most likely to occur to the incentive in the person's life settings.

Although no investigator has compared the brain's reaction to an insult denigrating an agent's family with the reaction to a serious threat of bodily harm, I suspect that these two events would produce distinct profiles, and the relations between these brain states would differ from comparable relations among behaviors or semantic descriptions. Thus, each source of evidence (words, acts, and biology) invites a different conclusion regarding the relation between rage and terror. It remains a possibility that these sources are incommensurable.

Some might argue that lawful correspondences among the three sources of evidence occur only when the magnitude of emotional arousal rises to extreme levels, a condition rarely actualized in a laboratory. Most languages, however, do not contain a sufficient number of terms capable of describing the full variation in an emotional state. English, for example, has the words *anxiety, worry, fear,* and *terror* to capture the entire range of feeling from concern over coming down with the flu to the state of a hostage who has just been told that he will be shot the next day.

The range of values for most biological reactions is considerably larger than the range for behaviors, and the range for behaviors is larger than the range for words. Because the magnitude of relation between two measures is always reduced when one or both has a restricted range, the inherent structure of the language available to describe emotions limits seriously the possibility of finding close correspondences between self-reports of emotion, on one hand, and behavioral and biological evidence, on the other.[6] This problem plagues the current strategy of looking for relations between a genetic polymorphism and a personality trait because there is a serious imbalance in the sensitivity of the biological and psychological measures. The former assessments require long hours of careful quantification of evidence whose rationale is based on many decades of research. The psychological measure, usually a questionnaire, can be gathered in thirty minutes, its rationale is less secure, and different biological states can yield similar scores. Thus, reliance on questionnaires in the search for the genetic bases of personality types is analogous to using an atomic clock to judge whether a person is walking rapidly, moderately quickly, at a normal pace, or slowly.

The main point is that each class of measurement used to infer an emotion relies on different metrics and reflects varying aspects of the phenomenon scientists want to understand. At the moment, we confront the frustration of three incompletely comparable meanings for an emotional state; hence, there are inconsistent and puzzling relations among them. Consider an analogy to the concept of illness. Physicians could rely on the patient's reported symptoms, physical appearance, physiology, or genetic features. Some patients who inherited the alleles for a disease might not report any symptoms or provide any clues in behavior, blood tests, or X-rays. Others might report distressing symptoms but fail to show any signs of disease in physiology or genes. This is the state of affairs in emotion research. The frequency of shy behaviors with strangers is not a proxy for verbal reports of social anxiety; activation of the amygdala while thinking about encountering crowds is not a proxy for reports of social anxiety or shy behavior with a stranger.

The concept of inclusive fitness in biology supplies a second analogy. The richness of the food supply, the number of predators, and mean annual temperature contribute to the inclusive fitness of a species. However, the relations among the three measures, and their separate contribution to fitness, vary with the species under consideration, and there is no rational way to combine them. Like brain profiles, behaviors, and verbal reports, they are incommensurable. Imagine a scientist who measured in one hundred adults the amount of blood flow to the amygdala, duration of body immobility, and a rating of the salience of felt anxiety to the sight of a caged tarantula. No current theory would permit investigators to decide whether the person who displayed large magnitudes on the first two measures but denied feeling anxious was more or less anxious than one who reported intense anxiety but showed minimal blood flow and no body immobility. Students of emotion do not have the advantage of metrics, such as energy and dollars, that allow physicists and economists to reduce diverse phenomena to a common scale.

An important reason for the apparent lack of commensurability of the three types of evidence is that each is influenced by its own set of unique factors. Variation in blood flow, for example, is affected by the person's breathing and heart rate while lying in the scanner. Verbal reports are always modulated by the individual's available vocabulary and his or her estimate of the scientist's purposes and the motivation to please or impress the investigator. Given these constraints, it would seem wise first to explore each source of information extensively in order to understand its principles, rather than to assume ahead of time that one knows what each procedure measures. Readers familiar with the history of twentieth-century physics will recall that the former strategy led to the unexpected discovery of facts that motivated the theory of quantum mechanics. Max Planck's patient study of the radiation frequencies emanating from a black body, which no one understood, led him to posit the quantum. I suspect that if scientists interested in emotional phenomena followed a similar plan, they would recognize the need for a new set of concepts, and the current terms that ignore origin and context, such as *fear*, *sad*, and *happy*, would be relegated to the ash heap of history where phlogiston, the ether, and animal magnetism lie buried.

## Are There Basic Emotions?

Humans are capable of an extraordinary variety of emotions. The demands, threats, economy, moral values, and social structure of a society select from the large number of possibilities a smaller number for elaboration. The size of the potential set and the scientist's desire for parsimony motivate theorists to invent a rationale that might legitimize a privileged list of "basic emotions." Psychologists have nominated six criteria that might define membership in this elite category: (1) prevalent across all societies; (2) derived from a salient feeling; (3) associated with a biologically prepared brain, autonomic, or motor reaction; (4) possesses a pleasant or unpleasant valence; (5) necessary for survival; and (6) contributes to social relationships and/or community harmony.

The deprivation states of hunger, thirst, excessive cold or heat, and lack of rest meet all six criteria, but many other emotional states meet only some of them. American and European investigators favor prevalence across cultures and valence when they nominate the emotional families of fear, anger, sadness, joy, and disgust as basic. A second reason for this set is that these societies celebrate the talents, motives, feelings, and private consciences of the solitary individual striving for personal achievement, an ascent in status, and private states of pleasure. Hence, fear of failing these missions, anger toward those who block gratification of these desires, sadness over losing relationships that contribute to their attainment, joy following their realization, and disgust at those who disregard these imperatives are frequently named as basic emotions.

The attractiveness of the above list of basic emotions ignores the fact, noted earlier, that many incentives produce coherent states that are blends of two or more elementary ones. One of the most prevalent blends combines worry over a harsh evaluation by a legitimate authority figure with shame over a social or task error. If Thomas Hobbes's seventeenth-century description of human nature was accurate, a feeling of intimidation in the presence of others who have more wealth, strength, or status, called *malu* by citizens of Sumatra, should be a basic emotion. Humans continually compare self's properties with those of select others, and a subtle feeling is produced when one of these comparisons leads the person to feel diminished. This emotion is rarely considered as basic, even though it must be among the most prevalent in all societies. It is especially common between siblings, members of closely collaborating dyads, and of course marriage partners because one member of the dyad is often more talented, attractive, courageous, empathic, popular, or moral than the other. Benjamin Franklin recognized that the younger diplomatic colleagues stationed with him in Paris during the

Revolutionary War, including John Adams, envied the extraordinary fame he enjoyed with the French populace. After several years of malicious gossip detailing his pursuit of women and incomplete record-keeping, these colleagues were able to persuade Congress to replace him because he was a perfect scapegoat for George Washington's failure to defeat the British after three years of war. This state may be less common in egalitarian cultures committed to the proposition that all individuals are entitled to equal dignity and more prevalent in hierarchical settings that assume some social categories are naturally entitled to respect. When the less adequate member appraises his or her feeling state correctly, it is reasonable to label the emotion "jealousy," "envy," or "intimidation." American and European wives regard this state as inconsistent with the contemporary ethic of equal dignity for all, and it contributes to the increased divorce rate over the past half-century. This feeling often escapes a correct appraisal because the person who detects a slight change in body tone often dismisses the sensation or misinterprets it as fatigue, frustration, or concern with a responsibility. Some might call this state "unconscious intimidation," but, as I argued earlier, this solution ignores the fact that the brain profile, salience, and consequences of the conscious and unconscious states are different. Cain would not have killed Abel if he were unaware of his feelings of intimidation by and resentment toward his brother. It is not obvious, therefore, that restricting the basic emotions to their simpler components is wise. Although experts claim that there are only ten basic facial types, humans can distinguish among the thousands of faces belonging to the same type.[7]

Traditional Japanese, who are more communitarian than Americans, regard *amae*, an emotion experienced by those who place their complete trust in the reliable nurture of another, as basic. The early Christians celebrated *agape*, a selfless love of God, as a fundamental emotion. The texts of ancient Greek myths and the biographical sketches in Plutarch's *Lives*, written almost two thousand years ago, imply that shame over an incestuous sexual experience and courage in the face of potential harm were basic emotions. Devout Hindu Brahmins regard a sense of purity and equanimity when a loved one dies as primary emotions, albeit less prevalent and harder to attain than shame or envy.[8]

Thus, an emotional state, like the burgeoning or extinction of a species as a function of changes in the local ecology, can become more or less prevalent depending on historical conditions within a particular cultural setting. The scientific advances that made it possible to tell a mother that her genes were responsible for her infant's motor paralysis created a new source of maternal guilt. Consider four incentives capable of evoking the unpleasant feeling of uncertainty: threat of harm to the body, the loss of a satisfying social relationship, a discrepant event or idea that is not immediately understood, and the choice of an ideology or life course. The first three events had to be present in all ancient societies. But the fourth, which requires the belief that everyone in the community is free to choose a philosophy and a career, was probably denied to most hunter-gatherers and many members of the great agricultural civilizations. Europeans had to wait until the nineteenth century for the philosopher Søren Kierkegaard to suggest that freedom of choice could be a significant origin of anxiety.

The emotions surrounding a desire for enhanced recognition provide a second example of history's power to alter the prevalence and salience of common states. Although humanists and scientists have always wanted recognition from their peers or the general public, the extraordinary increase in the number of professional scholars since the end of the Second World War has made this motive more salient because many feel an anonymity that was muted in earlier generations. Newton, Maxwell, Darwin, and Pasteur, along with Bach, Voltaire, Tolstoy, and Whitehead, were known and honored by a majority who labored in their vineyard. By contrast, most contemporary scientists, writers, historians, and philosophers do not know and are not known by most of their colleagues and probably 99 percent of the public. As a result, the emotion that blends a desire for recognition with a feeling of anonymity has acquired enhanced salience, and many seek celebrity with an intensity that would have provoked severe criticism a hundred years earlier.

It is useful to reflect on the following three facts. The first humans lived in groups of sixty to seventy individuals; fewer than 1 percent of the world's population lived in a city with more than a million inhabitants in 1800, but one in five do so today; and contemporary technological societies, with instant communication to distant places, have existed for only the last of the five thousand generations of our species. These changes have been accompanied by variation on an emotional state that has cycled throughout history every time the moral order became ambiguous. It was probably present after the age of Pericles in Greece, during the last century of the Roman Empire, and the years following the First World War, and it has returned today. But each time it surfaced, it had special features because of the historical context.

I suspect that a reasonable proportion of contemporary Americans and Europeans, reflecting on the events of the past six decades, experience a unique emotion whose origins are the recognition of life's unpredictability, the need to be vigilant toward and suspicious of the motives of all strangers, and a questioning of the meaningfulness of existence because of the fraying of moral certitude over the values entitled to unquestioned commitment. This state, which does not yet have a name, was made possible by the historical events that created bureaucratic economies, densely populated cities, easy geographic mobility, diverse values, but a demand for tolerance toward all ethical positions. In addition, the information technologies make it possible for individuals across the world to learn about a German law legislating imprisonment for denial of Nazi gas chambers at the same time an international conference in Tehran was questioning the existence of these chambers; genocide in Rwanda; the horrors of September 11; the danger of innocent-looking mail that might contain anthrax; impoverished parents selling their young daughters into prostitution; high school girls performing oral sex on boys they met for the first time several hours earlier; adolescent mothers dumping their newborns into trash cans; surrogate mothers carrying to term a fetus conceived in a petri dish with an egg and sperm donated by adults who would not be the infant's parents; priests sexually abusing boys; high government officials and movie stars stealing merchandise from department stores; company executives defrauding stockholders; surgeons abandoning patients on the operating table in order to make a bank deposit; scientists making fraudulent claims; Chinese government officials promising a cash reward to scientists who published a paper in *Nature* or *Science*; journalists inventing stories; celebrated writers plagiarizing others' prose; articles urging physicians to show empathic care for their patients; editors of medical journals complaining of the corrupting influence of the pharmaceutical industry; college presidents confessing to the confusion surrounding the purpose of a college education; books telling young scientists how "to survive and get

ahead" rather than how to make a discovery; and religious scholars interrupt-
ing their normal duties to write magazine essays refuting the claim in the
pulp-fiction novel *The Da Vinci Code* that Jesus had a sexual relationship
with Mary Magdalene. No nineteenth-century biologist would have thought
it necessary to inform the public of the impossibility of a Frankenstein or
Alice's experiences in Wonderland.

This emotion, for which words like *confused, rudderless, uncertain,* and
*spiritually empty* approximate, but do not fully capture, its meaning, is a coherent state and not the sum of several elementary or basic emotions. Pas-
cal was unusually prescient when he sensed, in the seventeenth century,
a personal mood that eventually became widespread three hundred years
later following two world wars, the Vietnam and Iraq fiascoes, the youth-led
rebellion against legitimate authority, and newspapers telling readers that
yesterday's scientific truth had just been overturned. Jean-Paul Sartre described it as a feeling of "inescapable nothingness," which W. H. Auden tried
to capture in his poem "The Age of Anxiety." Ben Bradlee, the editor of the
*Washington Post* during the Watergate episode that led to Richard Nixon's
resignation, previously served in the Pacific during the Second World War
and wrote in a 2006 issue of the *New Yorker* that his wartime experiences
"were years when you could get involved in something beyond yourself—
something that connected you to your times in ways that no longer seem so
natural, or expected."[9]

The *New Yorker* cartoons date the origin of the widespread acceptance
of this new mood in middle-class America to the decade between 1955 and
1965 when, for the first time, cartoonists satirized the boredom of work and
the spiritual vacuum of modern life. One illustration depicted an older man
declaring to another, "I did my job and grabbed my pile but no voice at even-
tide has cried, 'Well done.'" This theme had become undisguised by the
mid-1970s, when an artist had a wife say to her husband, "The only time we
meet each other's needs is when we fight." In another cartoon a group of
young men in business suits enclosed, like cattle, in a corral is described by
a man standing outside the corral, "In 6 months these MBAs will be ready
for market." By contrast, the cartoons of 1929–1939 satirized the snobbery
of class, the elite attitude of graduates of Ivy League colleges, the sexual
assertiveness of women, and the attempts by older men to seduce younger

women. These early cartoons made fun of desires, not the absence or emptiness of desire. It took only a little more than one generation, from the depression of Franklin D. Roosevelt's era to the security of Dwight D. Eisenhower's
presidency, to produce an extraordinary increase in the number of college
graduates with secure jobs, nice homes, and two automobiles and, as a result,
no pressing needs. The generation born between 1930 and 1960, who found
it easier than their parents or grandparents to obtain what they thought they
were supposed to work for, confronted an unexpected boredom and apathy
they did not understand when they reached midlife. Without some internal-
ized imperatives to obey or to resist, the vitality that gives self a shape dissi-
pates, and individuals look for an affirmation of self in the reactions of others.
Fortunately, evolution awarded humans the capacity to suppress this state, at
least temporarily, when it is necessary to proceed with the day's responsibilities.

The mood contrasts sharply with that of Jil Ker Conway, the first female
president of Smith College, who spent her childhood on an isolated farm in
Australia. Conway noted in her memoir, *The Road from Coorain*, that her
world was idyllic because it was comprehensible.[10] She was certain of her
parents' affection, could witness the products of her efforts, and believed the
truth of her mother's declaration that each life had meaning and that each
individual was able to control his or her future.

The style of contemporary Hollywood movies with broad acclaim are
characterized by two properties that distinguish them from American films
of the 1940s as well as from current films made by Asian or Middle Eastern
filmmakers. The scenes shift rapidly, each usually lasting less than a minute,
and many viewers are never completely certain of the coherence between
the scenes. The celebrated film *Syriana* (2005) is a prototype of this category.
Viewers wonder why an actor or actress did or said something as the scene
shifts from Washington, D.C., to an Arab oil state to a cricket game on a sand
lot to a motorcade in the desert.

The implicit message (it is not clear whether the screenwriter intended it
consciously) is that life consists of unconnected events with each person unaware of the behaviors of others in faraway places that will, nonetheless, have
profound implications for their lives. Such films, which depict modern life

as a series of disconnected experiences that each mind perceives as coherent, mirror Kurt Vonnegut's description of existence in his novel *Slaughterhouse Five*. Films like *Syriana* imply that each of us is a sailor in a small rowboat without a compass on a choppy sea trying to get to a safe port, unaware of the invisible events that will disrupt our plans. No metaphysical force is watching over us, and no level of talent or virtue will guarantee that our journey will not be disrupted. This was not Jil Ker Conway's conception of her life.

The idea of the solitary individual confronting a cruel, unjust, uncaring world, which has permeated the American mind, is captured by a short, silent film depicting a young man in an isolated area who needs help in extricating his leg from a hole in the ground. By the time several cars have sped by without stopping, the man has sunk farther into the hole and a passerby has stolen some of his clothing. When only the head of our hero is visible in the final scene, another stranger stamps his foot on the hapless man, immersing him completely in the hole. No English word captures the emotion felt by many viewers of this brutally skeptical film, which would have offended most Americans just a century ago.

The final day in the lives of the last Russian czar and his family, who had been placed under house arrest by the Bolsheviks, is illustrative of our condition. Although the czar told his family that this was the day he was sure they would be released, his captors had decided twelve hours earlier that they would be executed that evening. And they were. It is too early to tell what psychological defenses humans will develop to cope with these changes in daily life. We are still in the middle of the storm.

There are four possible reactions to this state of affairs: anger, joining a reform movement, hedonism, or religion. Belief in a spiritual force that wishes benevolent outcomes for humans is a helpful strategy under these social conditions. It is not surprising, therefore, that four of every ten Americans say they believe in a metaphysical entity. The adolescents described previously as high-reactive, who experienced salient uncertainty over the future, were more likely to be deeply religious than those who had been low-reactive as infants. A majority of Europeans experiencing the same uncertainty, however, are agnostics or atheists. Apparently, their strategy is an acceptance of the current state of affairs. The European understanding seems to share features with John von Neumann's description of the attitude of mathematicians toward the arcane intellectual products of their discipline. One does not understand mathematical ideas, one simply gets used to them.

All humans are vulnerable to a large number of emotions. The culture-historical warp selects the states that will have salience. Freud, trained as a physician and caught in the wake of the Darwinian wave, did not fully appreciate the power of history and culture. The prevalence of various infectious diseases over time and societies provides an analogy to the prevalence of specific emotions. Humans are vulnerable to many infections. Time and setting determine whether the predominant disease will be cholera, plague, malaria, influenza, small pox, or AIDS. The number of emotions that human biology permits is also analogous to the complete set of motor skills humans could, in principle, perfect. Historical and cultural contexts select or amplify the large, but nonetheless limited, number of conscious feelings into a hierarchy of possible emotions. Each society exploits only some of these states. The emotions that English names *fear, anger, disgust, sadness, joy, jealousy, pride, shame, guilt, empathy, sexual arousal,* and *love* are more prevalent across societies than a*gape* or *amae* because all human environments continually present incentives that provoke one or more members of these emotional families. But this does not mean that these dozen states are biologically more prepared, more often accompanied by a behavior, or more easily assigned a valence than agape, amae, surprise, confusion, loneliness, or alienation. The competence needed to pick up and throw a stone is not more basic, in a biological sense, than the ability to climb a ladder and prune a tree's top limbs. But not all cultures have ladders and pruning shears.

Agape would be nominated as a basic emotion if everyone had a deep faith in a spiritual force they believed was concerned with their welfare. Members of most ancient, and some modern, societies believed that supernatural forces were either protecting or plotting against them, suggesting that the emotions accompanying this belief are part of our biological competence. If neuroscientists were able to measure the brain states of individuals in a state of agape or amae, I suspect that they would discover neuronal profiles as distinct as those accompanying fear of attack, anger over an insult, sadness over loss of a friend, or joy following affection from a beloved. Prevalence should not be equated with biological primacy or psychological significance.

The prevalence of a gene depends on its location, whether in the nucleus or in the cytoplasm's mitochondria, but prevalence is not an index of a gene's significance for a phenotype. There are more molecules than atoms, more genes than nucleotides, more proteins than amino acids, more synapses than neurons, and more pigs than penguins. No biologist suggests that the flu is a more basic illness than polio, pine a more basic tree than peach, or ants more basic than antelope, even though the first member of these pairs is more common than the second.

Discoveries by scientists studying early development provide an analogy. The variation in the embryological development of different species is due in part to genes that regulate the expression of the DNA sequences in the exons that are the origins of amino acids and proteins. These regulatory genes, called promoters and enhancers, enhance or suppress the expression of the exon component of the gene in each bodily site. This process explains why humans and chimpanzees, who share over 98 percent of the same exons, have such different features.

Distinct chemical gradients in each bodily location select the genes that will be expressed or silenced in that place as the embryo develops. The consequences of bodily location for the expression of a gene are analogous to cultures selecting particular emotions from a larger set. The principle that local contexts select particular outcomes from a range of possibilities is also seen in the pruning of many millions of synapses during the postnatal years as a function of the child's experiences. Ecological selection of inherited traits is the central idea in Darwin's explanation of the changing variety of plants and animals. Dogs, but not apes, for example, have been selected to orient to human faces.[11]

Social environments, which change over time, create or amplify the emotional profiles that are adaptive in a particular community during a historical era. The Greeks and Romans selected courage as especially praiseworthy because threat of physical attack was common and both societies required this mood in their soldiers. The culture of the Utku Eskimo selected the emotion of *naklik* (concern with the physical and psychological welfare of another) as a frequent state.[12] The culture of medieval Europe selected fear of God's wrath as a prevalent interpretation of feelings of uncertainty. When, during the late fourteenth century, some citizens began to question God's power over each life, the unforgivable sin for the new skeptics was to allow another to take advantage of oneself. As a result, the emotions of shame or anger at self for permitting this exploitation rose in the hierarchy. Peter Abelard, whose famous love relationship with Héloïse produced a child and incurred the wrath of her uncle and the medieval religious community whose respect he courted for advancement, confessed, "What a figure should I cut in public! How the world would point its finger at me." Héloïse, who was deeply ashamed of her participation in an affair that cost Abelard his reputation, conveyed in a letter an emotion that few, if any, American women could experience. "The more I lowered myself before thee, the more I hoped to gain thy favor."[13]

The first generations of New England Puritans relied on shame to preserve civility. Punishments were usually public affairs in which the offender was whipped or put in a stock in a location visible to all in the village. Moreover, fines, which were used as punishments, were larger for slandering a person's reputation than for a physical assault.[14] Contemporary American communities, which are larger and more impersonal, find it harder to use shame to preserve civil order. The historical events that created large urban centers with transient residents holding different values led, inevitably, to a muting of concern with the opinions of neighbors and therefore less frequent occasions for shame or worry over one's social acceptability. Adam Smith and his eighteenth-century colleagues would have been surprised by this historical change because they were certain that concern with one's reputation with neighbors was innate and universal. About 70 percent of conversations are essentially gossip about another person's character; the more isolated from the local community an agent feels, the weaker the concern with gossip.[15]

Further, because geographically mobile, urban societies try to separate each individual's reputation and future status from the familial, ethnic, and religious groups to which they belong, these settings select the emotional states induced by the increasing psychological isolation from others, the continual possibility of academic, social, or occupational failure, and insufficient certainty over the absolute moral imperatives that should guide daily decisions. Few residents of ancient Babylon, Alexandria, Sparta, or Xian who kept a diary would have written, as did the poet Sylvia Plath, "What I fear worst is failure."[16]

Observers of modern Japanese society have noted with alarm a serious increase over the past two decades in an emotional and behavioral profile in older adolescent and young adult males characterized by apathy, withdrawal from academic or vocational responsibilities, and long, solitary periods in the bedroom. This new syndrome, called *hikikomori* and affecting close to 20 percent of youth, is the result of the dissemination of American and European values favoring autonomy and independence from the family.[17] The American values provoke questioning of the validity of the traditional Japanese posture of conformity to family pressure for achievement in sons and a subsequent state of response uncertainty. The emotional apathy and behavioral withdrawal, reflecting the youths' reaction to these inconsistent ideals, represent a persuasive example of the cultural selection of a mood.

The attraction to a tidy list of basic emotions shares features with the belief held by Paracelsus, the famous sixteenth-century physician-alchemist who argued that the properties of all material phenomena were derived from the basic qualities of sulfur (flammable), mercury (liquid), and salt (solidity).[18] Nineteenth-century physicists believed that atoms were the basic elements of matter. Early-twentieth-century scientists nominated electrons, neutrons, and protons. Contemporary theorists tell us that quarks, leptons, gluons, and the mysterious Z and W bosons are the basic forms. New evidence has led to a new list of basic components. The same is true for emotions. The search for basic emotional states is reminiscent of the wish to celebrate the authentic states of nature as opposed to human artifacts. Thomas Jefferson, along with most eighteenth-century Americans, regarded the countryside as more authentic and ethically purer than the city because the city transformed nature. These intuitions, which children share, have not proven useful in science and therefore should probably be excluded from discussions of emotions. The transformations of nature that assume the form of vaccines, chlorinated water, and antibiotics have prolonged human lives by at least thirty years over the past dozen centuries, suggesting that untransformed natural states are not always the most benevolent.

The belief in a set of basic emotions that transcends time and culture may be the result of a misplaced admiration for physics rather than biology. Although physicists search for the ultimate foundations of the observable, life scientists, who view nature from the opposite direction, continue to posit more, rather than fewer, categories for natural phenomena. The concept of a gene, whose structure Crick and Watson described in 1953, has been supplemented with haplotypes, exons, introns, enhancers, promoters, and transposons. Emotions are biological phenomena.

Darwin's profound insight was to recognize that there is no best exemplar of any species, only changes in the form of a species over long periods. The first horse was not more basic than the modern animal preparing to race in next year's Kentucky Derby. Similarly, history has transformed the emotion a Greek youth experienced when he was erotically aroused by the older man embracing him to the emotion a modern Greek adolescent feels when he recognizes that he is poor, uneducated, and marginalized in his society. Neither emotion is more basic, although both share enough features to be categorized as members of a family that differ from the exemplars of the family of emotions provoked by the unexpected receipt of high praise or an embrace from a beloved.

### Rescuing Basic Emotions: Fitness or Coherence

Two rationales are worth considering before we reject completely the contrast between more and less basic emotions. One argument awards special significance to the emotions that contribute to the evolutionary biologists' concept of inclusive fitness. Most students of human nature would agree that the following psychological functions contribute to fitness: (1) orienting, anticipating, or preparing to act in order to avoid events that might cause bodily harm or psychic distress; (2) learning new associations, representations, and habits that contribute to health and reproductive success; (3) maintaining the motivation for actions intended to gain a goal in the distant future; (4) inhibiting behaviors that would injure others, disrupt community harmony, or compromise self's belief in its virtue; (5) establishing bonds of loyalty toward and responsibility for select others; (6) defending self's property and dignity; and (7) guaranteeing reproduction of the next generation. Although these functions are not synonyms for emotional terms, the English names for the emotional families constructed from them are called *fear, anxiety, surprise, disgust, hope, joy, shame, guilt, sadness, anger, pride, love,* and *sexual arousal.* Thus, if one accepts the criterion of fitness as primary, one can argue that some emotional families are more basic than others. I recognize that this admission renders consequences a useful criterion for parsing emotions into categories of more or less psychological importance.

However, humans have other motives beside survival to reproductive maturity and maximizing the health and fecundity of one's relatives. Humans strive to match their qualities to an ideal because, like a hawk soaring in the sky, they can do so. Attending religious services, spending public funds to prolong the lives of older citizens, and making donations of money or blood to strangers who are victims of a disaster are inconsistent with acting to maximize fitness. There are several reasons why the principle of fitness as a guide to action has attracted advocates.

First, historical changes over the past two hundred years forced many to place self's interests ahead of the needs of others. A naked, lactating woman was a popular symbol for nature in sixteenth-century Europe. A lion killing a gazelle is the contemporary symbol. This harshly competitive and aggressive metaphor for nature, which evolutionary biologists claim is a scientific truth, is a product of history rather than a profound insight into the core quality of human nature. Many more Europeans donated blood last year than committed rape, robbery, or murder. Martin Luther's philosophy became popular in a short time because sixteenth-century Europeans were eager for a religion that freed them from paying avaricious priests for every service, replaced doing good acts with the simpler assignment of simply having faith, and removed moral taint from marital sex. Had the Catholic Church not created this trio of oppressive conditions there might have been no need for Luther's reformation.

Second, scientists have attained a moral authority that rivals the books of Leviticus, the New Testament, and the Koran because their discoveries have prolonged life and made each day less onerous. The lack of consensus on the actions that are right or wrong motivates a retreat to scientific facts which guarantee that a decision will at least be correct, even if it might harm another or weaken the cohesiveness of the community. But the biological principle of maximizing fitness is not always a useful guide for deciding what to do in times of conflict because the desire to regard self as virtuous, which is a unique property of our species, takes precedence over inclusive fitness much of the time. More than 40 percent of French adults in 1993 donated blood to a blood bank without receiving any payment for a charitable act that exacted a cost and did not benefit the donor materially. Chinese-American parents would give more resources to their adopted African-American infant than to a distant cousin in Beijing, even though their action would violate a strict interpretation of the principle of fitness. The biological urge to maximize fitness, like a shark cast up on a sandy beach or a lion struggling in the middle of a lake, is often impotent for humans with sufficient food and shelter trying to find a persuasive rationale for deciding what to do between breakfast and bedtime.

A second strategy for ranking the differential significance of emotions is the magnitude of covariation, or coherence, among the elements of the cascade that includes an incentive, a brain state, a feeling, and a meaningful appraisal. If this measure were treated as a continuum, the emotions nominated as basic would possess a high degree of coherence. That is, knowledge of the incentive permits a confident prediction of the subsequent brain profile, feeling, and emotional state. This strategy would separate the emotions associated with the biological appetites from others. There should be substantial correlations among changes in blood levels of glucose and lipids following six hours without food, the state of the hypothalamus, detected sensations from the gut, the decision that one is hungry, and the seeking of food. The emotions provoked by unexpected and unfamiliar events, which usually activate the brain stem, parahippocampal region, and amygdala to produce an orienting response, should also possess high coherence.

The emotions at the other end of this continuum are far less predictable from knowledge of the incentive because they vary within and across cultures and therefore have lower coherence. These states include the emotions evoked by a command, a greeting, a hostile thought, chamber music, a snowcapped mountain, and a sermon. I noted that although each brain state excludes a very large number of possible feelings, a brain state is nonetheless the foundation of more than one possible feeling and appraisal. Remember, possession of the two short alleles in the promoter region of the serotonin transporter gene can be associated with social anxiety, asocial behavior, or depression. The potential psychological meanings of a brain state resemble the possible meanings of an incomplete sentence, such as "The girl ran . . ."

The brain state created by the pheromone *androstadienone*, for example,

like the potentiality of a stem cell, can be followed by a number of psychological states, depending on the cultural and local setting, as well as the
agent's gender, temperament, and personal history. An appreciation of the
indeterminism of a brain state is conveyed with still another hypothetical
example. Suppose we wanted to know how likely a person would be to experience pride after unexpectedly receiving praise from a respected friend.
Let us be generous once again and assume unrealistically high probabilities
of 0.9 between each of the three phases of the cascade from the incentive
to the emotion—that is, 90 percent of the time one could predict the specific brain state produced by receipt of the praise, the feeling provoked by
the brain state, and the appraisal that followed the feeling. Nonetheless, the
probability that an emotion of pride will occur to the comment is only 0.73.
(This is the value obtained by multiplying the three 0.9 probabilities.) A scientist would be unable to predict the occurrence of pride from the praiseworthy comment 27 percent of the time. The error rate would be considerably higher for less salient incentives, such as a friendly greeting, a war scene
on television, or a person coughing at a concert. The extraordinary degree of
variation in temperaments and life histories guarantees indeterminacy in the
emotion that might follow the brain's response to a provocative event.

Although there is no known principle capable of parsing the emotions
that fall in different places on the continuum of coherence into discrete categories, this idea should motivate investigators to gather the evidence needed
to compute the necessary correlations. It remains a possibility that when this
information becomes available a brilliant scholar will detect a structure as
meaningful as the insight that the continuum of physical wavelengths that
defines the visible color spectrum can be divided into the color categories
red, yellow, green, blue, and violet.

Although this book does not provide a pleasing or constructive theory of
human emotions, it is useful to state as clearly as possible the conclusions
that deserve attention. The first is a reminder that in the study of emotions,
as in all the empirical sciences, robust relations between, or among, observations are the foundation of theory. The goal of research is to find relations
characterized by high probabilities between experimental conditions and
observations or between observations. The probability that a ball will fall to

the ground if dropped from a roof is 1.0, even though Newton and Einstein had very different explanations of this event. Newton inferred a gravitational force acting on the object; Einstein assumed that the ball altered space-time curvature. Even though the mathematical equations describing the observation, and their sense meanings, are different, the event remains the same.

A major problem in current research on the biological bases for emotions is that the probability that a specific feeling or appraisal will follow a particular brain state is low, whether we assess a thousand people or one person a thousand times. Hence, there is minimal determinism between most incentives and the cascade of processes representing a brain profile, a feeling, an appraisal, and an action. The goal we seek is to discover probability estimates that approach 0.7 or 0.8. Because this victory has not been achieved, scientists are forced to be satisfied with mean differences between conditions, or persons, that are statistically significant at probabilities of 0.05 or 0.01. Most of the time, however, significant mean differences do not permit investigators to predict the relevant observation more than 25 to 40 percent of the time. For example, although the magnitude of blood flow to the amygdala or intensity of reported anxiety to a scene of bloodied soldiers is higher in veterans with post-traumatic stress disorder than in veterans without this diagnosis, it is usually the case that no more than a quarter of the stressed veterans have scores that are higher than any one of the healthier individuals. When a scientist is lucky enough to discover a correlation between a genetic marker and an emotional state, the relation usually accounts for less than 10 percent of the variation.

Second, the metrics appropriate for each level of the cascade are different and not easily translatable from one to another. This fact implies that scientists must offer a strong rationale before they assign the same emotional label to distinct members of the cascade. Moreover, the popular emotional terms are not "states of nature" but constructs invented to explain a relation between observations. The term *fear*, for example, is exploited to explain the fact that presentation of a light predictive of electric shock is usually followed by activation of the amygdala and body immobility in rats. This term is not intended to describe the same psychological state in rats, chimps, and humans.

The twin notions of biological and psychological preparedness are also ideas deserving attention. Biological preparedness refers to the fact that species, as well as individuals within a species, differ in their receptivity or susceptibility to particular brain states to the same incentive. When we compare species we talk of biological preparedness; when we compare humans we talk of temperamental biases. Psychological preparedness refers to the fact that members of varied socially defined categories vary in the appraisals of their feelings. I suggested that the most influential categories are gender, ethnicity, class, religion, and culture, and always within a historical era. A harsh evaluation of one's career as two hundred thousand hours of useless work, which was the confession in 1969 of the admired English intellectual and political activist Leonard Woolf, was far more likely for those who spent their adult years in twentieth-century Europe than for those of equal stature who lived two centuries earlier.

The theme permeating every chapter of this book is the claim that every observation in this domain has more than one interpretation. Hence, the investigator needs a few guiding a priori premises that permit selection of one account over another because observations do not usually announce their meaning and, on some occasions, invite an incorrect interpretation. Consider a person with no knowledge of pencils, or the consequences of light striking a glass of water in which a pencil rests, who observes that the segment of the pencil resting in the water appears bent. This unambiguous perception invites three interpretations: water has the power to bend pencils that are usually straight; air has the power to straighten pencils that are usually bent; or, third, pencils are always straight and the observation is inaccurate. The last account could be verified by gathering a second source of evidence—namely, feeling the pencil in the water and discovering that it is straight. Every scientist needs some premises to protect against a misinterpretation of an observation.

My premises include the beliefs that language is a far better measure of appraisal processes than of detected feelings and that the semantic descriptions of feelings can be as distorting as the appearance of a bent pencil in a glass of water. Discussions of emotion based only on language are like the perceptions of a person wearing prisms that cause objects to appear thirty degrees to the right or left of where they appear to someone not wearing prisms. I also believe that cultures vary in appraisals of similar feelings, that animals and young infants are not capable of many emotions that human adults experience, that a changed brain state following an incentive does not always generate a feeling, and that detected feelings are critical components of, but not synonymous with, their appraisals. In spite of the many available options for classification, the invariant phenomena, analogous to phonemes in speech, are consciously detected changes in feeling that vary in origin, quality, salience, expectedness, and familiarity. If this class of events is removed, the concept of emotion dissolves into proposals for categories of semantic terms, behaviors, or profiles of brain activation, each with a metric and structure different from those appropriate for feelings, and each possible without the presence of a feeling. Hence, detected feelings, although opaque and difficult to quantify, invite serious empirical attention. The gravitational force between the Sun and the Earth is also invisible. Gottfried Leibniz, the seventeenth-century philosopher and mathematician, rejected Newton's inverse square law as a description of the motion of our planet around the Sun because he was certain that every effect had a material cause that could be observed or imagined. Although physicists have not yet found gravity waves, Newton's intuition was right. Feelings are not yet amenable to accurate measurement, but that fact should not be a reason for ignoring them.

The study of emotion is not mature enough to allow confidence in a great many premises. Investigators should always gather more than one source of evidence as a protection against incorrect inferences from one class of observation. The neuroscientist who insists that a particular brain state represents an emotion, even if it did not generate a feeling or appraisal, resembles that of the physicist loyal to quantum mechanics who denies the reality of the pen I am holding because the interpretation of the mathematics of quantum mechanics rejects the existence of stable objects. It is useful to know the elementary foundations of both psychological and physical phenomena. But these fundamental origins are only the beginning of a complex cascade of transitions, each possessing distinct properties and requiring distinct metrics and principles. Even though the special properties of human sensory, motor, and conceptual systems mean that we can never be certain of the nature of *Reality*, nonetheless, it is not foolish for me to believe that the pen I am holding has a shape, length, and texture. Although my brain state changed as I wrote this paragraph, I am certain that I did not experience any change in emotional state.

In light of the evidence pointing to the utility of examining the specific relations among the components of emotions, it is appropriate to ask why both social scientists and biologists have been reluctant to descend deeper into the empirical trenches to ferret out the facts necessary for theoretical advances. Two factors seem relevant. First, social scientists lack methods sensitive enough to measure the relevant phenomena, but acknowledging this fact would provoke an uncomfortable state of response uncertainty. Second, the fragmentation of specializations means that many investigators who are expert at measuring event-related potentials or brain activity in a scanner are less skilled at quantifying behaviors or semantic products, and many who know how to measure and analyze behaviors and self-reports are not expert at gathering information on the brain. Thus, each group continues to do what it knows best, and we remain in doubt over three profound questions. How does a person's past history, temperamental biases, and the local context combine to create a baseline brain state? How does that baseline state affect the biological reactions to an emotional incentive? How does any brain profile give rise to a psychological process?

The primary message in this book is a plea for accommodation to the rich complexity of this domain. It is an error to restrict the investigations of emotions to the small number of states that happen to have popular English names, certain facial expressions, behavioral consequences, or histories of rewarding or punishing experiences. The exclusion of the emotions provoked by seeing a blood-red sunset over a tropical lagoon, listening to the opening chords of a Brahms symphony, wondering whether life has a purpose, passing a stranded motorist on an isolated road, noticing a stranger dropping garbage on a neighbor's lawn, or realizing that self holds logically inconsistent beliefs about personal freedom has no sound basis in theory or empirical fact.

Declarations about emotions must always append the source of evidence, whether semantic report, behavior, or biology, and acknowledge that the meaning of a conclusion based on only one of these classes of information is restricted to that evidence. Current schemes, which resemble Galen's melancholic, choleric, phlegmatic, and sanguine types, or Cicero's quartet of desire, fear, distress, and pleasure, remain popular because, being free of cumbersome detail, they are parsimonious. But they have outlived their usefulness. Let us agree to a moratorium on the use of single words, such as *fear*, *anger*, *joy*, and *sad*, and write about emotional processes with full sentences rather than ambiguous, naked concepts that burden readers with the task of deciding who, whom, why, and especially what.

1 **What Are Emotions?**

1. H. Pearson, "What Is a Gene?" *Nature* 441 (2006): 399–401.

2. M. Macht and D. Dettmer, "Everyday Mood and Emotions after Eating a Chocolate Bar or an Apple," *Appetite* 46 (2006): 332–336.

3. J. M. Cooper, *Reason and Emotion: Essays on Ancient Moral Psychology and Ethical Theory* (Princeton, NJ: Princeton University Press, 1999).

4. R. Smith, *Inhibition* (Berkeley: University of California Press, 1992).

5. N. McCall, *Makes Me Wanna Holler* (New York: Vintage Books, 1995), 312.

6. J. C. Hupka, A. P. Lenton, and K. A. Hutchison, "Universal Development of Emotion Categories in Natural Language," *Journal of Personality and Social Psychology* 77 (1999): 247–278; A. O. Hirschman, *The Passions and the Interests: Political Arguments for Capitalism before Its Triumph* (Princeton, NJ: Princeton University Press, 1977); P. T. Young, *Motivation of Behavior: The Fundamental Determinants of Human and Animal Activity* (New York: Wiley, 1936).

7. J. S. Brown, H. I. Kalish, and I. E. Farber, "Conditioned Fear as Revealed by Magnitude of Startle Response to an Auditory Stimulus," *Journal of Experimental Psychology* 41 (1951): 317–328.

8. D. L. Neumann and A. M. Waters, "The Use of an Unpleasant Sound as an Unconditional Stimulus in a Human Aversive Pavlovian Conditioning Procedure," *Biological Psychology* 73 (2006): 175–185.

9. R. E. Adamec, J. Blundell, and A. Collins, "Neural Plasticity and Stress Induced Changes in Defense in the Rat," *Neuroscience and Biobehavioral Reviews* 25 (2001): 721–744.

10. J. Kagan and N. Snidman, *The Long Shadow of Temperament* (Cambridge, MA: Belknap Press of Harvard University Press, 2004).

11. W. James, "What Is an Emotion?" *Mind* 9 (1884): 188–205; J. Dewey, *Psychology*, 3rd rev. ed. (New York: American Book, 1891).

12. P. Ekman and R. J. Davidson, eds., *The Nature of Emotion: Fundamental Questions* (New York: Oxford University Press, 1994); J. Le Doux, *Synaptic Self: How Our Brains Become Who We Are* (New York: Viking, 2001).

13. J. Updike, *Self-Consciousness: Memoirs* (New York: Knopf, 1989), 27.

14. S. Braund and G. W. Most, *Ancient Anger: Perspectives from Homer to Galen* (New York: Cambridge University Press, 2003); R. A. Kaster, *Emotion, Restraint, and Community in Ancient Rome* (New York: Oxford University Press, 2005).

15. M. L. Reymert, *Feelings and Emotions* (New York: McGraw-Hill, 1950); G. C. Gonzaga, R. A. Turner, D. Keltner, B. Campos, and M. Altemus, "Romantic Love and Sexual Desire in Close Relationships," *Emotion* 6 (2006): 163–179.

16. J. T. Cacioppo and W. L. Gardner, "Emotion," *Annual Review of Psychology* 50 (1999): 191–234; A. Bain, *The Emotion and the Will* (London: Parker, 1859).

17. B. A. Woike, "Most Memorable Experiences," *Journal of Personality and Social Psychology* 68 (1995): 1081–1091; L. A. Penner, S. Shiffman, J. A. Paty, and B. A. Fritzsche, "Individual Differences in Intraperson Variability in Mood," *Journal of Personality and Social Psychology* 66 (1994): 712–721.

18. T. J. Strauman, "Self-Guides and Emotionally Significant Childhood Memories," *Journal of Personality and Social Psychology* 59 (1990): 869–880.

19. W. G. Parrott and J. Sabini, "Mood and Memory under Natural Conditions," *Journal of Personality and Social Psychology* 59 (1990): 321–326; D. M. Sanbonmatsu, S. Shavitt, and B. D. Gibson, "Salience, Set Size, and Illusory Correlation," *Journal of Personality and Social Psychology* 66 (1994): 1020–1033.

20. K. R. Scherer, "Feelings Integrate the Central Representation of Appraisal-Driven Response Organization in Emotion," in A. S. R. Manstead, N. Frijda, and A. Fischer, eds., *Feelings and Emotions*, 136–157 (New York: Cambridge University Press, 2004); R. Buck, "The Biological Affects: A Typology," *Psychological Review* 106 (1999): 301–336; J. J. Prinz, *Gut Reactions: A Perceptual Theory of Emotion* (New York: Oxford University Press, 2004).

21. A. M. Owen, M. R. Coleman, M. Boly, M. H. Davis, S. Laureys, and J. D. Pickard, "Detecting Awareness in the Vegetative State," *Science* 313 (2006): 1402; D. Chen, A. Katdare, and N. Lucas, "Chemosignals of Fear Enhance Cognitive Performance in Humans," *Chemical Senses* 415 (2006): 415–423; A. Holmes, S. Parmigiani, F. Ferrari, P. Palanza, and R. J. Rodgers, "Behavioral Profile of Wild Mice in the Elevated Plus-Maze for Anxiety," *Physiology and Behavior* 71 (2000): 509–516.

22. R. A. Shweder, "The Cultural Psychology of the Emotions," in M. Lewis and J. M. Haviland, eds., *Handbook of Emotions*, 417–431 (New York: Guilford, 1993); S. Schacter and J. E. Singer, "Cognitive, Social and Physiological Determinants of Emotional States," *Psychological Review* 69 (1962): 379–399; B. Mellers, "Choice and the Relative Pleasure of Consequences," *Psychological Bulletin* 126 (2000): 910–924; L. A. King, J. A. Hicks, J. L. Krull, and A. K. Del Gaiso, "Positive Affect and the Experience of Meaning in Life," *Journal of Personality and Social Psychology* 90 (2006): 179–196; F. M. E. Grouzet, T. Kasser, A. Ahuvia, J. M. F. Dols,

Y. Kim, S. Lau, R. M. Ryan, S. Saunders, P. Schmuck, and K. M. Sheldon, "The Structure of Goal Contents across Fifteen Cultures," *Journal of Personality and Social Psychology* 89 (2005): 800–816.

23. G. Mandler, *Mind and Emotion* (New York: Wiley, 1975); L. F. Barrett, "Are Emotions Natural Kinds?" *Perspectives on Psychological Science* 1 (2006): 28–58; L. F. Barrett and T. D. Wager, "The Structure of Emotion," *Current Directions in Psychological Science* 15 (2006): 79–83; R. B. Zajonc, "Feeling and Thinking: Preferences Need No Inferences," *American Psychologist* 35 (1980): 151–175; A. R. Damasio, *Looking for Spinoza: Joy, Sorrow, and the Feeling Brain* (London: Heinemann, 2003), 51; M. Lewis, "The Emergence of Human Emotions," in Lewis and Haviland, eds., *Handbook of Emotions*, 223–235; F. Perrin, C. Schnakers, M. Schabus, C. Degueldre, S. Goldman, S. Bredart, M. E. Faymonville, M. Lamy, G. Moonen, G. Luxen, P. Maquet, and S. Laurey, "Brain Responses to One's Own Name in Vegetative State, Minimally Conscious State, and Locked-in Syndrome," *Archives of Neurology* 63 (2006): 562–569; R. Buck, "The Biology of Affects: A Typology," *Psychological Review* 106 (1999): 301–336.

24. M. J. Miresco and L. J. Kirmayer, "The Persistence of Mind-Brain Dualism in Psychiatric Reasoning about Clinical Scenarios," *American Journal of Psychiatry* 163 (2006): 913–918; R. Plutchik, "Emotions and Their Vicissitudes: Emotions and Psychopathology," in Lewis and Haviland, eds., *Handbook of Emotions*, 53–66; R. C. Solomon, "The Philosophy of Emotions," in Lewis and Haviland, eds., *Handbook of Emotions*, 3–15.

25. F. Sperli, L. Spinelli, C. Pollo, and M. Seeck, "Contralateral Smile and Laughter, but No Mirth, Induced by Electrical Stimulation of the Cingulate Cortex," *Epilepsia* 47 (2006): 440–443; R. Hoehn-Saric and D. R. McLeod, "Anxiety and Arousal," *Journal of Affective Disorders* 61 (2000): 217–224; I. B. Mauss, R. W. Levenson, L. McCarter, F. H. Wilhelm, and J. J. Gross, "The Tie That Binds? Coherence among Emotion Experience, Behavior, and Physiology," *Emotion* 5 (2005): 175–190; S. H. Fairclough and L. Venables, "Prediction of Subjective States from Psychophysiology: A Multivariate Approach," *Biological Psychology* 71 (2006): 100–110.

26. J. P. Sartre, *The Emotions* (New York: Wisdom Library, 1948); M. C. Nussbaum, *Upheavals of Thought: The Intelligence of Emotions* (New York: Cambridge University Press, 2001); J. Campos, C. Frankel, and L. Camras, "On the Nature of Emotion Regulation," *Child Development* 75 (2004): 377–394; R. S. Lazarus, "Emotions and Interpersonal Relationships," *Journal of Personality and Social Psychology* 74 (2006): 9–46; E. T. Rolls, *Emotion Explained* (New York: Oxford University Press, 2005).

27. A. Ortony and T. J. Turner, "What's Basic about Basic Emotions?" *Psychological Review* 97 (1990): 315–331; D. L. Cairns, "Ethics, Ethology, Terminology," in Braund and Most, eds., *Ancient Anger*, 11–49.

28. M. Eimer and A. Holmes, "Event-Related Brain Potential Correlates of Emotional Face Processing," *Neuropsychologia* 45 (2007): 15–31.

29. S. Sakuragi and Y. Sugiyama, "Effects of Daily Walking on Subjective Symptoms, Mood and Autonomic Nervous Function," *Journal of Physical Anthropology* 25 (2006): 281–289; J. R. Bemporad, E. Beresin, and P. K. Rauch, "Psychodynamic Theories and Treatment of Childhood Anxiety Disorders," in H. L. Leonard, ed., *Child and Adolescent Psychiatric Clinics of North America*, 763–778 (Philadelphia: W. B. Saunders, 1993), 763.

30. C. T. Murphy, K. Guinagh, and W. J. Oates, *Greek and Roman Classics in Translation* (New York: Longmans, Green, 1947), 847.

31. C. Darwin, "A Biographical Sketch of an Infant," *Mind* 2 (1877): 285–294; M. J. Sabatini, P. Ebert, D. A. Lewis, P. Levitt, J. L. Cameron, and K. Mirnics, "Amygdala Gene Expression Correlates of Social Behavior in Monkeys Experiencing Maternal Separation," *Journal of Neuroscience* 27 (2007): 3295–3304.

32. B. Levine, "Autobiographical Memory and the Self in Time," *Brain and Cognition* 55 (2004): 54–68.

33. A. R. Caffe, P. C. Van Ryen, T. P. Van Der Woude, and F. W. Van Leeuwen, "Vasopressin and Oxytocin Systems in the Brain and Upper Spinal Cord of *Macaca fascicularis*," *Journal of Comparative Neurology* 287 (2004): 302–325; K. N. Ochsner, D. H. Ludlow, K. Knierim, J. Hanelin, T. Ramachandran, G. C. Glover, and S. C. Mackey, "Neural Correlates of Individual Differences in Pain-Related Fear and Anxiety," *Pain* 120 (2006): 69–77.

34. R. C. MacLean and I. Gudelj, "Resource Competition and Social Conflict in Experimental Populations of Yeast," *Nature* 441 (2006): 498–501; A. Weiss, J. E. King, and R. M. Enns, "Subjective Well-Being Is Heritable and Genetically Correlated with Dominance in Chimpanzees (*Pan troglodytes*)," *Journal of Personality and Social Psychology* 83 (2002): 1141–1149; A. Thornton and K. McAuliffe, "Teaching in Wild Meerkats," *Science* 313 (2006): 227–229.

35. P. Ball, *The Devil's Doctor: Paracelsus and the World of Renaissance Magic and Science* (London: Heinemann, 2006).

36. S. N. Moses, C. Villate, and J. D. Ryan, "An Investigation of Learning Strategy Supporting Transitive Inference Performance in Humans Compared to Other Species," *Neuropsychologia* 44 (2006): 1370–1387.

37. J. A. Gray and N. McNaughton, *The Neuropsychology of Anxiety: An Enquiry into the Function of the Septo-Hippocampal System*, 2nd ed. (New York: Oxford University Press, 2000).

38. Seneca, "On Anger" [ca. 40–50 CE], in J. W. Basore, ed., *Moral Essays* (Cambridge, MA: Harvard University Press, 1963).

39. S. Moskovitz, *Love Despite Hate: Child Survivors of the Holocaust and Their Adult Lives* (New York: Schocken Books, 1983), 217; P. Stallard and E. Smith, "Appraisals and Cognitive Coping Styles Associated with Chronic Post-Traumatic Symptoms in Child Road Traffic Accident Survivors," *Journal of Child Psychology and Psychiatry* 48 (2007): 194–201; N. Kar, P. K. Mohapatra, K. C. Nayak, P. Pattanaik, S. P. Swain, and H. C. Kar, "Post-Traumatic Stress Disorder in Children and Adolescents One

Year after a Super-Cyclone in Orissa, India: Exploring Cross-Cultural Validity and Vulnerability Factors," *BMC Psychiatry* (2007): in press.

40. H. Giles and N. Coupland, *Language: Contexts and Consequences* (Pacific Grove, CA: Brooks/Cole, 1991); S. W. Gregory and S. Webster, "A Nonverbal Signal in Voices of Interview Partners Effectively Predicts Communication Accommodation and Social Status Perceptions," *Journal of Personality and Social Psychology* 70 (1996): 1231–1240.

41. J. Kagan, "On the Nature of Emotions," in "The Development of Emotional Regulation: Biological and Behavioral Considerations," *Monographs of the Society for Research in Child Development* 59 (1994): 7–24; V. Woolf, *The Virginia Woolf Reader: An Anthology of Short Stories, Essays, Fiction, and Nonfiction* (San Diego: Harcourt Brace Jovanovich, 1984); L. Wittgenstein, *Philosophical Investigations* (New York: Macmillan, 1953).

42. A. R. Damasio, *Descartes' Error: Emotion, Reason, and the Human Brain* (New York: Grossett/Putnam, 1994); C. E. Izard, "Emotion-Cognition Relationships and Human Development," in C. Izard, J. Kagan, and R. B. Zajonc, eds., *Emotions, Cognition, and Behavior*, 17–37 (New York: Cambridge University Press, 1984); O. G. Cameron, "Interoception," *Psychosomatic Medicine* 63 (2001): 697–710; A. Wierzbicka, *Emotions across Languages and Cultures: Diversity and Universals* (New York: Cambridge University Press, 1999).

43. L. Weiskrantz, *Consciousness Lost and Found: A Neuropsychological Exploration* (New York: Oxford University Press, 1997); M. Montaigne, *Essays* (New York: Penguin, 1958), 381; Damasio, *Descartes' Error*; Young, *Motivation and Behavior*.

44. B. O. Olatunji, B. J. Deacon, J. S. Abramowitz, and D. F. Tolin, "Dimensionality of Somatic Complaints: Factor Structure and Psychometric Properties of the Self-Rating Anxiety Scale," *Journal of Anxiety Disorders* 20 (2006): 543–561; R. Melzack and P. D. Wall, *The Challenge of Pain* (New York: Basic Books, 1983), 50 (quotation); N. B. Schmidt, J. A. Richey, and K. K. Fitzpatrick, "Discomfort Intolerance," *Journal of Anxiety Disorders* 20 (2006): 263–280; R. Kalisch, K. Wiech, H. D. Critchley, and R. T. Dolan, "Levels of Appraisal," *Neuroimage* 30 (2006): 1458–1466; G. N. Martin, "The Effect of Exposure to Odor on the Perception of Pain," *Psychosomatic Medicine* 68 (2006): 613–616; A. Hernandez and N. Sachs-Ericsson, "Ethnic Differences in Pain Reports and the Modulating Role of Depression in a Community Sample of Hispanic and Caucasian Participants with Serious Health Problems," *Psychosomatic Medicine* 68 (2006): 121–128.

45. C. Mohr, F. Binkofski, C. Erdmann, C. Buchel, and C. Helmchen, "The Anterior Cingulate Cortex Contains Distinct Areas Dissociating External from Self-Administered Painful Stimulation: A Parametric fMRI Study," *Pain* 14 (2005): 347–357; M. St. Onge, M. Lortie-Lussier, P. Mercier, J. Grenier, and J. De Koninck, "Emotions in the Diary and REM Dreams of Young and Late Adulthood Women and Their Relation to Life Satisfaction," *Dreaming* 15 (2005): 116–128; J. N. Lundstrom and M. J. Olsson, "Subthreshold Amounts of Social Odorant Affect Mood,

but Not Behavior, in Heterosexual Women When Tested by a Male, but Not a Female, Experimenter," *Biological Psychiatry* 70 (2005): 197–204; M. K. Mc-Clintock, S. Bullivant, S. Jacob, N. Spencer, B. Zelano, and C. Ober, "Human Body Scents: Conscious Perceptions and Biological Effects," *Chemical Senses* 30 (2005): 135–137; R. Soussignon and B. Schall, "Children's Facial Responsiveness to Odors," *Developmental Psychology* 32 (1996): 367–379; J. Kagan, *The Nature of the Child* (New York: Basic Books, 1984).

46. M. Brune, H. Bahramali, M. Hennessy, and A. Snyder, "Are Angry Male and Female Faces Represented in Opposite Hemispheres of the Female Brain? A Study Using Repetitive Transcranial Magnetic Stimulation (rTMS)," *Journal of Integrative Neuroscience* 5 (2006): 187–197.

47. K. Kim, M. Uchiyama, X. Liu, K. Shibui, T. Ohida, R. Ogihara, and M. Okawa, "Somatic and Psychological Complaints and Their Correlates with Insomnia in the Japanese General Population," *Psychosomatic Medicine* 63 (2001): 441–446; W. Rief, A. Hessel, and E. Braehler, "Somatization Symptoms and Hypochondrical Features in the General Population," *Psychosomatic Medicine* 63 (2001): 595–602.

48. E. P. Vianna and D. Tranel, "Gastric Myoelectrical Activity as an Index of Emotional Arousal," *International Journal of Psychophysiology* 61 (2006): 70–76; C. Saarni, J. J. Campos, L. A. Camras, and D. Witherington, "Emotional Development: Action, Communication, and Understanding," in N. Eisenberg (volume editor), W. Damon and R. M. Lerner (editors-in-chief), *Handbook of Child Psychology*, 6th ed., vol. 3, 226–299 (New York: Wiley, 2006), 227.

49. J.-J. Rousseau, *The Confessions* [1781], trans. J. M. Cohen (New York: Penguin, 1953).

50. J. T. Cacioppo, G. G. Bernston, and D. J. Klein, "What Is an Emotion?" *Review of Personality and Social Psychology* 14 (1992): 63–98.

51. P. Dunckley, R. G. Wise, M. Fairhurst, P. Hobden, Q. Aziz, L. Chang, and I. Tracey, "A Comparison of Visceral and Somatic Pain Processing in the Human Brainstem Using Functional Magnetic Resonance Imaging," *Journal of Neuroscience* 25 (2005): 7333–7341; I. A. Strigo, G. H. Duncan, M. Boivin, and M. C. Bushnell, "Differentiation of Visceral and Cutaneous Pain in the Human Brain," *Journal of Neurophysiology* 89 (2006): 3294–3303.

52. D. Tsao, "A Dedicated System for Processing Faces," *Science* 314 (2006): 72–73.

53. S. M. Breugelmans, Z. Ambadar, J. B. Vaca, Y. H. Poortinga, B. Setiadi, and P. Widiyanto, "Body Sensations Associated with Emotions in Raramuri Indians, Rural Javanese, and Three Student Samples," *Emotion* 5 (2005): 166–174; J. A. Russell and L. F. Barrett, "Core Affect, Prototypical Emotional Episodes, and Other Things Called Emotion," *Journal of Personality and Social Psychology* 76 (1999): 805–819.

54. S. E. Taylor, J. S. Lerner, D. K. Sherman, R. M. Sage, and N. K. McDowell, "Are Self-Enhancing Cognitions Associated with Healthy or Unhealthy Biological

Profiles?" *Journal of Personality and Social Psychology* 85 (2003): 605–615; L. F. Barrett, K. S. Quigley, E. Bliss-Moreau, and K. R. Aronson, "Interoceptive Sensitivity and Self Reports of Emotional Experience," *Journal of Personality and Social Psychology* 87 (2004): 684–697; G. A. Bonanno, C. B. Wortman, D. R. Lehrman, R. G. Tweed, M. Haring, J. Sonnega, D. Carr, and R. M. Nesse, "Resilience to Loss and Chronic Grief," *Journal of Personality and Social Psychology* 83 (2002): 1150–1164; C. D. Murray and J. Fox, "Dissociated Body Experiences," *British Journal of Psychology* 96 (2005): 441–456; R. Schandry, "Heart Beat Perception and Emotional Experience," *Psychophysiology* 18 (1981): 483–488; Kagan and Snidman, *Long Shadow of Temperament.*

55. C. Peyrin, M. Baciu, C. Segebarth, and C. Marendaz, "Cerebral Regions and Hemispheric Specialization for Processing Spatial Frequencies during Natural Scene Recognition," *Neuroimage* 23 (2004): 698–707.

56. F. M. Cancian and S. C. Gordon, "Changing Emotion Norms in Marriage," *Gender and Society* 2 (1988); J. L. Tsai, B. Knutson, and H. H. Fung, "Cultural Variation in Affect Valuation," *Journal of Personality and Social Psychology* 90 (2006): 288–307; J. R. Timm, "The Celebration of Emotion," *Philosophy of East and West* 41 (1991): 59–75; J. Gledhill, "A Qualitative Study of the Characteristics and Representation of Fatigue in a French Speaking Population of Cancer Patients and Healthy Subjects," *European Journal of Oncological Nursing* 9 (2005): 294–312.

57. Z. Kaplan, M. A. Matar, R. Kamin, T. Sadan, and H. Cohen, "Stress-Related Responses after Three Years of Exposure to Terror in Israel," *Journal of Clinical Psychiatry* 66 (2005): 1146–1154; N. Laor, L. Wolmer, M. Alon, J. Siev, E. Samuel, and P. Toren, "Risk and Protective Factors Mediating Psychological Symptoms and Ideological Commitment of Adolescents Facing Continuous Terrorism," *Journal of Nervous and Mental Disease* 194 (2006): 279–286; M. Schiff, "Living in the Shadow of Terrorism," *Social Science and Medicine* 62 (2006): 2301–2312; M. Basoglu, M. Paker, O. Paker, E. Ozmen, I. Marks, C. Incesu, D. Sahin, and N. Sarimurat, "Psychological Effects of Torture," *American Journal of Psychiatry* 151 (1994): 76–81.

58. C. G. Jung, *Memories, Dreams, Reflections,* ed. A. Jaffe (New York: Vintage, 1961), 36; J. Siev and A. B. Cohen, "Is Thought-Action Fusion Related to Religiosity? Differences between Christians and Jews," *Behaviour Research and Therapy* 45 (2007): 829–837.

59. P. A. Frazier, "Victim Attributions and Post-Rape Trauma," *Journal of Personality and Social Psychology* 59 (1990): 298–304; L. M. Conoscenti and R. J. McNally, "Health Complaints in Acknowledged and Unacknowledged Rape Victims," *Journal of Anxiety Disorders* 20 (2006): 372–379; B. Andrews, C. R. Brewin, S. Rose, and M. Kirk, "Predicting PTSD Symptoms in Victims of Violent Crime," *Journal of Abnormal Psychology* 109 (2000): 69–73; A. Ehlers, R. A. Mayou, and B. Bryant, "Psychological Predictors of Chronic Posttraumatic Stress Disorder after Motor Ve-

hicle Accidents," *Journal of Abnormal Psychology* 107 (1998): 508–519; R. B. Weisberg, B. A. Brown, J. P. Wincze, and D. H. Barlow, "Causal Attributions and Male Sexual Arousal," *Journal of Abnormal Psychology* 110 (2001): 324–334.

60. K. J. Dover, *Greek Homosexuality* (Cambridge, MA: Harvard University Press, 1978); O. Murray, *Early Greece* (Cambridge, MA: Harvard University Press, 1993); J. W. Baldwin, *The Language of Sex: Five Voices from Northern France around 1200* (Chicago: University of Chicago Press, 1994); E. L. R. Ladourie, *Montaillou: The Promised Land of Error,* trans B. Bray (London: Scolar Press, 1978), 151 (quotation).

61. D. A. Clark, A. Cook, and D. Snow, "Depressive Symptom Differences in Hospitalized, Medically Ill, Depressed Psychiatric Inpatients and Nonmedical Controls," *Journal of Abnormal Psychology* 107 (1998): 38–48; S. R. Stader and J. E. Hokanson, "Psychosocial Antecedents of Depressive Symptoms," *Journal of Abnormal Psychology* 107 (1998): 17–26; I. J. Roseman, C. Wiest, and C. S. Swartz, "Phenomenology, Behaviors, and Goals Differentiate Discrete Emotions," *Journal of Personality and Social Psychology* 67 (1994): 206–221; H. S. Mayberg, J. A. Silva, S. K. Brannan, J. L. Tekell, R. K. Mahurin, S. McGinnis, and P. A. Jerabek, "The Functional Neuroanatomy of the Placebo Effect," *American Journal of Psychiatry* 159 (2002): 728–737; R. de la Fuente-Fernandez, T. J. Ruth, V. Sossi, M. Schulzer, D. B. Caine, and A. J. Stoessl, "Expectation and Dopamine Release: Mechanism of the Placebo Effect in Parkinson's Disease," *Science* 293 (2001): 1164; P. Petrovic, E. Kalso, K. M. Petersson, and M. Ingvar, "Placebo and Opioid Analgesia: Imaging a Shared Neuronal Network," *Science* 295 (2002): 1737.

62. H. Weiner, *Perturbing the Organism: The Biology of Stressful Experience* (Chicago: University of Chicago Press, 1992); F. A. Wilson and E. T. Rolls, "The Effect of Stimulus Novelty and Familiarity on Neuronal Activity in the Amygdala of Monkeys Performing Recognition Memory Tasks," *Experimental Brain Research* 93 (1993): 267–382; P. S. Bearman and H. Bruckner, "Promising the Future: Virginity Pledges and First Intercourse," *American Journal of Sociology* 106 (2001): 859–912.

## 2 Classifying Human Emotions

1. S. Hampshire, *Innocence and Experience* (Cambridge, MA: Harvard University Press, 1989).

2. B. Dohrenwend, "Inventorying Stressful Life Events as Risk Factors for Psychopathology," *Psychological Bulletin* 132 (2006): 477–495.

3. D. L. Cairns, "Ethics, Ethology, Terminology," in S. Braund and G. W. Most, eds., *Ancient Anger: Perspectives from Homer to Galen,* 11–49 (New York: Cambridge University Press, 2003); C. Lutz, "The Domain of Emotional Words in Ifaluk," *American Ethnologist* 9 (1982): 113–128; G. K. Paster, "Melancholic Cats, Lugged Bears and Early Modern Cosmology," in G. K. Paster, K. Rowe, and M. Floyd-Wilson, eds., *Reading the Early Modern Passions: Essays in the Cultural History of Emotion,* 113–129 (Philadelphia: University of Pennsylvania Press, 2004).

4. R. S. Herz, "A Naturalistic Analysis of Autobiographical Memories Triggered by

Olfactory Visual and Auditory Stimuli," *Chemical Senses* 29 (2004): 217–224; E. P. Koster, J. Degel, and D. Piper, "Proactive and Retroactive Interference in Implicit Odor Memory," *Chemical Senses* 27 (2002): 191–206; J. Willander and M. Larsson, "Smell Your Way Back to Childhood: Autobiographical Odor Memory," *Psychonomic Bulletin and Review* 13 (2006): 240–244; B. Ditto, "Familial Influences on Heart Rate, Blood Pressure, and Self-Report Anxiety Responses to Stress: Results from One Hundred Twin Pairs," *Psychophysiology* 30 (1993): 635–645; E. E. Wilkens and I. L. Bernstein, "Conditioning Method Determines Patterns of c-fos Expression Following Novel Taste-Illness Pairing," *Behavioral Brain Research* 169 (2006): 93–97.

5. R. W. Walker, J. Skowronski, J. Gibbons, R. Vogl, and R. Thompson, "On the Emotions That Accompany Autobiographical Memories," *Cognition and Emotion* 17 (2003): 703–724.

6. J. L. Briggs, *Never in Anger: Portrait of an Eskimo Family* (Cambridge, MA: Harvard University Press, 1970); Lutz, "Domain of Emotional Words."

7. B. Deacon and J. Abramowitz, "Anxiety Sensitivity and Its Dimensions across the Anxiety Disorders," *Journal of Anxiety Disorders* 20 (2006): 837–857.

8. S. M. Sherman, "What Is the Function of the Thalamus?" in J. L. v. Hemmen and T. J. Sejnowski, eds., *Twenty-Three Problems in Systems Neuroscience*, 65–82 (New York: Oxford University Press, 2006); E. T. Rolls, A. S. Browing, K. Inoue, and I. Hernadi, "Novel Visual Stimuli Activate a Population of Neurons in the Primate Orbitofrontal Cortex," *Neurobiology of Learning and Memory* 84 (2005): 111–123; P. Michelon, A. Z. Snyder, R. I. Buckner, M. McAvoy, and J. M. Zacks, "Neural Correlates of Incongruous Visual Information," *Neuroimage* 19 (2003): 1612–1626; N. Bunzeck and F. Duzel, "Absolute Coding of Stimulus Novelty in the Human Substantia Nigra/VTA," *Neuron* 51 (2006): 369–379; W. Schultz, "Behavioral Theories and the Neurophysiology of a Reward," in S. T. Fiske, A. E. Kazdin, and D. L. Schacter, eds., *Annual Review of Psychology*, 87–115 (Palo Alto, CA: Annual Reviews, 2006); H. S. Schaefer, K. M. Putnam, R. M. Benca, and R. J. Davidson, "Event-Related Functional Magnetic Resonance Imaging Measures of Neural Activity to Positive Social Stimuli in Pre- and Post-Treatment Depression," *Biological Psychiatry* 60 (2006): 974–986; F. Bermpohl, A. Pascual-Leone, A. Amedi, L. B. Merabet, F. Fregni, N. Gaab, D. Alsop, G. Schlaug, and G. Northoff, "Dissociable Networks for the Expectancy and Perception of Emotional Stimuli in the Human Brain," *Neuroimage* 30 (2006): 588–600; I. Savic and H. Berglund, "Right-Nostril Dominance in Discrimination of Unfamiliar, but Not Familiar, Odours," *Chemical Senses* 25 (2000): 517–523; G. Horstmann, "Latency and Duration of the Action Interruption in Surprise," *Cognition and Emotion* 20 (2006): 242–273; F. Dolcos and G. McCarthy, "Brain Systems Mediating Cognitive Interference by Emotional Distraction," *Journal of Neuroscience* 26 (2006): 2072–2079; D. C. Rubin and M. Kozin, "Vivid Memories," *Cognition* 16 (1984): 81–95.

9. A. P. Atkinson, J. Tipples, D. Burt, and A. W. Young, "Asymmetric Interference

between Sex and Emotion in Face Perception," *Perception and Psychophysics* 67 (2005): 1189–1213; J. C. Hsieh, S. Stone-Elander, and M. Ingvar, "Anticipatory Coping of Pain Expressed in the Human Anterior Cingulate Cortex: A Positron Emission Tomography Study," *Neuroscience Letters* 262 (1999): 61–64; P. Petrovic, K. Carlsson, K. M. Petersson, P. Hansson, and M. Ingvar, "Content Dependent Deactivation of the Amygdala during Pain," *Journal of Cognitive Neuroscience* 16 (2004): 1289–1301; J. D. Rollnik, N. Schmitz, and J. Kugler, "Cardiovascular Reactions Induced by Unpredictable, Predictable, and Controllable Painful Stimuli during Sphygmomanometry," *International Journal of Psychophysiology* 40 (2001): 161–165.

10. P. Ball, *The Devil's Doctor: Paracelsus and the World of Renaissance Magic and Science* (London: Heinemann, 2006).

11. N. Christenfeld, D. P. Phillips, and L. M. Glynn, "What's in a Name," *Journal of Psychosomatic Research* 47 (1999): 241–254.

12. P. Schäfer, *Judeophobia: Attitudes toward the Jews in the Ancient World* (Cambridge, MA: Harvard University Press, 1997).

13. P. Rozin, R. Rozin, B. Appel, and C. Wachtel, "Documenting and Explaining the Common AAB Pattern in Music and Humor: Establishing and Breaking Expectations," *Emotion* 6 (2006): 349–355.

14. O. Paz, *Itinerary* (New York: Harcourt, 1999).

15. J. D. Miller, E. C. Scott, and S. Okamoto, "Public Acceptance of Evolution," *Science* 313 (2006): 765–766.

16. I. Biederman and E. A. Vessel, "Perceptual Pleasure and the Brain," *American Scientist* 94 (2006): 247–253.

17. F. A. Wilson and E. T. Rolls, "The Effect of Stimulus Novelty and Familiarity on Neuronal Activity in the Amygdala of Monkeys Performing Recognition Memory Tasks," *Experimental Brain Research* 93 (1993): 267–382; U. Rutishauser, A. N. Mamelak, and E. M. Schuman, "Single-Trial Learning of Novel Stimuli by Individual Neurons of the Human Hippocampus-Amygdala Complex," *Neuron* 49 (2006): 805–813; L. Pessoa, S. Japee, D. Sturman, and L. G. Ungerleider, "Target Visibility and Visual Awareness Modulate Amygdala Responses to Fearful Faces," *Cerebral Cortex* 16 (2006): 366–371; A. L. Adkin, S. Quant, B. E. Maki, and W. E. McIlroy, "Cortical Responses Associated with Predictable and Unpredictable Compensatory Balance Reactions," *Experimental Brain Research* 172 (2006): 85–93; B. D. Bartholow, B. J. Bushman, and M. A. Sestir, "Chronic Violent Video Game Exposure and Desensitization to Violence: Behavioral and Event-Related Brain Potential Data," *Journal of Experimental Social Psychology* 42 (2006): 532–539.

18. K. Buhr and M. J. Dugas, "Investigating the Construct Validity of Intolerance of Uncertainty and Its Unique Relationship with Worry," *Journal of Anxiety Disorders* 20 (2006): 222–236.

19. K. Buhr and M. J. Dugas, "The Intolerance of Uncertainty Scale," *Behaviour Research and Therapy* 40 (2002): 931–945; R. E. Cooney, L. Y. Atlas, J. Joorman,

F. Eugene, and I. H. Gotlib, "Amygdala Activation in the Processing of Neutral Faces in Social Anxiety Disorder: Is Neutral Really Neutral?" *Psychiatry Research: Neuroimaging* 148 (2006): 55–59.

20. P. J. Whalen, J. Kagan, R. G. Cook, I. C. Davis, H. Kim, S. Polis, D. G. McLaren, L. H. Somerville, A. A. McLean, J. S. Maxwell, and T. Johnstone, "Human Amygdala Responsivity to Masked Fearful Eye-Whites," *Science* 306 (2004): 2061.

21. Q. Luo, T. Holroyd, M. Jones, T. Hendler, and J. Blair, "Neural Dynamics for Facial Threat Processing as Revealed by Gamma Band Synchronization Using MEG," *Neuroimage* 34 (2006): 839–847.

22. A. Holmes, J. S. Winston, and M. Eimer, "The Role of Spatial Frequency Information for ERP Components Sensitive to Faces and Emotional Facial Expression," *Brain Research: Cognitive Brain Research* 25 (2005): 508–520; Pessoa et al., "Target Visibility"; C. I. Hooker, L. T. Germine, R. T. Knight, and M. D'Esposito, "Amygdala Response to Facial Expressions Reflects Emotional Learning," *Journal of Neuroscience* 26 (2006): 8915–8922; M. Brand, F. Grabenhorst, K. Starcke, M. M. Vandekerckove, and H. J. Markowitsch, "Role of the Amygdala in Decisions under Ambiguity and Decisions under Risk," *Neuropsychologia* 45 (2007): 1305–1317; C. Grillon, J. M. P. Baas, B. Cornwell, and L. Johnson, "Context Conditioning and Behavioral Avoidance in a Virtual Reality Environment," *Biological Psychiatry* 60 (2006): 752–759; U. Herwig, B. Abler, H. Walter, and S. Erk, "Expecting Unpleasant Stimuli: An fMRI Study," *Psychiatry Research: Neuroimaging* 154 (2007): 1–12.

23. L. Nummenmaa, J. Hyona, and M. G. Calvo, "Eye Movement Assessment of Selective Attentional Capture by Emotional Pictures," *Emotion* 6 (2006): 257–268; O. V. Lipp, "Of Snakes and Flowers," *Emotion* 6 (2006): 296–308; R. Righart and B. de Gelder, "Context Influences Early Perceptual Analysis of Faces—An Electrophysiological Study," *Cerebral Cortex* 16 (2006): 1249–1257; R. Palermo and M. Coltheart, "Photographs of Facial Expression: Accuracy, Response Times, and Ratings of Intensity," *Behavior Research Methods, Instruments and Computers* 36 (2000): 634–638; A. Simmons, M. B. Stein, S. C. Matthews, J. S. Feinstein, and M. P. Paulus, "Affective Ambiguity for a Group Recruits Ventromedial Prefrontal Cortex," *Neuroimage* 29 (2006): 655–661.

24. J. E. Joseph, D. K. Powell, A. H. Andersen, R. S. Bhatt, M. K. Dunlap, S. T. Foldes, E. Forman, N. A. Steinmetz, and Z. Zhang, "fMRI in Alert, Behaving Monkeys," *Journal of Neuroscience Methods* 15 (2006): 10–24; C. E. Schwartz, C. I. Wright, L. M. Shin, J. Kagan, P. J. Whalen, K. G. McMullin, and S. L. Rauch, "Differential Amygdalar Response to Novel vs. Newly Familiar Neutral Faces," *Biological Psychiatry* 53 (2003): 854–862; D. A. Fitzgerald, M. Angstadt, L. M. Jelsone, P. J. Nathan, and K. L. Phan, "Beyond Threat: Amygdala Reactivity across Multiple Expressions of Facial Affect," *Neuroimage* 30 (2005): 1441–1448; J. C. Britton, S. F. Taylor, K. D. Sudheimer, and I. Liberzon, "Facial Expressions and Complex IAPS Pictures," *Neuroimage* 31 (2006): 906–919; T. Straube, H. J. Mentzel, and W. H. Miltner, "Common and Distinct Brain Activation to Threat and Safety Signals

in Social Phobia," *Neuropsychobiology* 52 (2005): 163–168; E. A. Kensinger and D. L. Schacter, "Amygdala Activity Is Associated with the Successful Encoding of Item, but Not Source, Information for Positive and Negative Stimuli," *Journal of Neuroscience* 26 (2006): 2564–2570; J. P. Royet, D. Zald, R. Versace, N. Costes, F. Lavenne, O. Koenig, and R. Gervais, "Emotional Responses to Pleasant and Unpleasant Olfactory, Visual, and Auditory Stimuli," *Journal of Neuroscience* 20 (2000): 7752–7759; D. M. Small, M. D. Gregory, Y. E. Mak, D. Gitelman, M. M. Mesulam, and T. Parrish, "Dissociation of Neural Representation of Intensity and Affective Valuation in Human Gustation," *Neuron* 39 (2003): 701–711; R. Stark, A. Schienle, C. Girod, B. Walter, P. Kirsch, C. Blecker, U. Ott, A. Schafer, G. Sammer, M. Zimmerman, and D. Vaitl, "Erotic and Disgust-Inducing Pictures—Differences in the Hemodynamic Responses of the Brain," *Biological Psychology* 70 (2005): 19–29; E. R. Gizewski, E. Krause, S. Karama, A. Baars, W. Senf, and M. Forsting, "There Are Differences in Cerebral Activation between Females in Distinct Menstrual Phases during Viewing of Erotic Stimuli," *Experimental Brain Research* 174 (2006): 101–108; K. J. Pallesen, E. Brattico, C. Bailey, A. Korvenoja, J. Koivisto, A. Gjedde, and S. Carlson, "Emotion Processing of Major, Minor, and Dissonant Chords," *Annals of the New York Academy of Sciences* 1060 (2005): 450–453; S. Koelsch, "Investigating Emotion with Music," *Annals of the New York Academy of Sciences* 1060 (2005): 412–418; J. Grezes, S. Berthoz, and R. E. Passingham, "Amygdala Activation When One Is the Target of Deceit," *Neuroimage* 30 (2006): 601–608; Y. Cheng, A. N. Meltzoff, and J. Decety, "Motivation Modulates the Activity of the Human Mirror-Neuron System," *Cerebral Cortex* (2007): in press; S. Berthoz, J. Grezes, J. L. Armony, R. E. Passingham, and R. S. Dolan, "Affective Response to One's Own Moral Violations," *Neuroimage* 31 (2006): 945–950; L. Cahill, N. M. Weinberger, B. Roozendaal, and J. L. McGaugh, "Is the Amygdala the Focus of Conditioned Fear?" *Neuron* 23 (1999): 227–228; P. A. Lewis, H. D. Critchley, P. Rotshtein, and R. J. Dolan, "Neural Correlates of Processing Valence and Arousal in Affective Words," *Cerebral Cortex* 17 (2007): 742–748.

25. W. M. Mason, J. P. Capitanio, C. J. Machado, S. P. Mendoza, and D. G. Amaral, "Amagdalectomy and Responsiveness to Novelty in Rhesus Monkeys (*Macaca mulatta*): Generality and Individual Consistency of Effects," *Emotion* 6 (2006): 73–81.

26. M. D. Bauman, J. E. Poscano, W. A. Mason, P. Lavenex, and D. G. Amaral, "The Expression of Social Dominance Following Neonatal Lesions of the Amygdala or Hippocampus in Rhesus Monkeys (*Macaca mulatta*)," *Behavioral Neuroscience* 120 (2006): 749–760; C. J. Machado and J. Bachevalier, "The Impact of Selective Amygdala, Orbital Frontal Cortex, or Hippocampal Formation Lesions on Established Social Relationships in Rhesus Monkeys (*Macaca mulatta*)," *Behavioral Neuroscience* 120 (2006): 761–786.

27. A. Izquierdo and E. A. Murray, "Combined Unilateral Lesions of the Amygdala and Orbital Prefrontal Cortex Impair Affective Processing in Rhesus Monkeys," *Journal of Neurophysiology* 91 (2004): 2023–2035.

28. K. P. Lewis and R. A. Barton, "Amygdala Size and Hypothalamus Size Predict Social Play Frequently in Nonhuman Primates," *Journal of Comparative Psychology* 129 (2006): 31–37.

29. J. S. Winston, J. M. Gottfried, J. M. Kilner, and R. J. Dolan, "Integrated Neural Representations of Odor Intensity and Affective Valence in Human Amygdala," *Journal of Neuroscience* 25 (2005): 8903–8907; H. Garavan, J. C. Pendergrass, T. J. Ross, E. A. Stein, and R. C. Risinger, "Amygdala Response to Both Positively and Negatively Valenced Stimuli," *Neuroreport* 28 (2001): 2779–2783; A. K. Anderson, K. Christoff, I. Stappen, D. Panitz, D. G. Ghahremani, G. Glover, J. D. Gabrieli, and N. Sobel, "Dissociated Neural Representations of Intensity and Valence in Human Olfaction," *Nature Neuroscience* 6 (2003): 196–202; A. Ishai, "Sex, Beauty and the Orbitofrontal Cortex," *International Journal of Psychophysiology* 63 (2007): 181–185; Y. Moriguchi, T. Ohnishi, T. Kawachi, T. Mori, M. Hirakata, M. Yamada, H. Matsuda, and G. Komali, "Specific Brain Activation in Japanese and Caucasian People to Fearful Faces," *Neuroreport* 16 (2005): 133–136.

30. R. Paz, J. G. Pelletier, E. P. Bauer, and D. Pare, "Emotional Enhancement of Memory via Amygdala-Driven Facilitation of Rhinal Interactions," *Nature Neuroscience* 9 (2006): 1321–1329.

31. H. G. Walbott and K. R. Scherer, "Stress Specificities: Differential Effects of Coping Style, Gender, and Type of Stressor on Autonomic Arousal, Facial Expression, and Subjective Feeling," *Journal of Personality and Social Psychology* 61 (1991): 147–156; N. Eisenberg, R. A. Fabes, B. Murphy, and M. Karbon, "The Relations of Emotionality and Regulation to Dispositional and Situational Empathy-Related Responding," *Journal of Personality and Social Psychology* 66 (1994): 776–797; M. Bensafi, C. Rouby, V. Farget, B. Bertrand, M. Vigouroux, and A. Holley, "Autonomic Nervous System Responses to Odours," *Chemical Senses* 27 (2002): 703–709; A. Popma, L. M. C. Jansen, R. Vermeiren, H. Steiner, A. Raine, S. H. M. Van Goozen, H. van Engeland, and A. H. Doreleijers, "Hypothalamus Pituitary Adrenal Axis and Autonomic Activity during Stress in Delinquent Male Adolescents and Controls," *Psychoneuroendocrinology* 31 (2006): 948–957.

32. M. Sarlo, D. Palomba, A. Angrilli, and L. Stegagno, "Blood Phobia and Spider Phobia," *Biological Psychology* 60 (2002): 91–108.

33. R. Caldara, M. L. Seghier, B. Rossion, F. Lazeyras, C. Michel, and C. A. Hauret, "The Fusiform Face Area Is Tuned for Curvilinear Patterns with More High-Contrasted Elements in the Upper Part," *Neuroimage* 31 (2006): 313–319; O. J. Hulme and S. Zeki, "The Sightless View: Neural Correlates of Occluded Objects," *Cerebral Cortex* 17 (2007): 1197–1205.

34. K. M. Dalton, B. M. Nacewicz, A. L. Alexander, and R. J. Davidson, "Gaze-Fixation, Brain Activation, and Amygdala Volume in Unaffected Siblings of Individuals with Autism," *Biological Psychiatry* (2007): in press.

35. A. Ohman and S. Wiens, "The Concept of an Evolved Fear Module and Cognitive Theories of Anxiety," in A. S. R. Manstead, N. Frijda, and A. Fischer, eds., *Feelings*

*and Emotions*, 58–80 (New York: Cambridge University Press, 2004); V. Lo Bue and J. De Loache, "Finding the Snake in the Grass," Paper presented at meeting of Society for Research in Child Development, Boston, March 2007.

36. V. Paquette, J. Levesque, B. Mensour, J. M. Leroux, G. Beaudoin, P. Bourgouin, and M. Beauregard, "Change the Mind and You Change the Brain," *Neuroimage* 18 (2003): 401–418.

37. K. Lacey, M. D. Zaharia, J. Griffiths, A. V. Ravindran, Z. Merali, and H. Anisman, "A Prospective Study of Neuroendocrine and Immune Alterations Associated with the Stress of an Oral Academic Examination among Graduate Students," *Psychoneuroendocrinology* 25 (2000): 339–356.

38. D. R. Lara and H. S. Akiskal, "Toward an Integrative Model of the Spectrum of Mood, Behavioral, and Personality Disorders Based on Fear and Anger Traits," *Journal of Affective Disorders* 94 (2006): 89–103.

39. J. Pripfl, S. Robinson, U. Leodolter, E. Moser, and H. Bauer, "EEG Reveals the Effect of fMRI Scanner Noise on Noise-Sensitive Subjects," *Neuroimage* 31 (2006): 332–341; K. M. Allen, J. Blascovich, J. Tomaka, and R. M. Kelsey, "Presence of Human Friends and Pet Dogs as Moderators of Autonomic Responses to Stress in Women," *Journal of Personality and Social Psychology* 61 (1991): 582–589.

40. M. Costa, C. Braun, and N. Birbaumer, "Gender Differences in Response to Pictures of Nudes," *Biological Psychology* 63 (2003): 129–147; D. Sabatinelli, P. J. Lang, A. Keil, and M. M. Bradley, "Emotional Perception: Correlation of Functional MRI and Event-Related Potentials," *Cerebral Cortex* 17 (2007): 1085–1091.

41. D. G. Nair, "About Being BOLD," *Brain Research Reviews* 50 (2005): 229–243; M. Peper, "Imaging Emotional Brain Functions," *Journal of Physiology-Paris* 99 (2006): 293–307.

42. G. S. Berns, J. Chapelow, M. Cekic, C. F. Zink, G. Pagnoni, and M. E. Martin-Skurski, "Neurobiological Substrates of Dread," *Science* 312 (2006): 754–758; Wilson and Rolls, "Stimulus Novelty."

43. A. Ferretti, M. Caulo, C. Del Gratta, R. Di Matteo, A. Merla, F. Montorsi, V. Pizzella, P. Pompa, P. Rigatti, P. M. Rossini, A. Salonia, A. Tartaro, and G. L. Roman, "Dynamics of Male Sexual Arousal," *Neuroimage* 26 (2005): 1086–1096; H. Kim, L. H. Somerville, T. Johnstone, S. Polis, A. L. Alexander, L. M. Shin, and P. J. Whalen, "Contextual Modulation of Amygdala Responsivity to Surprised Faces," *Journal of Cognitive Neuroscience* 16 (2004): 1730–1745.

44. B. Krasnow, L. Tamm, M. D. Greicius, T. T. Yang, G. H. Glover, A. L. Reiss, and V. Menon, "Comparison of fMRI Activation at 3 and 1.5 T during Perceptual, Cognitive, and Affective Processing," *Neuroimage* 18 (2003): 813–826; M. Vuga, N. A. Fox, J. F. Cohn, C. J. George, R. M. Levenstein, and M. Kovacs, "Long-Term Stability of Frontal Electroencephalographic Asymmetry in Adults with a History of Depression and Controls," *International Journal of Psychophysiology* 59 (2006): 107–115; J. Gaab, N. Rohleder, U. M. Nater, and U. Ehlert, "Psychological Determinants of the Cortisol Stress Response," *Psychoneuroendocrinology* 30 (2005): 599–

610; L. M. Soravia, M. Heinrichs, A. Aerni, C. Maroni, G. Schelling, U. Ehlert, B. Roozendaal, and D. J. de Quervain, "Glucocorticoids Reduce Phobic Fear in Humans," *Proceedings of the National Academy of Sciences* 103 (2006): 5585–5590; M. E. Raichle and M. A. Mintun, "Brain Work and Brain Imaging," in S. E. Hyman, T. M. Jessell, C. J. Shatz, and C. F. Stevens, eds., *Annual Review of Neurophysiology*, 449–476 (Palo Alto, CA: Annual Reviews, 2006).

45. R. Stark, A. Schienle, B. Walter, P. Kirsch, C. Blecker, U. Ott, A. Schafer, G. Sammer, M. Zimmerman, and D. Vaitl, "Hemodynamic Effects of Negative Emotional Pictures—a Test-Retest Analysis," *Neuropsychobiology* 50 (2004): 108–118; E. J. Hermans, P. Putman, J. M. Baas, H. P. Koppeschaar, and J. van Honk, "A Single Administration of Testosterone Reduces Fear-Potentiated Startle in Humans," *Biological Psychiatry* 59 (2006): 872–874; E. J. Hermans, P. Putman, and J. van Honk, "Testosterone Administration Reduces Empathetic Behavior," *Psychoneuroendocrinology* 31 (2006): 859–866.

46. Gizewski et al., "Differences in Cerebral Activation"; S. Karama, A. R. Lecours, J. M. Leroux, P. Bourgouin, G. Beaudoin, S. Joubert, and M. Beauregard, "Areas of Brain Activation in Males and Females during Viewing of Erotic Film Excerpts," *Human Brain Mapping* 16 (2002): 1–13.

47. L. Zadro, C. Boland, and R. Richardson, "How Long Does It Last? The Persistence of the Effects of Ostracism in the Socially Anxious," *Journal of Experimental Social Psychology* 42 (2006): 692–697.

48. L. M. Williams, K. J. Brown, D. Palmer, B. J. Liddell, A. H. Kemp, G. Olivieri, A. Peduto, and E. Gordon, "The Mellow Years? Neural Basis of Improving Emotional Stability over Age," *Journal of Neuroscience* 26 (2006): 6422–6430.

49. Ball, *Devil's Doctor*.

50. K. C. Berridge and P. Winkielman, "What Is an Unconscious Emotion?" *Cognition and Emotion* 17 (2003): 181–212; S. T. Murphy and R. B. Zajonc, "Affect, Cognition, and Awareness," *Journal of Personality and Social Psychology* 64 (1993): 723–739; R. Gaillard, A. Del Cul, L. Naccache, F. Vinckier, L. Cohen, and S. Dehaene, "Nonconscious Semantic Processing of Emotional Words Modulates Conscious Access," *Proceedings of the National Academy of Science* 103 (2006): 7524–7529.

51. J. N. Lundstrom, M. J. Olsson, B. Schaal, and T. Hummel, "A Putative Social Chemosignal Elicits Faster Cortical Responses Than Perceptually Similar Odorants," *Neuroimage* 30 (2006): 1340–1346; B. I. Grosser, L. Monti-Bloch, C. Jennings-White, and D. L. Beliner, "Behavioral and Electrophysiological Effects of Androstadienone, a Human Pheromone," *Psychoneuroendocrinology* 25 (2000): 289–299; M. G. Haselton, M. Mortezaie, E. G. Pillsworth, A. Bleske-Rechek, and D. A. Frederick, "Ovulatory Shifts in Human Female Ornamentation," *Hormones and Behavior* 51 (2007): 40–45.

52. L. K. Paul, A. Lautzenheimer, W. S. Brown, A. Hart, D. Neumann, M. Spezio, and R. Adolphs, "Emotion Arousal in Agenesis of the Corpus Callosum," *International Journal of Psychophysiology* 61 (2006): 47–56.

53. B. J. Liddell, K. J. Brown, A. H. Kemp, M. J. Barton, P. Das, A. Peduto, E. Gordon, and L. M. Williams, "A Direct Brainstem-Amygdala-Cortical Alarm System for Subliminal Signals of Fear," *Neuroimage* 24 (2005): 235–243.

54. J. Storbeck, M. D. Robinson, and M. E. McCourt, "Semantic Processing Precedes Affect Retrieval," *Review of General Psychology* 10 (2006): 41–55.

55. Rutishauser, Mamelak, and Schuman, "Single-Trial Learning"; S. M. Daselaar, M. S. Fleck, S. E. Prince, and R. Cabeza, "The Medial Temporal Lobe Distinguishes Old from New Independently of Consciousness," *Journal of Neuroscience* 26 (2006): 5835–5839.

56. A. Burt and R. Trivers, *Genes in Conflict: The Biology of Selfish Genetic Elements* (Cambridge, MA: Harvard University Press, 2006).

57. C. Padoa-Schioppa and J. A. Assad, "Neurons in the Orbitofrontal Cortex Encode Economic Value," *Nature* 441 (2006): 223–226.

58. S. S. Tomkins, "Affect, Imagery, Consciousness," in *The Positive Affects* (New York: Springer, 1962); S. S. Tomkins, "Affect, Imagery, Consciousness," in *The Negative Affects* (New York: Springer, 1963); P. Ekman, "An Argument for Basic Emotions," *Cognition and Emotion* 6 (1992): 169–200; C. E. Izard, *The Face of Emotion* (New York: Appleton-Century-Crofts, 1971).

59. P. Rozin, L. Lowery, and R. Ebert, "Varieties of Disgust Faces and the Structure of Disgust," *Journal of Personality and Social Psychology* 66 (1994): 870–881; R. Reisenzein, S. Bordgen, T. Holtbernd, and D. Matz, "Evidence of Strong Dissociation between Emotion and Facial Displays," *Journal of Personality and Social Psychology* 91 (2006): 295–315; E. Greimel, M. Macht, E. Krumhuber, and H. Ellgring, "Facial and Affective Reactions to Tastes and Their Modulation by Sadness and Joy," *Physiology and Behavior* 89 (2006): 261–269.

60. R. Thompson, S. Gupta, K. Miller, S. Mills, and S. Orr, "The Effects of Vasopressin on Human Facial Responses Related to Social Communication," *Psychoneuroendocrinology* 29 (2004): 35–48; B. Parkinson, "Do Facial Movements Express Emotions or Communicate Motives?" *Personality and Social Psychology Review* 9 (2005): 278–311; J. M. Fernandez-Dols, and M. A. Ruiz-Belda, "Are Smiles a Sign of Happiness? Gold Medal Winners at the Olympic Games," *Journal of Personality and Social Psychology* 69 (1995): 1113–1119; M. Ruiz-Belda, J. Fernandez-Dols, and K. Barchard, "Spontaneous Facial Expressions of Happy Bowlers and Soccer Fans," *Cognition and Emotion* 17 (2003): 315–327; S. Sarra and E. Otta, "Different Types of Smiles and Laughter in Preschool Children," *Psychological Reports* 89 (2001): 547–558; Hermans, Putman, and van Honk, "Testosterone Administration"; J. M. Carroll and J. A. Russell, "Facial Expressions in Hollywood's Portrayal of Emotion," *Journal of Personality and Social Psychology* 72 (1997): 164–176; G. Peleg, G. Katzir, O. Peleg, M. Kamara, L. Brodsky, H. Hel-Or, D. Keren, and E. Nevo, "Hereditary Family Signature of Facial Expression," *Proceedings of the National Academy of the United States* 103 (2006): 15021–15026.

61. U. Fischer, C. W. Hess, and K. M. Rosler, "Uncrossed Cortico-Muscular Projections

in Humans Are Abundant to Facial Muscles of the Upper and Lower Face, but May Differ between the Sexes," *Journal of Neurology* 252 (2005): 21–26; U. Dimberg and M. Petterson, "Facial Reactions to Happy and Angry Facial Expressions," *Psychophysiology* 37 (2000): 693–696; J. Kagan and N. Snidman, *The Long Shadow of Temperament* (Cambridge, MA: Harvard University Press, 2004); M. de Wied, A. van Boxtel, R. Zaalberg, P. P. Goudena, and W. Matthys, "Facial EMG Responses to Dynamic Emotional Facial Expressions in Boys with Disruptive Behavior Disorders," *Journal of Psychiatric Research* 40 (2006): 121–122.

62. A. Wierzbicka, *Emotions across Languages and Cultures: Diversity and Universals* (New York: Cambridge University Press, 1999); J. Aronoff, B. A. Woike, and L. M. Hyman, "Which Are the Stimuli in Facial Displays of Anger and Happiness?" *Journal of Personality and Social Psychology* 62 (1992): 1050–1066.

63. A. Ortony and T. J. Turner, "What's Basic about Basic Emotions?" *Psychological Review* 97 (1990): 315–331; M. B. Arnold, *Emotion and Personality* (New York: Columbia University Press, 1960).

64. H. Distel and R. Hudson, "Judgment of Odor Intensity Is Influenced by Subjects' Knowledge of the Odor Source," *Chemical Senses* 26 (2001): 247–251; B. Dresp, A. Marcellini, and E. de Leseleuc, "What a Beautiful Stump!" *Perception* 34 (2005): 86; D. A. Zellner, D. Allen, M. Henley, and S. Parker, "Hedonic Contrast and Condensation: Good Stimuli Make Mediocre Stimuli Less Good and Less Different," *Psychonomic Bulletin and Review* 13 (2006): 235–239.

65. M. D. Schulkind and G. M. Woldorf, "Emotional Organization of Autobiographical Memory," *Memory and Cognition* 33 (2005): 1025–1035; K. Spronk, "Good Death and Bad Death in Ancient Israel According to Biblical Lore," *Social Science and Medicine* 58 (2004): 987–995; M. Eid and E. Diener, "Norms for Experiencing Emotions in Different Cultures: Inter- and Intranational Differences," *Journal of Personality and Social Psychology* 81 (2001): 869–885.

66. R. A. Kaster, *Emotion, Restraint, and Community in Ancient Rome* (New York: Oxford University Press, 2005).

67. M. V. Saarela, Y. Hlushchuk, A. C. Williams, M. Schurmann, E. Kalso, and R. Hari, "The Compassionate Brain," *Cerebral Cortex* 17 (2006): 230–237; M. L. Kringelbach, J. O'Doherty, E. T. Rolls, and C. Andrews, "Activation of the Human Orbitofrontal Cortex to a Liquid Food Stimulus Is Correlated with Its Subjective Pleasantness," *Cerebral Cortex* 13 (2003): 1064–1071; L. Dube and J. L. Le Bel, "The Content and Structure of Laypeople's Concept of Pleasure," *Cognition and Emotion* 17 (2003): 263–296.

68. E. Bernat, C. J. Patrick, S. D. Benning, and A. Tellegen, "Effects of Picture Content and Intensity on Affective Physiological Responses," *Psychophysiology* 43 (2006): 93–103.

69. J. A. Russell and L. F. Barrett, "Core Affect, Prototypical Emotional Episodes, and Others Things Called Emotion," *Journal of Personality and Social Psychology* 76 (1999): 805–819; Bensafi et al., "Responses to Odours"; P. Shaver, J. Schwartz,

D. Kirson, and C. O'Connor, "Emotion Knowledge," *Journal of Personality and Social Psychology* 52 (1987): 1061–1086.

70. A. Brancucci, C. Babiloni, P. M. Rossini, and G. L. Romani, "Right Hemisphere Specialization for Intensity Discrimination of Musical and Speech Sounds," *Neuropsychologia* 43 (2005): 1916–1923.

71. D. Kahneman, personal communication, 2003.

72. A. Wunsch, P. Philippot, and L. Plaghki, "Affective Associative Learning Modifies the Sensory Perception of Nocioceptive Stimuli without Participant's Awareness," *Pain* 102 (2003): 27–38; E. Diener, C. R. Colvin, W. G. Pavot, and A. Allman, "The Psychic Costs of Intense Positive Affect," *Journal of Personality and Social Psychology* 61 (1991): 492–503; P. A. McGraw, B. A. Mellers, and P. E. Tetlock, "Expectations and Emotions of Olympic Athletes," *Journal of Experimental Social Psychology* 41 (2005): 438–446; D. A. Pizarro, E. Uhlmann, and P. Bloom, "Causal Deviance and the Attribution of Moral Responsibility," *Journal of Experimental Social Psychology* 39 (2003): 653–660.

73. U. Schimmack and D. Diener, "Affect Intensity: Separating Intensity and Frequency in Repeatedly Measured Affect," *Journal of Personality and Social Psychology* 73 (1997): 1313–1329; O. Pollatos, W. Kirsch, and R. Schandry, "On the Relationship between Interoceptive Awareness, Emotional Experience, and Brain Processes," *Cognitive Brain Research* 25 (2005): 948–962.

74. Paster, "Melancholic Cats."

75. J. N. Lundstrom, J. A. Boyle, and M. Jones-Gotman, "Sit Up and Smell the Roses Better: Olfactory Sensitivity to Phenyl Ethyl Alcohol Is Dependent on Body Position," *Chemical Senses* 31 (2006): 249–252; A. Raz, B. Lieber, F. Soliman, J. Buhle, J. Posner, B. S. Peterson, and M. I. Posner, "Ecological Nuances in Functional Magnetic Resonance Imaging (fMRI)," *Neuroimage* 25 (2005): 1–7.

76. R. A. Shweder, *Why Do Men Barbecue?* (Cambridge, MA: Harvard University Press, 2003); V. S. Ramachandran and E. M. Hubbard, "Synesthesia," in J. L. v. Hemmen and T. J. Sejnowski, eds., *Twenty-Three Problems in Systems Neuroscience*, 432–473 (New York: Oxford University Press, 2006).

77. M. Friedman, H. C. Chen, and J. Vaid, "Proverb Preferences across Cultures: Dialecticality or Poeticality?" *Psychonomic Bulletin and Review* 13 (2006): 353–359.

78. N. H. Frijda, "The Laws of Emotion," *American Psychologist* 33 (1988): 349–358; R. Buck, "The Biological Affects: A Typology," *Psychological Review* 106 (1999): 301–336; C. Saarni, J. J. Campos, L. A. Camras, and D. Witherington, "Emotional Development: Action, Communication, and Understanding," in N. Eisenberg (volume editor), W. Damon and R. M. Lerner (editors-in-chief), *Handbook of Child Psychology*, 6th ed., vol. 3, 226–299 (New York: Wiley, 2006), 227.

79. Schultz, "Behavioral Theories"; R. A. Rescorla, "Comparison of the Rates of Associative Change during Acquisition and Extinction," *Journal of Experimental Psychology: Animal Behavior Processes* 28 (2002): 406–415.

80. N. Eisenberg, J. Liew, and S. U. Pidada, "The Longitudinal Relations of Regulation

and Emotionality to Quality of Indonesian Children's Socioemotional Functioning," *Developmental Psychology* 40 (2004): 790–804.

81. C. E. Izard, *The Psychology of Emotions* (New York: Plenum, 1991).

82. W. V. Quine, *Theories and Things* (Cambridge, MA: Harvard University Press, 1981).

83. J. Mainland and N. Sobel, "The Sniff Is Part of the Olfactory Percept," *Chemical Senses* 31 (2006): 181–196.

84. J. L. McGaugh and L. Cahill, "Emotion and Memory," in R. J. Davidson, K. R. Scherer, and H. H. Goldsmith, eds., *Handbook of Affective Science*, 93–116 (New York: Oxford University Press, 2003).

85. R. A. Shweder, "The Cultural Psychology of the Emotions," in M. Lewis and J. M. Haviland, eds., *Handbook of Emotions*, 417–431 (New York: Guilford, 1993).

3 **Language and Emotions**

1. H. R. Schlosberg, "Three Dimensions of Emotion," *Psychological Review* 61 (1954): 81–88; C. C. Moore, A. K. Romney, T. L. Hsia, and C. D. Rusch, "The Universality of the Semantic Structure of Emotion Terms: Methods for the Study of Inter- and Intra-Cultural Variability," *American Anthropologist* 101 (1999): 529–546; J. R. J. Fontaine, Y. H. Poortinga, B. Setiadi, and S. S. Markham, "Cognitive Structure of Emotion Terms in Indonesia and the Netherlands," *Cognition and Emotion* 16 (2002): 61–87; K. R. Scherer, "On the Nature and Function of Emotion," in K. R. Scherer and P. Ekman, eds., *Approaches to Emotion*, 293–318 (Hillsdale, NJ: L. Erlbaum, 1984); J. L. Tsai, B. Knutson, and H. H. Fung, "Cultural Variation in Affect Valuation," *Journal of Personality and Social Psychology* 90 (2006): 288–307; R. Mauro, K. Sato, and J. Tucker, "The Role of Appraisal in Human Emotions," *Journal of Personality and Social Psychology* 62 (1992): 301–317.

2. J. T. Larsen, A. P. McGraw, and J. T. Cacioppo, "Can People Feel Happy and Sad at the Same Time?" *Journal of Personality and Social Psychology* 81 (2001): 684–696; G. Saucier, "Factor Structures of English-Language Personality Type-Nouns," *Journal of Personality and Social Psychology* 85 (2003): 695–708; C. E. Osgood, G. J. Suci, and P. H. Tannenbaum, *The Measurement of Meaning* (Urbana: University of Illinois Press, 1957).

3. S. Wiens, "Interoception in Emotional Experience," *Current Opinion in Neurology* 18 (2005): 442–447; A. K. Anderson and E. A. Phelps, "Is the Human Amygdala Critical for the Subjective Experience of Emotion?" *Journal of Cognitive Neuroscience* 14 (2002): 709–720.

4. M. Henle, ed., *The Selected Papers of Wolfgang Kohler* (New York: Liveright, 1971); W. V. Quine, *Theories and Things* (Cambridge, MA: Harvard University Press, 1981).

5. G. Buzsáki, *Rhythms of the Brain* (New York: Oxford University Press, 2006); J. O'Doherty, E. T. Rolls, S. Francis, R. Bowtell, and F. McGlone, "Representation of Pleasant and Aversive Taste in the Human Brain," *Journal of Neurophysiology* 85

(2001): 1315–1321; J. S. Winston, J. M. Gottfried, J. M. Kilner, and R. J. Dolan, "Integrated Neural Representations of Odor Intensity and Affective Valence in Human Amygdala," *Journal of Neuroscience* 25 (2005): 8903–8907.

6. C. B. Zhang and K. Liljenquist, "Washing Away Your Sins: Threatened Morality and Physical Cleansing," *Science* 313 (2006): 1451–1452.

7. C. Chrea, D. Valentin, C. Sulmont-Rosse, D. H. Nguyen, and H. Abdi, "Semantic Typicality and Odor Representation: A Cross-Cultural Study," *Chemical Senses* 30 (2005): 37–49; E. M. Saffran, H. B. Coslett, and M. T. Keener, "Differences in Word Associations to Pictures and Words," *Neuropsychologia* 41 (2003): 1541–1546.

8. A. J. Tindell, K. S. Smith, S. Pecina, K. C. Berridge, and J. W. Aldridge, "Ventral Pallidum Firing Codes Hedonic Reward," *Journal of Neurophysiology* 96 (2006): 2399–2409.

9. D. Kemmerer, "The Semantics of Space," *Neuropsychologia* 44 (2006): 1607–1621.

10. L. F. Barrett, "Are Emotions Natural Kinds?" *Perspectives on Psychological Science* 1 (2006): 28–58.

11. P. Shaver, J. Schwartz, D. Kirson, and C. O'Connor, "Emotion Knowledge," *Journal of Personality and Social Psychology* 52 (1987): 1061–1086; G. C. Davey, A. S. McDonald, U. Hirisave, G. G. Prabhu, S. Iwawaki, C. I. Jim, H. Merckelbach, P. J. de Jong, P. W. Leung, and B. C. Reiman, "A Cross-Cultural Study of Animal Fears," *Behaviour Research and Therapy* 36 (1998): 735–750; J. M. Sundet, I. Skre, J. J. Okkenhaug, and K. Tambs, "Genetic and Environmental Causes of the Interrelationships between Self-Reported Fears," *Scandinavian Journal of Psychology* 44 (2003): 97–106.

12. G. E. Hardie, S. Janson, W. M. Gold, V. Carrieri-Kohlman, and H. A. Boushey, "Ethnic Differences: Word Descriptors Used by African-American and White Asthma Patients during Induced Bronchoconstriction," *Chest* 117 (2000): 928–929; S. R. Clarvit, F. R. Schneier, and M. R. Liebowitz, "The Offensive Subtype of Taijin-Kyofu-sho in New York City," *Journal of Clinical Psychiatry* 57 (1996): 523–527.

13. Y. Matsumoto, "Reexamination of the Universality of Face: Politeness Phenomena in Japanese," *Journal of Pragmatics* 12 (1988): 403–426.

14. N. L. Etcoff and J. J. Magee, "Categorical Perception of Facial Expressions," *Cognition* 44 (1992): 227–240.

15. J. Faggot, J. Goldstein, J. Davidoff, and A. Pickering, "Cross-Species Differences in Color Categorization," *Psychonomic Bulletin and Review* 13 (2006): 275–280.

16. N. Vriends, E. S. Becker, A. Meyer, S. L. Williams, R. Lutz, and J. Margraf, "Recovery from Social Phobia in the Community and Its Predictors," *Journal of Anxiety Disorders* (2007): in press.

17. A. Azizian, T. D. Watson, M. A. Parvaz, and N. K. Squires, "Time Course of Processes Underlying Picture and Word Evaluation," *Brain Topography* 18 (2006): 213–222.

18. R. O'Kearney and M. R. Dadds, "Language for Emotions in Adolescents with

Externalizing and Internalizing Disorders," *Development and Psychopathology* 17 (2005): 529–548; P. Bauer, L. Stennes, and J. Haight, "Representation of the Inner Self in Autobiography," *Memory* 11 (2003): 27–42.

19. P. de Jong, M. van den Hout, H. Rietbroek, and J. Huijding, "Dissociations between Implicit and Explicit Attitudes toward Phobic Stimuli," *Cognition and Emotion* 17 (2003): 521–546; T. Ellwart, M. Rinck, and E. S. Becker, "From Fear to Love: Individual Differences in Implicit Spider Associations," *Emotion* 6 (2006): 18–27; B. A. Teachman, A. P. Gregg, and S. R. Woody, "Implicit Associations for Fear-Relevant Stimuli among Individuals with Snake and Spider Fears," *Journal of Abnormal Psychology* 110 (2001): 226–235; E. C. Pinel, "Stigma Consciousness," *Journal of Personality and Social Psychology* 76 (1999): 114–128; L. M. Sankis, E. M. Corbitt, and T. A. Widiger, "Gender Bias in the English Language," *Journal of Personality and Social Psychology* 77 (1999): 1289–1296; C. R. Ember and M. Ember, "Psychosexual Predictors of the Gender of Objective Nouns in French," *Ethos* 7 (1979): 51–67.

20. A. Innes-Ker and P. M. Niedenthal, "Emotion Concepts and Emotional States in Social Judgment and Categorization," *Journal of Personality and Social Psychology* 83 (2002): 804–816; R. Gaillard, A. Del Cul, L. Naccache, F. Vinckier, L. Cohen, and S. Dehaene, "Nonconscious Semantic Processing of Emotional Words Modulates Conscious Access," *Proceedings of the National Academy of Science* 103 (2006): 7524–7529; S. T. Murphy and R. B. Zajonc, "Affect, Cognition, and Awareness," *Journal of Personality and Social Psychology* 64 (1993): 723–739.

21. J. Storbeck, M. D. Robinson, and M. E. McCourt, "Semantic Processing Precedes Affect Retrieval," *Review of General Psychology* 10 (2006): 41–55; N. C. Carroll and A. W. Young, "Priming of Emotion Recognition," *Quarterly Journal of Experimental Psychology* 58 (2005): 1173–1197; H. C. Heims, H. D. Critchley, R. Dolan, C. J. Mathias, and L. Cipolotti, "Social and Motivational Functioning Is Not Critically Dependent on Feedback of Autonomic Responses," *Neuropsychologia* 42 (2004): 1979–1988.

22. B. Mesquita, "Emotions in Collectivist and Individualist Contexts," *Journal of Personality and Social Psychology* 80 (2001): 68–74; A. Wierzbicka, "Talk about Emotions: Semantics, Culture, and Cognition," *Cognition and Emotion* 6 (1992): 285–319; W. V. Quine, *From a Logical Point of View: Nine Logico-Philosophical Essays* (Cambridge, MA: Harvard University Press, 1953); J. Li, L. Wang, and K. W. Fischer, "The Organization of Chinese Shame Concepts?" *Cognition and Emotion* 18 (2004): 767–797.

23. M. E. Brandt and J. D. Boucher, "Concepts of Depression in Emotion Lexicons of Eight Cultures," *International Journal of Intercultural Relations* 10 (1986): 321–346; B. Fehr and J. A. Russell, "The Concept of Love Viewed from a Prototype Perspective," *Journal of Personality and Social Psychology* 60 (1991): 425–438; A. Wierzbicka, *Emotions across Languages and Cultures: Diversity and Universals* (New York: Cambridge University Press, 1999).

24. S. Oishi, E. Diener, C. Napa-Scollon, and R. Biswas-Diener, "Cross-Situational Consistency of Affective Experience across Cultures," *Journal of Personality and Social Psychology* 86 (2004): 460-472.

25. Moore et al., "Universality"; Fontaine et al., "Cognitive Structure."

26. H. Frank, O. I. Harvey, and K. Verdun, "American Responses to Five Categories of Shame in Chinese Culture," *Personality and Individual Differences* 28 (2000): 887-896.

27. A. Mechelli, G. Sartori, P. Orlandi, and C. J. Price, "Semantic Relevance Explains Category Effects in Medial Fusiform Gyrus," *Neuroimage* 30 (2006): 992-1002; G. M. Manguno-Mire and J. H. Geer, "Network Knowledge Organization," *Sex Roles* 39 (1998): 705-729; D. G. Dillon, J. J. Cooper, T. Grent-t-Jong, M. G. Woldorff, and K. S. La Bar, "Dissociation of Event-Related Potentials Indexing Arousal and Semantic Cohesion during Emotional Word Encoding," *Brain and Cognition* 62 (2006): 43-57.

28. R. Wilkins and E. Gareis, "Emotion Expression and the Locution 'I Love You': A Cross-Cultural Study," *International Journal of Intercultural Relations* 30 (2006): 51-75; E. Ofek and H. Pratt, "Neurophysiological Correlates of Subjective Significance," *Clinical Neurophysiology* 116 (2005): 2354-2362.

29. J. A. Russell, "Culture and the Categorization of Emotions," *Psychological Bulletin* 110 (1991): 426-450; W. T. Jones, *The Medieval Mind*, 2nd ed. (New York: Harcourt, Brace and World, 1969), 106; D. Jacquart and C. Thomasset, *Sexuality and Medicine in the Middle Ages* (Princeton, NJ: Princeton University Press, 1988).

30. I. Choi and R. E. Nisbett, "Cultural Psychology of Surprise," *Journal of Personality and Social Psychology* 79 (2000): 890-905; C. Lutz, "The Domain of Emotional Words in Ifaluk," *American Ethnologist* 9 (1982): 113-128.

31. L. J. Ji, Z. Zhang, and R. E. Nisbett, "It Is Culture or Is It Language?" *Journal of Personality and Social Psychology* 87 (2004): 57-65.

32. F. Yu-Lan, *A History of Chinese Philosophy*, trans. D. Bodde (Princeton, NJ: Princeton University Press, 1953).

33. S. Sakuragi and Y. Sugiyama, "Effects of Daily Walking on Subjective Symptoms, Mood and Autonomic Nervous Function," *Journal of Physical Anthropology* 25 (2006): 281-289.

34. C. Nakane, *Japanese Society* (Berkeley: University of California Press, 1970).

35. K. M. Douglas and R. M. Sutton, "When What You Say about Others Says Something about You: Language Abstraction and Inferences about Describers' Attitudes and Goals," *Journal of Experimental Social Psychology* 42 (2006): 500-508.

36. S. Yokoyama, T. Miyamoto, J. Riera, J. Kim, Y. Akitsuki, K. Iwata, K. Yoshimoto, K. Harie, S. Satao, and R. Kawashima, "Cortical Mechanism Involved in the Processing of Verbs," *Journal of Cognitive Neuroscience* 18 (2006): 1304-1313.

37. Y. Miyamoto and N. Schwarz, "When Conveying a Message May Hurt the Relationship: Cultural Differences in the Difficulty of Using an Answering Machine," *Journal of Experimental Social Psychology* 42 (2006): 540-547.

38. M. Roberts, ed., *Chinese Fairy Tales and Fantasies* (New York: Pantheon, 1979).

39. U. Rudolph and F. Fosterling, "The Psychological Causality Implicit in Verbs: A Review," *Psychological Bulletin* 121 (1997): 192–218; Y. Kashima, E. S. Kashima, U. Kim, and M. Gelfand, "Describing the Social World: How Is a Person, a Group, and a Relationship Described in the East and the West?" *Journal of Experimental Social Psychology* 42 (2006): 389–396.

40. A. Najib, J. P. Lorberbaum, S. Kose, D. E. Bohning, and M. S. George, "Regional Brain Activity in Women Grieving a Romantic Relationship Breakup," *American Journal of Psychiatry* 161 (2004): 2245–2256.

41. S. D. Gosling, O. P. John, K. H. Craik, and R. W. Robins, "Do People Know How They Behave?" *Journal of Personality and Social Psychology* 74 (1998): 1337–1349.

42. R. A. Shweder, "The Cultural Psychology of the Emotions," in M. Lewis and J. M. Haviland, eds., *Handbook of Emotions*, 417–431 (New York: Guilford, 1993); A. Singh-Manoux, M. G. Marmot, and N. E. Adler, "Does Subjective Social Status Predict Health and Change in Health Status Better than Objective Status?" *Psychosomatic Medicine* 67 (2005): 855–861; M. Schredl and E. Doll, "Emotion in Diary Dreams," *Consciousness and Cognition* 7 (1998): 634–646.

43. R. Faggen, *Striving toward Being* (New York: Farrar, Straus, and Giroux, 1997), 89.

44. S. Moratti, A. Keil, and G. A. Miller, "Fear but Not Awareness Predicts Enhanced Sensory Processing in Fear Conditioning," *Psychophysiology* 43 (2006): 216–226.

45. H. Weiner, *Perturbing the Organism: The Biology of Stressful Experience* (Chicago: University of Chicago Press, 1992); A. Schwerdtfeger, "Predicting Autonomic Reactivity to Public Speaking: Don't Get Fixed on Self-Report Data!" *International Journal of Psychophysiology* 52 (2004): 217–224; H. R. Riggio and R. E. Riggio, "Emotional Expressiveness, Extraversion, and Neuroticism: A Meta-Analysis," *Journal of Nonverbal Behavior* 26 (2002): 195–218.

46. E. J. Hermans, P. Putman, J. M. Baas, H. P. Koppeschaar, and J. van Honk, "A Single Administration of Testosterone Reduces Fear-Potentiated Startle in Humans," *Biological Psychiatry* 59 (2006): 872–874; J. J. Gross and R. W. Levenson, "Emotional Suppression," *Journal of Personality and Social Psychology* 64 (1993): 970–986; J. L. Tsai, R. W. Levenson, and K. McCoy, "Cultural and Temperamental Variation in Emotional Response," *Emotion* 6 (2006): 484–497; P. M. Di Bartolo and A. E. Grills, "Who Is Best at Predicting Children's Anxiety in Response to a Social Evaluative Task?" *Journal of Anxiety Disorders* 20 (2006): 630–645; C. M. Philpott, C. R. Wolstenholme, P. C. Goodenough, A. Carl, and G. E. Murty, "Comparison of Subjective Perception with Objective Measurement of Olfaction," *Otolaryngology and Head and Neck Surgery* 134 (2006): 488–490.

47. D. Matsumoto and P. Ekman, "The Relationships among Expressions, Labels, and Descriptions of Contempt," *Journal of Personality and Social Psychology* 87 (2004): 529–540.

48. M. Groosman and W. Wood, "Sex Differences in Intensity of Emotional Experience," *Journal of Personality and Social Psychology* 65 (1993): 1010–1022; M. M.

Carter, T. Sbrocco, O. Miller, S. Suchday, E. L. Lewis, and R. E. K. Freedman, "Factor Structure, Reliability, and Validity of the Penn State Worry Questionnaire," *Journal of Anxiety Disorders* 19 (2005): 827–843.

49. D. C. Funder, "Personality," in S. T. Fiske, D. L. Schacter, and C. Zahn-Waxler, eds., *Annual Review of Psychology*, 197–222 (Palo Alto, CA: Annual Reviews, 2001), 213.

50. G. Wyszecki and W. S. Stiles, *Color Science: Concepts and Methods, Qualitative Data and Formulae*, 2nd ed. (New York: Wiley, 1982).

51. E. Bernat, C. J. Patrick, S. D. Benning, and A. Tellegen, "Effects of Picture Content and Intensity on Affective Physiological Responses," *Psychophysiology* 43 (2006): 93–103.

52. F. Petty, P. R. Padala, S. Ramaswamy, M. Almeida, M. Monnahan, and D. R. Wilson, "Predictors of Treatment Response in PTSD: Childhood Trauma, Social Rank, Defeat, and Entrapment," *Biological Psychiatry* 59 (2006): 156S; G. E. Bruder, J. P. Sedoruk, C. E. Tenke, J. W. Stewart, P. J. McGrath, and F. M. Quitkin, "Regional Hemisphere Activity Predicts Clinical Response to an SSRI Antidepressant," *Biological Psychiatry* 59 (2006): 136S; G. C. Blackhart, J. A. Minnix, and J. P. Kline, "Can EEG Asymmetry Patterns Predict Future Development of Anxiety and Depression?" *Biological Psychology* 72 (2006): 46–50; M. B. Tome, C. R. Cloninger, J. P. Watson, and M. T. Isaac, "Serotonergic Autoreceptor Blockade in the Reduction of Antidepressant Latency," *Journal of Affective Disorders* 44 (1997): 101–109.

53. J. L. McGaugh and L. Cahill, "Emotion and Memory," in R. J. Davidson, K. R. Scherer, and H. H. Goldsmith, eds., *Handbook of Affective Science*, 93–116 (New York: Oxford University Press, 2003).

## 4 Variation in Emotional Experience

1. M. Schiff, "Living in the Shadow of Terrorism," *Social Science and Medicine* 62 (2006): 2301–2312; T. L. Gruenewald, M. E. Kemeny, and N. Aziz, "Subjective Social Status Moderates Cortisol Responses to Social Threat," *Brain Behavior and Immunity* 20 (2006): 410–419.

2. B. Doosje, N. R. Branscombe, R. Spears, and A. S. R. Manstead, "Guilty by Association," *Journal of Personality and Social Psychology* 75 (1998): 872–886.

3. G. C. Homans, *Coming to My Senses: The Autobiography of a Sociologist* (New Brunswick, NJ: Transaction Books, 1984).

4. E. T. Rolls, *Emotion Explained* (New York: Oxford University Press, 2005).

5. R. E. Roberts, Y. R. Chen, and C. R. Roberts, "Ethnocultural Differences in Prevalence of Adolescent Suicidal Behaviors," *Suicide and Life Threatening Behavior* 27 (1997): 208–217.

6. A. Firkowska, A. Ostrowska, M. Sokolwska, Z. Stein, and M. Susser, "Cognitive Development and Social Policy," *Science* 200 (1978): 1357–1362.

7. W. Wang, W. Du, P. Liu, J. Liu, and Y. Wang, "Five-Factor Personality Measures in Chinese University Students: Effects of One-Child Policy?" *Psychiatry Research*

109 (2002): 37–44; M. Bobak, H. Pikhart, A. Pajak, R. Kubinova, S. Malyutina, H. Sebakova, R. Topor-Madry, Y. Nikitin, and M. Marmot, "Depressive Symptoms in Urban Population Samples in Russia, Poland, and the Czech Republic," *British Journal of Psychiatry* 188 (2006): 359–365; R. W. Simm and L. E. Nath, "Gender and Emotion," *American Journal of Sociology* 109 (2004): 1137–1176; A. Steptoe, S. R. Kunz-Ebrecht, C. I. Wright, and P. J. Feldman, "Socioeconomic Position and Cardiovascular and Neuroendocrine Responses following Cognitive Challenge in Old Age," *Biological Psychology* 69 (2005): 149–166; S. B. Manuck, J. D. Flory, R. E. Ferrell, and M. F. Muldoon, "Socio-Economic Status Covaries with Central Nervous System Serotonergic Responsivity as a Function of Allelic Variation in the Serotonin Transporter Gene-Linked Polymorphic Region," *Psychoendocrinology* 29 (2004): 651–668; S. Cohen, W. J. Doyle, and A. Baum, "Socioeconomic Status Is Associated with Stress Hormones," *Psychosomatic Medicine* 68 (2006): 414–420; A. W. Gilbertson, L. A. Paulus, S. K. Williston, T. V. Guruits, N. B. Lasko, R. K. Pitman, and S. P. Orr, "Neurocognitive Function in Monozygotic Twins Discordant for Combat Experience," *Journal of Abnormal Psychology* 115 (2006): 484–495; D. L. Foley, D. B. Goldston, E. J. Costello, and A. Angold, "Proximal Psychiatric Risk Factors for Suicidality in Youth," *Archives of General Psychiatry* 63 (2006): 1017–1024; L. D. Barrett, "Achievement Values and Anomie among Women in a Low-Income Housing Project," *Social Forces* 49 (1970): 127–134.

8. R. Lampert, J. Ickovics, R. Horwitz, and F. Lee, "Depressed Autonomic Nervous System Function in African Americans and Individuals of Lower Social Class," *American Heart Journal* 150 (2005): 153–160.

9. J. G. Johnson, P. Cohen, B. P. Dohrenwend, B. G. Link, and J. S. Brook, "A Longitudinal Investigation of Social Causation and Social Selection Processes Involved in the Association between Socioeconomic Status and Psychiatric Disorders," *Journal of Abnormal Psychology* 108 (1999): 490–499; A. Bystritsky, "Treatment-Resistant Anxiety Disorders," *Molecular Psychiatry* 11 (2006): 805–814; R. A. Godoy, V. Reyes-Garcia, T. McDade, T. Huanca, W. R. Leonard, S. Tanner, and V. Vadez, "Does Village Inequality in Modern Income Harm the Psyche? Anger, Fear, Sadness, and Alcohol Consumption in a Pre-Industrial Society," *Social Science and Medicine* 63 (2006): 359–372; U. M. Staudinger, W. Fleeson and P. B. Baltes, "Predictors of Subjective Physical Health and Global Well-Being," *Journal of Personality and Social Psychology* 76 (1999): 305–319; S. W. Gregory and S. Webster, "A Nonverbal Signal in Voices of Interview Partners Effectively Predicts Communication Accommodation and Social Status Perceptions," *Journal of Personality and Social Psychology* 70 (1996): 1231–1240.

10. G. Cantor, *Quakers, Jews, and Science* (New York: Oxford University Press, 2005); J. Updike, *Self-Consciousness: Memoirs* (New York: Knopf, 1989), 27; F. Kermode, *Not Entitled* (New York: Farrar, Straus and Giroux, 1995), 50; R. Nozick, *Philosophical Explanations* (Cambridge, MA: Harvard University Press, 1981), vii.

11. M. Marmot, M. Bobak, and G. D. Smith, "Explanations for Social Inequalities in

Health," in A. R. Tarlov and D. C. Walsh, eds., *Society and Health*, 172–210 (New York: Oxford University Press, 1995); A. Steptoe and G. Willemsen, "The Influence of Low Job Control on Ambulatory Blood Pressure and Perceived Stress over the Working Day in Men and Women from the Whitehall II Cohort," *Journal of Hypertension* 22 (2004): 915–920.

12. K. T. Kivlighan, D. A. Granger, and A. Booth, "Gender Differences in Testosterone and Cortisol Response to Competition," *Psychoneuroendocrinology* 30 (2005): 58–71; V. Ruchkin, D. G. Sukhodolsky, R. Vermeiren, R. A. Koposov, and M. Schwab-Stone, "Depressive Symptoms and Associated Psychopathology in Urban Adolescents," *Journal of Nervous and Mental Disease* 194 (2006): 106–113; J. D. Buckner, M. A. Mallott, N. B. Schmidt, and J. Taylor, "Peer Influence and Gender Differences in Problematic Cannabis Use among Individuals with Social Anxiety," *Journal of Anxiety Disorders* 20 (2006): 1097–1102; E. Palagi, "Social Play in Bonobos (*Pan paniscus*) and Chimpanzees (*Pan troglodytes*)," *American Journal of Physical Anthropology* 129 (2005): 418–426.

13. J. K. Olofsson and S. Nordin, "Gender Differences in Chemosensory Perception and Event-Related Potentials," *Chemical Senses* 29 (2004): 629–637; D. M. Almeida and R. C. Kessler, "Everyday Stressors and Gender Differences in Daily Distress," *Journal of Personality and Social Psychology* 75 (1998): 670–680; J. J. Gross and O. P. Oliver, "Mapping the Domain of Expressivity," *Journal of Personality and Social Psychology* 74 (1998): 170–191; J. Vahtera, M. Kivimaki, A. Vaananen, A. Linna, J. Pentti, H. Helenius, and M. Elovainio, "Sex Differences in Health Effects of Family Death or Illness," *Psychosomatic Medicine* 68 (2006): 283–291.

14. A. Aloisi and M. Bonifazi, "Sex Hormones, Central Nervous System and Pain," *Hormones and Behavior* 50 (2006): 1–7; Y. R. Smith, C. S. Stohler, T. E. Nichols, J. A. Bueller, R. A. Koeppe, and J. K. Zubieta, "Proprioceptive and Antinociceptive Effects of Estradiol through Endogenous Opioid Neurotransmission in Women," *Journal of Neuroscience* 26 (2006): 5777–5785.

15. D. W. Birnbaum and B. E. Chemelski, "Preschoolers' Inferences about Gender and Emotion," *Sex Roles* 10 (1984): 505–511; J. Kagan, "Acquisition and Significance of Sex Typing and Sex Role Indentity," in M. Hoffman and L. Hoffman, eds., *Review of Child Development Research*, 137–167 (New York: Russell Sage, 1964); A. A. Albert and J. R. Porter, "Children's Gender-Role Stereotypes," *Sociological Forum* 3 (1988): 184–210; C. S. Farris, "Gender and Grammar in Chinese," *Modern China* 14 (1988): 277–308.

16. Y. Yamamoto, B. S. Cushing, K. M. Kramer, P. D. Epperson, G. E. Hoffman, and C. S. Carter, "Neonatal Manipulations of Oxytocin Alter Expression of Oxytocin and Vasopressin Immunoreactive Cells in the Paraventricular Nucleus of the Hypothalamus in a Gender-Specific Manner," *Neuroscience* 125 (2004): 947–955; C. S. Carter, "Sex Differences in Oxytocin and Vasopressin," *Behavioural Brain Research*

176 (2006): 170–186; E. F. Coccaro, R. J. Kavoussi, R. L. Hauger, T. B. Cooper, and C. F. Ferris, "Cerebrospinal Fluid Vasopressin Levels Correlates with Aggression and Serotonin Function in Personality-Disordered Subjects," *Archives of General Psychiatry* 55 (1998): 709–714; L. A. Weiss, L. Pan, M. Abney, and C. Ober, "The Sex-Specific Genetic Architecture of Quantitative Traits in Humans," *Nature Genetics* 38 (2006): 218–222.

17. R. R. Thompson, K. George, J. C. Walton, S. P. Orr, and J. Benson, "Sex-Specific Influences of Vasopressin on Human Social Communication," *Proceedings of the National Academy of Sciences* 103 (2006): 7889–7894.

18. L. A. Rosenblum, E. L. P. Smith, M. Altemus, B. A. Scharf, M. J. Owens, C. B. Nemeroff, J. M. Gorman, and J. D. Coplan, "Differing Concentrations of Corticotrophin-Releasing Factor and Oxytocin in the Cerebrospinal Fluid of Bonnet and Pigtail Macaques," *Psychoneuroendocrinology* 27 (2002): 651–660; D. D. Francis, L. J. Young, M. J. Meaney, and T. R. Insel, "Naturally Occurring Differences in Maternal Care Are Associated with the Expression of Oxytocin and Vasopressin (V1a) Receptors: Gender Differences," *Journal of Neuroscience* 14 (2002): 349–353.

19. S. E. Taylor, L. C. Klein, B. P. Lewis, T. L. Gruenewald, N. Guring, A. R. Regan, and J. A. Updegraff, "Biobehavioral Responses to Stress in Females: Tend—and Befriend, Not Fight—or Flight," *Psychological Review* 107 (2000): 411–429.

20. R. M. Ross and G. S. Losey, "Sex Change in a Coral Reef Fish," *Science* 221 (1989): 574–575.

21. M. K. Mullen, "Children's Classifications of Nature and Artifact Pictures into Female and Male Categories," *Sex Roles* 23 (1990): 577–587.

22. W. Gundersheimer, "The Green-Eyed Monster: Renaissance Conceptions of Jealousy," *Proceedings of the American Philosophical Society* 137 (1993): 321–331.

23. J. T. Manning, M. Callow, and P. E. Bundred, "Finger and Toe Ratios in Humans and Mice," *Medical Hypotheses* 60 (2003): 340–343; S. M. Van Anders, P. A. Vernon, and C. J. Wilbur, "Finger-Length Ratios Show Evidence of Prenatal Hormone-Transfer between Opposite-Sex Twins," *Hormones and Behavior* 49 (2006): 315–319; N. McDermott, R. Gandelman, and J. M. Reinisch, "Contiguity to Male Fetuses Influences Ano-Genital Distance and Time of Vaginal Opening in Mice," *Physiology and Behavior* 20 (1978): 661–663.

24. D. A. Putz, S. J. C. Gaulin, R. J. Sporter, and D. H. McBurney, "Sex Hormones and Finger Length: What Does 2D:4D Indicate?" *Evolution and Human Behavior* 25 (2004): 182–199; J. H. G. Williams, K. D. Greenhalgh, and J. T. Manning, "Second to Fourth Finger Ratio and Possible Precursors of Developmental Psychopathology in Preschool Children," *Early Human Development* 72 (2003): 57–65; H. J. Schneider, J. Pickel, and G. K. Stalla, "Typical Female 2nd-4th Finger Length (2D:4D) Ratios in Male-to-Female Transsexuals—Possible Implications for Prenatal Androgen Exposure," *Psychoneuroendocrinology* 31 (2006): 265–269; J. Hone-

kopp, M. Voracek, and J. T. Manning, "2nd to 4th Digit Ratio (2D:4D) and Number of Sex Partners," *Psychoneuroendocrinology* 31 (2006): 30–37; B. Fink, K. Grammer, P. Mitteroecker, P. Gunz, K. Schaefer, F. L. Bookstein, and J. T. Manning, "Second to Fourth Digit Ratio and Face Shape," *Proceedings of the Royal Society B* 272 (2005): 1995–2001; B. Fink, N. Neave, K. Laughton, and J. T. Manning, "Second to Fourth Ratio and Sensation Seeking," *Personality and Individual Differences* 41 (2006): 1253–1262; A. Csatho, A. Osvath, E. Bicsak, K. Karadi, J. Manning, and J. Kallai, "Sex Role Identity Related to the Ratio of Second to Fourth Digit Length in Women," *Biological Psychology* 62 (2003): 147–156; Q. Rahman, "Fluctuating Asymmetry, Second to Fourth Finger Length Ratios and Human Sexual Orientation," *Psychoneuroendocrinology* 30 (2005): 382–394; C. M. Falter, M. Arroyo, and G. J. Davis, "Testosterone: Activation or Organization of Spatial Cognition," *Biological Psychology* 73 (2006): 132–140; A. Verdonck, M. Gaethofs, C. Carels, and F. de Zegher, "Effect of Low-Dose Testosterone Treatment on Craniofacial Growth in Boys with Delayed Puberty," *European Journal of Orthodontics* 21 (1999): 137–143; P. S. Bearman and H. Bruckner, "Opposite-Sex Twins and Adolescent Same-Sex Attraction," *American Journal of Sociology* 107 (2002): 1179–1205.

25. W. Schultz, "Behavioral Theories and the Neurophysiology of a Reward," in S. T. Fiske, A. E. Kazdin, and D. L. Schacter, eds., *Annual Review of Psychology*, 87–115 (Palo Alto, CA: Annual Reviews, 2006); D. E. Comings and K. Blum, "Reward Deficiency Syndrome," *Progress in Brain Research* 126 (2000): 325–341; C. A. Munro, M. E. McCaul, D. F. Wong, L. M. Oswald, Y. Zhou, J. Brasic, H. Kuwabara, A. Kumar, M. Alexander, W. Ye, and G. S. Wand, "Sex Differences in Striatal Dopamine Release in Healthy Adults," *Biological Psychiatry* 59 (2006): 966–974; V. Kaasinen, K. Nagren, J. Hietala, L. Farde, and J. O. Rinne, "Sex Differences in Extrastriatal Dopamine D2-Like Receptors in the Human Brain," *American Journal of Psychiatry* 158 (2001): 308–311; D. E. Dluzen, "Unconventional Effects of Estrogen Uncovered," *Trends in Pharmacological Sciences* 26 (2005): 485–487.

26. I. Z. Ben Zion, R. Tessler, L. Cohen, E. Lerer, Y. Raz, R. Bachner-Melman, I. Gritsenko, L. Nemanov, A. H. Zohar, R. H. Belmaker, J. Benjamin, and R. P. Ebstein, "Polymorphisms in the Dopamine D4 Receptor Gene (DRD4) Contribute to Individual Differences in Human Sexual Behavior: Desire, Arousal, and Sexual Function," *Molecular Psychiatry* 11 (2006): 782–786; N. M. Lind, A. Gjedde, A. Moustgaard, A. K. Olsen, S. B. Jensen, S. Jakobsen, S. M. Arnfred, A. K. Hansen, R. P. Hemmingsen, and P. Cumming, "Behavioral Response to Novelty Correlates with Dopamine Receptor Availability in Striatum of Gottingen Minipigs," *Behavioral Brain Research* 164 (2005): 172–177.

27. C. Cajochen, M. Munch, S. Kobialka, K. Krauchi, R. Steiner, P. Oelhafen, S. Orgul, and A. Wirz-Justice, "High Sensitivity of Human Melatonin, Alertness, Thermoregulation, and Heart Rate to Short Wavelength Light," *Journal of Clinical Endocrinology and Metabolism* 90 (2005): 1311–1316; R. L. Cowan, B. d. B. Frederick, M. Rainey, J. M. Levin, L. C. Maas, J. Bang, J. Hennen, S. E. Lukas, and P. F.

Renshaw, "Sex Differences in Response to Red and Blue Light in Human Primary Visual Cortex," *Psychiatry Research: Neuroimaging* 100 (2000): 129–138.

28. E. E. Maccoby and C. N. Jacklin, *The Psychology of Sex Differences* (Stanford, CA: Stanford University Press, 1974); J. S. Hyde and M. C. Linn, "Gender Similarities in Mathematics and Science," *Science* 314 (2006): 599–600; I. Dar-Nimrod and S. J. Heine, "Exposure to Scientific Theories Affects Women's Math Performance," *Science* 314 (2006): 435; Falter, Arroyo, and Davis, "Testosterone."

29. F. Jacob, *The Statue Within: An Autobiography*, trans. F. Philip (New York: Basic Books, 1988).

30. J. A. Houck, *Hot and Bothered: Women, Medicine, and Menopause in Modern America* (Cambridge, MA: Harvard University Press, 2006).

31. F. D. Peat, *From Certainty to Uncertainty: The Story of Science and Ideas in the Twentieth Century* (Washington, DC: Joseph Henry Press, 2002), 153.

32. G. M. Carstairs, *The Twice Born: A Study of a Community of High-Caste Hindus* (Bloomington: University of Indiana Press, 1975), 231.

33. U. Halbreich and S. Karkun, "Cross-Cultural and Social Diversity of Prevalence of Postpartum Depression and Depressive Symptoms," *Journal of Affective Disorders* 91 (2006): 97–111.

34. D. Bhugra, "Mad Tales from Bollywood," *Acta Scandinavica Psychiatrica* 112 (2005): 250–256.

35. D. Malaspina, "Prenatal Exposure to Severe Social Threat," *Biological Psychiatry* 59 (2006): 100S.

36. K. E. Stabell, S. Andreson, S. J. Bakke, H. Bjornaes, H. M. Borchgrevink, E. Heminghyt, and G. K. Roste, "Emotional Responses during Unilateral Amobarbitol Anesthesia: Differential Hemispheric Contributions?" *Acta Neurologica Scandinavia* 110 (2004): 313–321; W. B. Whitehead, "Perception of Gastric Contractions and Self-Control of Gastric Motility," *Psychophysiology* 17 (1980): 552–558; J. L. Hansen, D. R. Reed, M. J. Wright, N. G. Martin, and P. A. Breslin, "Heritability and Genetic Covariation of Sensitivity to PROP, SOA, Quinine HCL, and Caffeine," *Chemical Senses* 31 (2006): 403–413; D. G. Liem, A. Westerbeek, S. Wolterwink, F. J. Kok, and C. de Graaf, "Sour Taste Preferences of Children Relate to Preference for Novel and Intense Stimuli," *Chemical Senses* 29 (2004): 713–720; L. F. Barrett, K. S. Quigley, E. Bliss-Moreau, and K. R. Aronson, "Interoceptive Sensitivity and Self Reports of Emotional Experience," *Journal of Personality and Social Psychology* 87 (2004): 684–697; O. Pollatos, K. Gramann, and R. Schandry, "Neural Systems Connecting Interoceptive Awareness and Feelings," *Human Brain Mapping* 28 (2006): 9–18; A. Bernstein, M. J. Zvolensky, S. H. Stewart, M. N. Comeau, and E. W. Leen-Feldner, "Anxiety Sensitivity Taxonicity across Gender among Youth," *Behaviour Research and Therapy* 44 (2006): 679–698; D. A. Seminowicz and K. D. Davis, "Cortical Responses to Pain in Healthy Individuals Depends on Pain Catastrophizing," *Pain* 120 (2006): 297–306.

37. Ben Zion et al., "Polymorphisms"; N. B. Schmidt, J. A. Richey, and K. K. Fitz-

patrick, "Discomfort Intolerance," *Journal of Anxiety Disorders* 20 (2006): 263–280; E. Diener, R. E. Lucas, and C. N. Scollon, "Beyond the Hedonic Treadmill," *American Psychologist* 61 (2006): 305–314.

38. T. Parker, *The Violence of Our Lives: Interviews with Life-Sentence Prisoners in America* (New York: Henry Holt, 1995), 66.

39. D. S. Jones and R. H. Perlis, "Pharmacogenetics, Race, and Psychiatry," *Harvard Review of Psychiatry* 14 (2006): 92–108.

40. D. Li and L. He, "Meta-Analysis Supports Association between Serotonin Transporter (5-HTT) and Social Behavior," *Molecular Psychiatry* 12 (2006): 47–54; J. T. Sakai, S. E. Young, M. L. Stallings, D. Timberlake, D. Smolen, G. L. Stetler, and T. J. Crowley, "Case-Control and within Family Tests of an Association between Conduct Disorder and 5HTTLPR," *American Journal of Medical Genetics B Neuropsychiatric Genetics* 141 (2006): 825–832; S. E. Taylor, B. M. Way, W. T. Welch, C. J. Hilmert, B. J. Lehman, and M. I. Eisenberger, "Early Family Environment, Current Adversity, the Serotonin Transporter Promoter Polymorphism, and Depressive Symptomatology," *Biological Psychiatry* 60 (2006): 671–676; P. Courtet, N. Franc, M. C. Picot, I. Jaussent, F. Jollant, S. Guillaume, and A. Malafosse, "Season of Birth Variations as Risk Factor of Suicide Attempts and Interaction with the Serotonin Transporter Gene," *Psychiatrica Danube* 18 (2006): 75.

41. L. Pezawas, A. Meyer-Lindenberg, E. M. Drabant, B. A. Verchinski, K. E. Munoz, B. S. Kolachana, M. F. Egan, V. S. Mattay, A. R. Hariri, and D. R. Weinberger, "5-HTTLPR Polymorphism Impacts Human Cingulate-Amygdala Interactions: A Genetic Susceptibility Mechanism for Depression," *Nature Neuroscience* 8 (2005): 828–834; A. Graff-Guerrero, C. De la Fuente-Sandoval, B. Camarena, D. Gomez-Martin, R. Apiquian, A. Fresan, A. Aguilar, J. C. Mendez-Nunez, C. Escalona-Huerta, R. Drucker-Colin, and H. Nicolini, "Frontal and Limbic Metabolic Differences in Subjects Selected according to Genetic Variation of the SLC6A4 Gene Polymorphism," *Neuroimage* 25 (2005): 1197–1204; X. Gonda, Z. Rihmer, T. Zsombok, G. Bagdy, K. K. Akiskal, and H. S. Akiskal, "The 5HTTLPR Polymorphism of the Serotonin Transporter Gene Is Associated with Affective Temperaments as Measured by TEMPS-A," *Journal of Affective Disorders* 91 (2006): 125–131; H. L. Urry, C. M. van Reekum, T. Johnstone, N. H. Kalin, M. E. Thurow, H. S. Schaefer, C. A. Jackson, C. J. Frye, L. L. Greischar, A. L. Alexander, and R. J. Davidson, "Amygdala and Ventromedial Prefrontal Cortex Are Inversely Coupled during Regulation of Negative Affect and Predict the Diurnal Pattern of Cortisol Secretion among Older Adults," *Journal of Neuroscience* 26 (2006): 4415–4425; M. Perez, J. S. Brown, S. Vrshek-Schallhorn, F. Johnson, and T. E. Joiner, "Differentiation of Obsessive-Compulsive-, Panic-, Obsessive-Compulsive Personality-, and Non-Disordered Individuals by Variation in the Promoter Region of the Serotonin Transporter Gene," *Journal of Anxiety Disorders* 20 (2006): 794–806.

42. B. C. Haberstick, A. Smolen, and J. K. Hewitt, "Family-Based Association Test of the 5HTTLPR and Aggressive Behavior in a General Population Sample of

Children," *Biological Psychiatry* 59 (2006): 836–843; J. Ormel and T. Wohlfarth, "How Neuroticism, Long-Term Difficulties, and Life Situation Change Influence Psychological Distress: A Longitudinal Model," *Journal of Personality and Social Psychology* 60 (1991): 744–755; S. C. Segerstrom, S. E. Taylor, M. E. Kemeny, and J. L. Fahey, "Optimism Is Associated with Mood, Coping and Immune Change in Response to Stress," *Journal of Personality and Social Psychology* 74 (1998): 1646–1655; W. J. Bouwsma, *John Calvin: A Sixteenth-Century Portrait* (New York: Oxford University Press, 1988).

43. J. H. Stubbe, D. Posthuma, D. I. Boomsma, and E. J. De Geus, "Heritability of Life Satisfaction in Adults," *Psychological Medicine* 35 (2005): 1581–1588; L. Harker and D. Keltner, "Expressions of Positive Emotion in Women's College Yearbook Pictures and Their Relationship to Personality and Life Outcomes across Adulthood," *Journal of Personality and Social Psychology* 80 (2001): 112–124; D. D. Danner, D. A. Snowdon, and W. V. Friesen, "Positive Emotions in Early Life and Longevity," *Journal of Personality and Social Psychology* 80 (2001): 804–813; A. L. Marsland, S. Cohen, B. S. Rabin, and S. B. Manuck, "Trait Positive Affect and Antibody Response to Hepatitis B Vaccination," *Brain, Behavior, and Immunity* 20 (2006): 261–269.

44. M. Bosquet and B. Egeland, "The Development and Maintenance of Anxiety Symptoms from Infancy through Adolescence in a Longitudinal Sample," *Development and Psychopathology* 18 (2006): 517–550; J. Kagan, "On the Nature of Emotions," *The Development of Emotional Regulation: Biological and Behavioral Considerations; Monographs of the Society for Research in Child Development* 59 (1994): 7–24; J. Kagan and N. Snidman, *The Long Shadow of Temperament* (Cambridge, MA: Harvard University Press, 2004).

45. B. M. Gutteling, C. de Weerth, and J. K. Buitelaar, "Prenatal Stress and Children's Cortisol Reaction to the First Day of School," *Psychoneuroendocrinology* 30 (2005): 541–549; B. R. Loney, M. A. Butler, E. N. Lima, C. A. Counts, and L. A. Eckel, "The Relation between Salivary Cortisol, Callous-Unemotional Traits, and Conduct Problems in an Adolescent Non-Referred Sample," *Journal of Child Psychology and Psychiatry* 47 (2006): 30–36.

46. J. Kagan, N. Snidman, V. Kahn, and S. Towsley, "The Preservation of Two Infant Temperaments through Adolescence," *Monographs of the Society for Research in Child Development* (2007); C. I. Wright, D. Williams, E. Feczko, L. F. Barrett, B. C. Dickerson, C. E. Schwartz, and M. M. Wedig, "Neuroanatomical Correlates of Extraversion and Neuroticism," *Cerebral Cortex* 16 (2006): 1809–1819.

47. X. Bornas, J. Llabres, M. Noguera, A. M. Lopez, F. Barcelo, M. Tortella-Feliu, and M. A. Fullana, "Looking at the Heart of Low and High Heart Rate Variability Fearful Flyers," *Biological Psychology* 70 (2005): 182–187; J. P. Sanchez-Navarro, J. M. Martinez-Selva, and F. Roman, "Uncovering the Relationship between Defence and Orienting in Emotion," *International Journal of Psychophysiology* 61 (2006): 34–46.

48. A. Buske-Kirschbaum, S. Fischbach, W. Rauh, J. Hanker, and D. Hellhammer,

"Increased Responsiveness of the Hypothalamus-Pituitary-Adrenal (HPA) Axis to Stress in Newborns with Atopic Disposition," *Psychoneuroendocrinology* 29 (2004): 705–711.

49. A. S. Waterman, "Two Conceptions of Happiness," *Journal of Personality and Social Psychology* 64 (1993): 678–691.

50. F. Ducci, T. K. Newman, S. Funt, G. L. Brown, M. Virkkunen, and D. Goldman, "A Functional Polymorphism in the MAOA Gene Promoter (MAOA-LPR) Predicts Central Dopamine Function and Body Mass Index," *Molecular Psychiatry* 11 (2006): 858–866.

51. J. T. Bromberger and K. A. Matthews, "A 'Feminine' Model of Vulnerability to Depressive Symptoms," *Journal of Personality and Social Psychology* 70 (1996): 591–598; M. E. Coles, C. A. Schofield, and A. S. Pietrefesa, "Behavioral Inhibition and Obsessive-Compulsive Disorder," *Journal of Anxiety Disorders* 20 (2006): 1118–1132; G. L. Gladstone and G. P. Parker, "Is Behavioral Inhibition a Risk Factor for Depression?" *Journal of Affective Disorders* 95 (2006): 85–94; W. E. Lee, M. E. J. Wadsworth, and M. Hotopf, "The Protective Role of Trait Anxiety," *Psychological Medicine* 36 (2006): 345–351.

52. L. L. Watkins, J. A. Blumenthal, J. R. T. Davidson, M. A. Babyak, C. B. McCants, and M. H. Sketch, "Phobic Anxiety, Depression, and Risk of Ventricular Arrhythmias in Patients with Coronary Heart Disease," *Psychosomatic Medicine* 68 (2006): 651–656.

53. D. E. Hinton, V. Pich, S. A. Safren, M. H. Pollack, and R. J. McNally, "Anxiety Sensitivity in Traumatized Cambodian Refugees," *Behaviour Research and Therapy* 43 (2005): 1631–1643.

54. S. A. Shankman, C. E. Tenke, G. E. Bruder, C. E. Durbin, E. P. Hayden, and D. N. Klein, "Low Positive Emotionality in Young Children," *Developmental Psychopathology* 17 (2005): 85–98.

55. Jones and Perlis, "Pharmacogenetics, Race, and Psychiatry"; J. Kagan, R. B. Kearsley, and P. R. Zelazo, *Infancy: Its Place in Human Development* (Cambridge, MA: Harvard University Press, 1978); D. G. Freedman, *Human Infancy: An Evolutionary Perspective* (New York: Halsted Press, 1974); J. Kagan, D. Arcus, N. Snidman, W. Yufeng, J. Hendler, and S. Green, "Reactivity in Infants: A Cross National Comparison," *Developmental Psychology* 30 (1994): 342–345; L. A. Camras, Y. Chen, R. Bakeman, K. Norris, and T. R. Cain, "Culture, Ethnicity, and Children's Facial Expressions," *Emotion* 6 (2006): 103–114; J. L. Tsai, R. W. Levenson, and K. McCoy, "Cultural and Temperamental Variation in Emotional Response," *Emotion* 6 (2006): 484–497; C. S. Huntsinger and P. E. Jose, "A Longitudinal Investigation of Personality and Social Adjustment among Chinese American and European American Adolescents," *Child Development* 77 (2006): 1309–1324; W. Kessen, ed., *Childhood in China: The American Delegation on Early Childhood Development in the People's Republic of China* (New Haven: Yale University Press, 1975), 107.

56. L. L. Cavalli-Sforza, P. Menozzi, and A. Piazza, *The History and Geography of*

*Human Genes* (Princeton, NJ: Princeton University Press, 1994); A. J. Redd, V. F. Chamberlain, V. S. Kearney, D. Stover, T. Karafet, K. Calderon, B. Walsh, and M. F. Hammer, "Genetic Structure among Thirty-Eight Populations from the United States Based on Eleven U.S. Core Y Chromosome STRs," *Journal of Forensic Science* 51 (2006): 580–585; T. Marui, O. Hasimoto, E. Nanba, C. Kato, M. Tochigi, T. Umekage, N. Kato, and T. Sasaki, "Gastrin-Releasing Peptide Receptor (GRPR) Locus in Japanese Subjects with Autism," *Brain and Development* 26 (2004): 5–7; N. C. Hong, T. R. Norman, K. O. Naing, I. Schweitzer, W. H. B. Kong, A. Fan, and S. Klimidis, "A Comparative Study of Sertraline Dosages, Plasma Concentrations, Efficacy and Adverse Reactions in Chinese versus Caucasian Patients," *International Journal of Clinical Psychopharmacology* 21 (2006): 87–92; T. Hanihara, "Frontal and Facial Flatness of Major Human Populations," *American Journal of Physical Anthropology* 111 (2000): 105–134; P. Saetre, J. Lindberg, J. A. Leonard, K. Olsson, U. Petterson, H. Ellegren, T. F. Bergstrom, C. Vila, and E. Jazin, "From Wild Wolf to Domestic Dog," *Brain Research Molecular Brain Research* 126 (2004): 198–206; M. H. McIntyre, B. Cohn, and P. T. Ellison, "Sex Dimorphism in Digital Formulae of Children," *American Journal of Physical Anthropology* 129 (2005): 143–150; S. R. Kardia, J. Chu, and M. R. Sowers, "Characterizing Variation in Sex Steroid Hormone Pathway Genes in Women of Four Races/Ethnicities," *American Journal of Medicine* 119 (2006): S3–15; M. A. Palmatier, A. M. Kang, and K. K. Kidd, "Global Variation in the Frequencies of Functionally Different Catechol-O-Methyltransferase Alleles," *Biological Psychiatry* 46 (1999): 557–567; R. S. Spielman, L. A. Bastone, J. T. Burdick, M. Morley, W. J. Evans, and V. G. Cheung, "Common Genetic Variants Account for Differences in Gene Expression among Ethnic Groups," *Nature Genetics* 39 (2007): 226–231.

57. M. Levin, G. A. Buznikov, and J. M. Lauder, "Of Minds and Embryos," *Developmental Neuroscience* 28 (2006): 171–185; S. R. Hansson, E. Mezey, and B. J. Hoffman, "Serotonin Transporter Messenger RNA Expression in Neural Crest-Derived Structures and Sensory Pathways of the Developing Rat Embryo," *Neuroscience* 89 (1999): 243–265; Taylor et al., "Early Family Environment"; J. Gelernter, H. Kranzier, and J. F. Cubells, "Serotonin Transporter Protein (SLC6A4) Allele and Haplotype Frequencies and Linkage Disequilibria in African- and European-American and Japanese Populations and in Alcohol-Dependent Subjects," *Human Genetics* 101 (1997): 243–246; J. Gelernter, J. F. Cubells, J. R. Kidd, A. J. Pakstis, and K. K. Kidd, "Population Studies of Polymorphisms of the Serotonin Transporter Protein Gene," *American Journal of Medical Genetics* 88 (1999): 61–66; M. Nakamura, S. Ueno, A. Sano, and H. Tanabe, "The Human Serotonin Transporter Gene Linked Polymorphism (5-HTTLPR) Shows Ten Novel Allelic Variants," *Molecular Psychiatry* 5 (2000): 32–38.

58. L. N. Trut, "Early Canid Domestication," *American Scientist* 87 (1999): 160–169.

59. B. J. Shen, L. R. Stroud, and R. Niaura, "Ethnic Differences in Cardiovascular Responses to Laboratory Stress," *International Journal of Behavioral Medicine* 11

(2004): 181–186; H. O. Rourke and J. L. Fudge, "Distribution of Serotonin Transporter Labeled Fibers in Amygdaloid Subregions," *Biological Psychiatry* 60 (2006): 479–490.

60. N. R. Marmorstein, "Generalized versus Performance-Focused Social Phobia: Patterns of Comorbidity among Youth," *Journal of Anxiety Disorders* 20 (2006): 778–793.

61. B. D. Weiss, L. Francis, J. H. Senf, H. K, and R. Hargraves, "Literacy Education as Treatment for Depression in Patients with Limited Literacy and Depression," *Journal of General Internal Medicine* 8 (2006): 823–828.

## 5 A Pair of Problems

1. S. L. Rossell and A. C. Nobre, "Semantic Priming of Different Affective Categories," *Emotion* 4 (2004): 354–363; N. Alvarado and K. A. Jameson, "Varieties of Anger," *Motivation and Emotion* 26 (2002): 153–182; I. J. Wambacq and J. F. Jerger, "Processing of Affective Prosody and Lexical-Semantics in Spoken Utterances as Differentiated by Event-Related Potentials," *Brain Research Cognitive Brain Research* 20 (2004): 427–437.

2. I. C. Christie and B. H. Friedman, "Autonomic Specificity of Discrete Emotion and Dimensions of Affective Space," *International Journal of Psychophysiology* 51 (2004): 143–153; L. Silvert, S. Delplanque, H. Bouwalerh, C. Verpoort, and H. Sequeira, "Autonomic Responding to Aversive Words without Conscious Valence Discrimination," *International Journal of Psychophysiology* 53 (2004): 135–145; J. S. Lerner and D. Keltner, "Fear, Anger, and Risk," *Journal of Personality and Social Psychology* 81 (2001): 146–159; D. Talmi and M. Moscovitch, "Can Memory Relatedness Explain the Enhancement of Memory for Emotional Words?" *Memory and Cognition* 32 (2004): 742–751.

3. S. Khalfa, D. Schon, J. L. Anton, and C. Liégeois-Chauvel, "Brain Regions Involved in the Recognition of Happiness and Sadness in Music," *Neuroreport* 16 (2005): 1981–1984.

4. G. S. Berns, J. Chapellow, M. Cekic, C. F. Zink, G. Pagnoni, and M. E. Martin-Skurski, "Neurobiological Substrates of Dread," *Science* 312 (2006): 754–758; S. W. Stirman and J. W. Pennebaker, "Word Use in the Poetry of Suicidal and Nonsuicidal Poets," *Psychosomatic Medicine* 63 (2001): 517–522.

5. J. Niessing, B. Ebisch, K. E. Schmidt, M. Niessing, W. Singer, and R. A. W. Galuske, "Hemodynamic Signals Correlate Tightly with Synchronized Gamma Oscillations," *Science* 309 (2005): 948–954.

6. A. H. Van Stegeren, R. Goekoop, W. Everaerd, P. Scheltens, F. Barkhof, J. P. A. Kuijer, and S. A. R. B. Rombouts, "Noradrenaline Mediates Amygdala Activation in Men and Women during Encoding of Emotional Material," *Neuroimage* 24 (2005): 898–909.

7. J. Fanghamel, T. Gedrange, and P. Pruff, "The Face—Physiognomic Expressiveness and Human Identity," *Annals of Anatomy* 188 (2006): 262–266.

8. A. Preti and P. Miotto, "Suicide in Classical Mythology," *Acta Psychiatrica Scandinavica* 111 (2005): 384–391; G. M. Carstairs, *The Twice-Born: A Study of a Community of High-Caste Hindus* (Bloomington: University of Indiana Press, 1975), 231; D. G. Mandelbaum, *Society in India* (Berkeley: University of California Press, 1970).

9. W. H. Auden, *Collected Poems*, ed. E. Mendelson (New York: Random House, 1976), 57; B. Bradlee, "A Return," *New Yorker*, October 2, 2006, 52–57, quotation at 57.

10. J. K. Conway, *The Road from Coorain* (New York: Knopf, 1989).

11. J. Brauer, J. Kaminski, J. Riedel, J. Call, and M. Tomasello, "Making Inferences about the Location of Hidden Food: Social Dog, Causal Ape," *Journal of Comparative Psychology* 120 (2006): 38–47.

12. J. L. Briggs, *Never in Anger: Portrait of an Eskimo Family* (Cambridge, MA: Harvard University Press, 1970).

13. H. O. Taylor, *The Mediaeval Mind*, 4th ed., vol. 2 (London: Macmillan, 1925), 36.

14. J. Demos, "Shame and Guilt in Early New England," in R. Harré and W. G. Parrott, eds., *The Emotions: Social, Cultural, and Biological Dimensions*, 74–88 (Thousand Oaks, CA: Sage, 1996).

15. R. I. M. Dunbar, *Grooming, Gossip, and the Evolution of Language* (London: Faber and Faber, 1996).

16. S. Plath, *The Unabridged Journals of Sylvia Plath* (New York: Anchor Books, 2000), 471.

17. A. Fogel and M. Kawai, "Hikikomori in Japanese Youth," in S. J. Chen, H. Murohashi, and Y. Fugino, eds., *Annual Report of Research and Clinical Center for Child Development, 2004-2005*, 1–12 (Sapporo, Japan: Hokkaido University, 2006).

18. P. Ball, *The Devil's Doctor: Paracelsus and the World of Renaissance Magic and Science* (London: Heinemann, 2006).